EDUCATION AND MUSIC

EDUCATION AND MUSIC

PETER FLETCHER

OXFORD NEW YORK
OXFORD UNIVERSITY PRESS

Oxford University Press, Walton Street, Oxford OX2 6DP

Oxford New York Toronto
Delhi Bombay Calcutta Madras Karachi
Petaling Jaya Singapore Hong Kong Tokyo
Nairobi Dar es Salaam Cape Town
Melbourne Auckland

and associated companies in
Berlin Ibadan

Oxford is a trade mark of Oxford University Press

Published in the United States
by Oxford University Press, New York

First published in hardback 1987
Reprinted in paperback 1989 (with additions), 1991

British Library Cataloguing in Publication Data

Fletcher, Peter, 1936–
Education and music.
1. Education. Curriculum subjects: music
I. Title
780'.7

ISBN 0–19–317420–0
ISBN 0–19–317425–1 (Pbk)

Library of Congress Cataloging in Publication Data

Fletcher, Peter, 1936–
Education and music.
Includes index.
1. Music in education.   I. Title.
MT1.F53   1989   780'.7   86–16358
ISBN 0–19–317420–0
ISBN 0–19–317425–1 (Pbk)

Printed in Great Britain by
The Alden Press, Oxford

PREFACE

Over the past thirty years, the nature and scope of school education has changed out of all recognition. During that period, music has come to occupy an increasingly important place within the school educational framework. In the process, its methodology and content have been influenced considerably by prevailing educational theory, sometimes with greatly beneficial results and sometimes at the expense of establishing musically satisfactory priorities. The purpose of this book is to analyse in some detail the components of education and music in relation to each other, historically and as they appear in current practice, and to draw such conclusions as may prove helpful in legislating for music within school education against a likely future background of severe financial restraint and unprecedented technological advance.

For the most part, this book deals with aspects of education and music that are not usually given prominence in educational writing. The beliefs and emphases put forward are the result of experience combined with observation and intuition and therefore represent a personal view of education and music and their inter-relationship. I have always been suspicious of educational rationales for music because, whenever I have tested relevant educational theory and dogma against my own musical intuition, I have frequently found that my musical intuition of what is educationally right has clashed with current educational reasoning of what is musically right. I make no apology for having followed, over some twenty years, my own musical intuitions on this matter for, having been privileged to observe the astonishingly beneficial effects that real musical achievement can have on the personal development of young people, I am convinced that music is too powerful a subject to compromise its individuality to educational theory. If the teaching of music is approached with the kind of expertise that is usually considered essential for the teaching of science and humanity subjects, and if challenging opportunities are presented to children who have been encouraged to avail themselves of that expertise, it is possible to reach that ultimate discovery that music is in fact about something more than music — about idealism, sharing, truth-seeking, and humanity.

This book is not, therefore, another treatise on musical method, nor is it another attempt to prove the importance of music in education. I do not believe it is possible to prove, other than empirically, the veracity of any educational rationale and, in any case, music — of all subjects within education — should, by virtue of its results, be its own best advocate. What I do believe is that it is possible for education to provide musical opportunities that can have a profound influence on many people's lives. I also believe that education has the power either to elevate or undermine the status and appreciation of musical art today. Rather than set out to analyse educational processes in music that can, ultimately, be subject only to empirical judgements, I have preferred to examine the historical and cultural practices that have determined our present attitudes to music and its place in education.

In Part One I have examined, historically, the interaction between education and music in their relationship to the development of European culture. From this I have attempted to establish criteria for aims that have some historical and cultural significance, if not validity. In Part Two, I have attempted to analyse the intrinsic nature of European art music, the problems that this has presented to musical artists in the twentieth century and the cultural benefits and problems arising from the perpetuation of Western art music in a predominantly multi-cultural society. From this I have attempted to establish musical objectives that, again, may have some historical and cultural significance. Part Three is the essential core of the book. In it I have examined aspects of current practice and have suggested the kinds of priorities in relation to resources that may assist with the realization of the aims and objectives outlined.

This book is addressed to general educators, music educators, and general musicians alike. One of the greatest handicaps facing education in the arts today is the misunderstanding among many general educators of the essential purpose of art. There is a corresponding ignorance among many professional artists of the nature of education and the problems it faces. Among musicians themselves, the very distance between the most complex educational problems and the most complex musical problems has tended to isolate musical performers from music teachers. The professional musician tends to be nervous of institutionalized education because he senses that its musical objectives are far removed from what he knows and understands to represent the living world of music. The professional music teacher is sometimes nervous of approaching the world of professional music if he senses that it involves knowledge and skills that outreach his more limited musical objectives within education. This book attempts to reconcile these disparities by approaching the subjects of education and music separately, and by insisting on the value of education as an *enabler* and of music as a source of *artistic* experience.

Although this book is intended to be read sequentially, readers with specific interests or limited time may wish to skip certain chapters. Most chapters can stand on their own, as can Part Three, particularly if taken in conjunction with Chapters 4 and 8. Some general educators could find Chapters 6 and 7 heavy going (though no more so than would a mathematically-ignorant musician facing a simple treatise on computer technology). Some may consider Chapters 1 to 3 as being of only peripheral significance to the issues facing educational institutions today. As, however, one purpose of this book is to counter the modern tendency to look straight for teaching methods before considering aims and objectives in the light of a sound knowledge of the subject itself, I hope that general educators and musicians alike may persevere with the more specialized parts of the book.

I should like to thank the Leicestershire Education Committee for allowing me a sabbatical term during Autumn 1982 and the Education Department of Exeter University for receiving me as an Honorary Research Fellow during that period. I should also like to thank the countless colleagues and students who have influenced and rejuvenated my thinking and understanding over the years. In particular, I should like to thank my colleague, Peter Easton, for patiently and painstakingly talking through this project with me and so helping me to clarify my own objectives in undertaking it; and I should also, as ever, like to thank the composer, Douglas Young, for constantly stimulating my musical thinking, as well as for making some valuable suggestions. Naturally, all confusions and errors remain my own. Finally, I should like to thank Sheila Norman for accepting the additional strain of typing much of the first draft and Shelley Anderson for undertaking the typing of the final version.

Peter Fletcher

CONTENTS

INTRODUCTION

> The growing paralysis of musical pedagogy, the
> ever widening gap between school music and the
> living art, explains why the musical side of Greek
> education, which had once been one of its really
> original and attractive features, gradually declined
> during Hellenistic times.[1]
>
> H. I. Marrou, *A History of Education in Antiquity*

Music education is approaching a state of crisis. This is a paradox,
for it has travelled a long way over the past twenty-five years. It has
increased its resources, improved its techniques and raised its
standards. Yet crisis looms; and it is not so much financial as
conceptual. It is an identity crisis.

Music in schools has become increasingly removed from music
outside schools. This is because the majority of school music takes
place in a classroom, and the sounds made by up to thirty
unselected children in a classroom tend to bear little resemblance to
sounds made anywhere else. They offer stark contrast to the sounds
made by the best of our youth orchestras, choirs, jazz orchestras,
and other ensembles, which show a sure dedication to standards,
eclecticism of taste, and awareness of the wider social context of
music. The difference between what educators refer to as the
curricular and extra-curricular aspects of music is not just one of
kind or even objective: it represents a fundamental clash between
the natural needs of music and the extenuating claims of education.

It is only in recent years that the word 'education' has been used
as a suffix to subject disciplines, and it has usually been added to
those subjects whose very nature makes precise definitions of aims
and objectives difficult. When we talk about 'education in music'
we simply mean that music of some kind will be taught, regardless
of where, by whom, and in what sized groups. However, when we
talk about 'music in education', we mean something very different:
we mean that music has a role to play in the educative process. The
term implies no assertion of roles: it simply implies that music has
an identity quite separate from that of education and that it has a

place in education without being subservient to it. But once we remove the vital preposition 'in', there is an immediate implication that music has been subsumed by education, that 'music education' has become a separate discipline with its own set of theories and objectives, capable of alienation from the practice of living music. Failure to distinguish between purely educational and purely musical components has resulted in serious confusion over aims and objectives in music education.

Aims themselves can be very difficult to define. It is relatively easy to describe, at least in terms of external factors, what *musical ability* does for people; it is very much harder to describe, in terms of external or internal factors, what a *love of music* does for people — or, indeed, why it should be encouraged to go on doing it. It is harder still to describe *why* some people should react to music so much more emotionally than others, and *why* these reactions should involve such a wide variety of style and expression. There have been attempts to do this but they have generally been inconclusive. Empirically, the purpose of music is clear — at least to sensitive souls; rationally, it remains elusive.

Music communicates in a way that is unique to itself. It can, and frequently does, function at a purely decorative level. But when its effect is cathartic, expressive of some deep psychological truth, it is one that can be achieved by no other means than music. This effect may be manifest spiritually or physically and it may be individual or collective: either way, it is essentially musical. Musical experience is its own description; words only confuse the issue. Words can describe predictive external causes, such as the social ambience and the style of the music. But words cannot describe the value of musical experience. Musical experience, too, is its own evaluation. The power of music is essentially irrational.

Yet because man has always shown a natural inclination to explain the irrational, to replace mystery with certainty, words have been written. Indeed, throughout its whole history, music has been a cause for endless and sometimes mind-boggling rationalization. This constant need for explanation has betrayed both recognition and fear of music's primordial power. It has also caused a gulf between musical theory and practice that has never been satisfactorily bridged.

The ancient Greeks believed that music was the primary influence on the soul and that the arithmetical proportions inherent in the harmonic series provided a vital link between science and aesthetics, mind and spirit. They therefore speculated that the proportions of musical intervals provided the basis upon which the universe was constructed. Musical practice and musical theory were therefore naturally regarded as two quite separate disciplines, to be taught by different people in different places. In general this belief and practice continued with little change until the end of the sixteenth century AD.

It took the Copernican revolution finally to discredit the Classical theory of musical astronomy, while Protestantism, a by-product of it, lent a new slant to the theory of musical ethics. During the seventeenth century, musical theorists began to speculate on the 'affectations' rather than the 'morality' that music could bring to the mind and spirit. Musical philosophy passed from church to university, while academies sprung up all over Europe to provide instruction in practical arts. In Britain, the *moral* role of education was eventually assumed by the Nonconformist church, whose prescription of the hymn as a simple and direct means of Christian unity ensured that this limited form of music would become an important part of education. It was only by the beginning of the twentieth century that music, *per se*, became a fundamental part of 'collective' education. There it retained its 'moral' overtones until the heyday of the Beatles, when musical theorists and educators were propelled into neo-Platonic discussion on the power of different modes of music to ennoble or corrupt the character. For the first time in the history of music, the Dionysians won the day and pop music entered school, eclipsing residual notions of music as a moral force and, at the same time, battering the rational Apollonian tradition of great art as the bequest of great minds and souls. The flood-gates were open for music to become a powerful source of social and cultural collision.

Since the advent of television, the sources of our musical awareness have increased greatly, throwing an entirely new perspective on that small part of Europe which had hitherto so largely conditioned it. Few people are unaware of the variety of musics with which we are beset, from didgeridoos to computer-controlled synthesizers, though few are aware that they tend to have very different functions and associations. Education has become a natural depository for these often conflicting musical functions and has responded by throwing them all into the same melting-pot. The results can be seen in many classrooms throughout the land: ill-digested facts, poorly-acquired skills, bored children, and, often, desperate teachers. Outside the classroom, it is still not impossible to hear steel bands thundering out 'Swan Lake' while bands of recorders pipe the 'Jamaican Rumba', or choirs regurgitating cant, imitation jazz, while ill-assorted orchestras churn out 'Hymn of Joy' — the received tradition.

The received tradition itself has been decried by many as a symbol of artistic 'elitism'. For the moral notion lingers still: music *must* be good for *everyone*: therefore it must be given to everyone. The need to popularize (and, in the process, to trivialize) the classical musical tradition is evident in our current concert life, much of which represents a mere travesty of 'art', as it succumbs to the social and financial pressures of a materialist society in which good PR can count for more than intrinsic worth. Concerts all too often require 'personalities' to ensure good ticket sales while new music is frequently avoided or chosen because of some temporary cult status that publicists can attach to a particular composer or circumstance. Like music in education, art music is approaching a state of crisis.

Because musical values have been largely subsumed by educational values, education has faced an unprecedentedly difficult task in sorting out its musical priorities. It has increasingly seen the received musical tradition (from Europe) as a threat to its obligation to be 'whole'; it has often bowed unreasonably to musical pop culture in its desire to be 'egalitarian'; it has generally accepted (and inevitably Europeanized) foreign musical cultures in its desire to be 'multi-cultural'. In attempting to dilute the European tradition, foreign styles have often been accepted without a proper understanding of the traditions from which they grew. In its determination to ensure that the mechanical processes of music are not pursued at the expense of development of the senses and understanding, it has even tended to abjure the one outstanding — if regionally uneven — achievement of the post-war years: providing *opportunity* for acquiring instrumental skills for *all* children, regardless of cultural background or financial circumstance.

It is of course entirely appropriate — and apposite to the general aims of education — that the mind should be educated in any subject before, or at least concurrently with, the inculcation of related skills. Over many years, there has been a growing sense of the inadequacy of instrumental lessons *per se*, partly because of egalitarian considerations and partly because they have often seemed to stress the importance of skill acquisition at the expense of musical imagination. Consequently, instrumental instruction has come to be regarded by some educators as an élitist activity, opposite to the general aims of education. For such people, the school classroom has come to be regarded as the principal means whereby training in the mechanical processes of music, and education in musical understanding and sensibility can be brought into an organic relationship.

As a result of this, the past fifteen years have witnessed a substantial body of research into methodology in the secondary school classroom. This research has provided some imaginative ideas on curriculum content and organization, which will prove very helpful to imaginative, if harassed, teachers regularly facing large classes of potentially uninterested children. There has also been an outpouring of research on the nature of aesthetic experience, intended to justify the place of music in schools. Much of all this research, however, has ignored the simple fact that, for all the motivation and support that the classroom can provide, the detailed mechanical processes involved in the playing of keyboard and orchestral instruments cannot be taught in the classroom — certainly not if good playing habits are to be developed. Consequently, the wider issues of the nature of musical ability, the place of music in society, and the role of education in music have been relatively neglected in this research, while the classroom has assumed an importance out of all proportion to its usefulness.

Perhaps we have expected too much of education and even of music education itself. When comprehensive education became widespread, it was confidently assumed that it could act as a social leavener; that it could provide equal opportunities for all, raise the standards of the less able through the general mix of ability, and continue improving standards at the top. The theory was and still is fine, but it outstripped the ability of many teachers to practise it. Few teachers are equally successful at stimulating the less able and teaching their subject to the highest standard. In many cases, teachers who had been secure in more academic teaching have become insecure when faced with the less able. Conversely, those able and experienced in teaching the less able have sometimes overestimated their ability to teach to the highest standards and undervalued the importance of this activity. It was similarly assumed that, through music education, child-centred musical techniques could bring meaningful experiences to all, developing imagination and a new awareness of sound. Again, the theory was and still is fine, but it has outstripped the ability of many teachers to practise it. Those who had been successful in bringing out the musically motivated have not necessarily proved good at engaging the unmotivated.

These issues have important implications within education, because they bear upon some of its cherished concepts. They challenge its subsuming nature. It is of crucial importance to music that its own special issues be detached from educational issues, in order that the two may be linked co-operatively rather than sealed in mutual conflict. It will then be seen that there is a place for the aesthetic approach to music in the classroom as well as for the exercise of real musical expertise outside the classroom. Should professional instruction in instrumental and vocal skills disappear, music in schools would become moribund. The music teacher who says 'Of course, the real music takes place *outside* the classroom' should not have to hang his head in shame. He may simply be indicating a natural preference, quite possibly shared by his pupils, for the living world of music rather than the pedagogy of the classroom.

We need to put *real* opportunities before all our children. Equality of *opportunity* is fundamental. Should the aesthetic, classroom argument subsume the musical argument, there will be no equality of opportunity. The opportunity to practise the living art of music will become the preserve of the privileged rich, while professionally competent and sensitive teachers will be banned from schools in favour of those whose mediocrity will prove equal to the mediocre sounds that will assault the ears. And then, as H. I. Marrou said of Hellenistic education, 'the growing paralysis of musical pedagogy and the ever widening gap between school music and the living art will cause the musical side of school, once one of its really original and attractive features, to decline.'

PART ONE

AIMS — The Educational Background

1

The Greek Legacy

It is a commonplace to say that European civilization (and therefore American too) has three roots,
Greek, Roman and Judaeo-Christian. But it has
become a commonplace because it is so obviously
true.[1]

M. I. Finley, *Aspects of Antiquity*

'Then what will this education be like?' asked Plato of Classical
Greek elementary education, 'for it seems difficult to discover a
better one than that which our forefathers adopted — gymnastics for
the body and "music" for the soul.'[2] Plato's reference to gymnastics
reflected the Archaic Greek belief in the 'moral' attributes of a fully
developed physique in which beauty and strength combine. His
reference to 'music' (of the Muses — the Goddesses of poetry and
music, dance and theatre) represented the same 'moral' element in
Greek culture, subsuming the artistic, the spiritual, and the intellectual. This notion of the 'whole man' whose physical beauty is
moral and whose morality is beautiful — 'a sound mind in a sound
body', as a more utilitarian Latin poet put it — was central to the
Greek, humanistic ideal, even after Hellenistic 'school' education
had incorporated rhetoric, logic, and other 'useful' arts. It arose
from the Archaic belief in the importance of valour — a highly
competitive concept requiring appropriate education of mind and
body, to produce a complete, well-rounded, and virtuous personality. When a recent government paper on curriculum set out a list
of educational aims 'related to development of mind, body and
spirit' incorporating the 'acquisition of knowledge, skills and
understanding'[3] it would seem to have been proselytizing a creed
very similar to that adopted by the Greeks.

The genius of Greek culture lay in its ability to separate and
rationalize the attributes of mind, body, and spirit in relation to the
acquisition of knowledge, skill, and understanding. Culture is
shaped, to a large extent, by the extent to which human action and
psychic development are conditioned by concept or precept, reason

3

or revelation. The ancient Greeks were unique in the importance they attached to the reasoning of concepts rather than the revealing of precepts. This ability to take a detached viewpoint, to pit one theory against another, was the thing that marked and elevated Greek culture above that of other Mediterranean civilizations; and it is this aspect, more than any other, that justifies a hard and serious investigation into our cultural roots.

The Greeks had a highly developed sense of *aisthēsis* (perception through the senses). Their appreciation of beauty was intense and they attached great importance to it. Devotion to the study of the Muses became a principal means of escaping the clutches of Hades for the astral spheres of the Elysian Fields. Supreme happiness was thus identified with the artist or man of letters. To the Greeks, beauty lay ultimately in man himself, with the physical and mental aspects as one. Throughout the Archaic period the Greeks had carved *kouroi*, statues of young men, recognizably Greek, but clearly betraying Egyptian origins. They were carved to a traditional formula by artisans whose work was called *technē*: art in the sense of skill or cunning, the work of a professional. By the end of the sixth century BC, the new Greek questioning spirit was applied to the *technē* of sculpture. Should sculpture not aspire to imitate the physical and moral beauty of man? For the first time in the history of Western 'art', it was recognized that its essence would lie in its relationship with the reality of nature. If perfect man was the supreme revelation of beauty, the Greeks argued, and if the attainment of beauty was the path to divine favour, art's logical response should surely be to represent man's *beauty* in idealistic form, thereby imitating the perfection of the Gods. The new artistic element that made possible the idealized statues of the Parthenon friezes, where Gods are indistinguishable from men, was *mimēsis*: a borrowing from, or mirroring of nature, for artistic purposes. Classical Greek sculpture presented heroic man in characterful poses and states of muscular stress, but personal individuality of expression was negated in the common portrayal of the ideal. When, in fact, art did become personalized, as the ideal of the city state withered following the Macedonian conquest, sculpture became vulgarized, precisely because it imitated successful man rather than ideal man. *Mimēsis* introduced the problem as to whether art should copy or interpret nature — a problem that is very much still with us.

Music was also subject to *mimēsis*, for the Greeks were musicians more than they were sculptors, architects, or playwrights. The ability to sing to the lyre was a necessity for any young gentleman. From the time of the Trojan war, music had been considered an indispensable comfort to the soul. The numerous 'rational' and sometimes contradictory prescriptions for its use arose from a keen awareness of its irrational power. By the middle of the fifth century BC, Damon of Athens set the tone for future debate when he declared that musical activity arises out of the activity of the soul; it could therefore be beneficial as a 'liberal' art (liberal in the sense of freeborn) in that it could affect the nature favourably or unfavourably. Indeed, changes in musical style were always accompanied by changes in the laws of the state. This kind of notion reflected music's inseparable connection with *ēthos*, for music was considered the primary means of conveying ethical (moral) states of mind. Music was therefore inseparable from education. The conviction that music could thus 'civilize' was enhanced by the observed correspondence between the laws of music and arithmetic.

There was nothing new in the understanding that music embodies numerical principles, for this was common knowledge to civilizations from China to Persia. The characteristic Greek element lay in subjecting the numerical laws of music to rational enquiry. It was this enquiry that gave music such close and long-lasting astronomical connections. It was also the basis for Plato's rationalization of music as an ethnic agent, that the character of the various musical modes, and the words that were inevitably associated with them, could be made to represent the character of the various Greek tribes. *Mousikē* combined the moral function of *ēthos* with the artistic function of the muses and thus incorporated what to the Greeks were the two all-important aspects of beauty — itself the basic preparation for divine favour. The *ēthos* of music was totally educational. The actual *practice* of music, divorced from arcane theory, lay *outside* education.

Education, until the latter part of the Classical period, was not 'collective'. It was individual, aristocratic, all male, and reflected the cultural concepts of valour and beauty. It was based on a loving relationship between master and pupil which caused the pupil to spare no effort in the emulation of his master and the master to spare no effort in setting the best possible example to his pupil,

in keeping with the high nature of his 'calling'. This highly
personal practice of 'education' was consistent with the notion of
'beauty' as the fount of divine commendation. Education and
pupil-teacher relationship, in this case, were synonymous and were
voluntary rather than prescribed. The aristocratic view that education should be reserved for those who were thought best able to
profit from it — or, more fundamentally, that inequality of
opportunity preserves arisocratic privilege — has many resonances
in British educational history of the past hundred years, which are
still by no means silent.

Democratization of education came to Classical Greece during
the fifth century BC, largely due to the democratization of the
gymnasium, formerly reserved for the aristocracy. Aristophanes
mourned the passing of the old education, with its basis in athletics
and music, and described the way the boys walked 'quietly and
decorously through the streets to their music master', where they
learnt the old songs by heart, singing them to the traditional tunes,
and not doing 'anything disreputable such as putting in chromatic
bits, all tied up in knots' — on pain of 'being given six of the best for
insulting the muses'.[4] The 'disreputable putting in of chromatic
bits' referred to the new style of music being pioneered by famous
composers like Timotheus of Miletus. These composers had found
a new function for music in the mastery of new and elaborate
instruments and the display of technical virtuosity. In order to
create music capable of containing such virtuosity, they were
obliged to reach beyond previously accepted constraints of harmony and rhythm. Thus, at the same time as sculpture was being
personalized, music was also becoming a means of personal
expression and, as was to happen in later times, was removing itself
from the centre to the periphery of human affairs. Musical 'artists',
combining former concepts of *techne* and *mimesis*, were pressing for
artistic innovations that statesmen preferred to ignore. It was
difficult for music to continue to occupy its traditional role as a
general moral force at the centre of education when its essential
stability was being challenged by forms that placed it among a
specialist élite. This conflict between the moral ideal and the
inherent competitiveness of personal endeavour lies at the very
heart of the 'art' process of modern times. It is embodied in the
notion of professionalism and is still a potential source of confusion
within education.

Simultaneously with these technical musical innovations, a new conflict was emerging in education, provoked initially by the Sophists. The Sophists were itinerant teachers and, because they taught for money rather than love, were the first professional educators. What they taught was neither arcane nor speculative but highly functional: how to get on in life. They were the progenitors of rhetoric, that form of public oratory which aims to *persuade* people of the truth of what is being said rather than to *seek* the truth itself. This skill has provided both means and justification for political duplicity ever since.

As a result of the Sophists and the arguments they aroused with Socratic philosophers, primary and secondary schools were formalized in the Hellenistic era of the fourth century BC. Educators were then faced with three fundamental problems that haunt us still. Firstly, as educational availability begins to extend from the higher to the lower orders, should it be assumed that the lower orders should aspire to the knowledge and skills of the higher orders? This question has obvious political overtones. Secondly, as the cult of professionalism tends not only to create an élite but to detract from the essence of the core, to what extent should it be the province of education? Thirdly, if education concentrates too exclusively on the production of the broadly-educated, well-rounded citizen, is there not a danger of producing superficiality and dilettantism? Conversely, if education concentrates too greatly on utilitarian sciences — the skills that the state needs and that provide citizens with an income — might this not lead to the creation of narrow-minded, selfish, and unworthy citizens? This latter point was largely proved by the utilitarian-minded Romans and is in danger of being proved again at this very time.

It says much for the Greeks that they were keenly aware of these fundamental problems over 2,200 years before us, and that they argued them with compassion, dignity, and candour while keeping open minds on the subjects. Nevertheless, it would be a mistake to carry comparisons too far. Greek education was 'collective' and democratic only in the sense that it was fundamentally provided for the children of freeborn ('liberal') men. For all the reasoning of the philosophers, Greek culture remained predominantly athletic rather than intellectual and often brutally so. Until the Romans finally annexed Greece in the second century BC, it also remained artistic rather than bookish. (The literary influence on education

came from monotheistic religions, by nature religions of the book.)
Greek philosophers turned their speculations into dramatic dia-
logue, just as playwrights concerned themselves with the burning
issues of the day, happily involving the Gods in justification of their
judgements. The competitive spirit, deriving from military
valour, remained a part of Greek culture. The festivals of music and
theatre in honour of Dionysus were competitive, and winners were
keen to erect stone epitaphs to their victories, to remind the Gods
of their artistic pre-eminence. Athletics were also fiercely competitive and became the more so as professionalism in all *technai*
developed. The specialized virtuosity that professionalism provoked was found incompatible with education. While technical
skills were taught *outside* school, the business of education became
more literary and intellectual. Schools (*scholē* = leisure) enabled the
aristocratic class to respond to the challenge of devoting leisure to
useful learning. They created an intellectual élite and were not
concerned with *practical* education in athletics or arts.

The genius — and the ultimate undoing — of the Greeks lay in the
fact that, as a group of city states, always quarrelsome, they never
attempted to remedy their recurrent problems by adherence to a
single theory. Where Plato had looked to an idealized education
based on rational truth, his pupil Aristotle, teacher of Alexander the
Great, perceived the need for a limited democracy. To Artistotle,
the purpose of education was first and foremost political, in the
sense of producing the ideal statesman and citizen. It should not, he
held, compete with artistic professionalism but provide only as
much technique as is needed to develop taste. Music is therefore no
longer to be at the core of the curriculum but is to be regarded as an
ancillary subject. In this way, Aristotle was able to rationalize the
point that the ideal statesman should still be a broadly-educated
person.

Such well-composed answers to perennial questions were no
more complete then than now. Throughout the Hellenistic period,
the Greeks appeared ambivalent in their approach to education,
alternating between the idea of education in the round as a
humanizing process and the idea of it as a specific preparation of the
mind for higher learning. Essentially, however, education came to
comprise the seven liberal arts which were at the root of Plato's
thinking, first clearly formulated in the first century BC, and subsequently taken up during the Carolingian renaissance and through

to the Middle Ages. They comprised three literary arts (the *trivium*): grammar, rhetoric, and dialectic; and four branches of mathematics (the *quadrivium*): geometry, arithmetic, astronomy, and music theory. The notion of Arts and Science and indeed of the Liberal Arts themselves still obtains today: it is the basis of much university education (particularly in North America) and it has necessarily influenced school education in the need to prepare for it.

The role of music within the liberal arts has remained as ambivalent as it was before the Roman Empire put a temporary stop to education in practical music. Theoretically, music provided vital links with astronomy and moral education. Yet the *practice* of music was indispensable for public occasions and, despite the growing professionalism of musical performance, it was common for choirs of boys to take part in the public festivals that played such a large part in the school calendar. However, the music performed was relatively simple and the teaching of it would not have encroached too greatly on the school curriculum.

The similarities between ancient Greek and modern British social, educational, and musical problems are too great to be coincidental. Much of the importance of historical scrutiny lies in the establishing of the universality or novelty of current concerns. The ancient Greeks may seem very remote from the pressures of modern education and musical practice and, indeed, we know very little of the actual music they performed. But the Greeks established the basic archetypes of Western civilization, and it takes some of the freneticism out of current arguments to know that similar arguments preoccupied our cultural forefathers over two thousand years ago. Above all, liberal education was devoted to humanism, the notion of the complete man. Humanism provided the impetus for the European renaissance, to which, despite the 'global village' in which we live and work, we are still the confused heirs. H. I. Marrou, has shrewdly and pertinently summed up the merits and dangers of the classical legacy:

The historical conditions of the period . . . did not really know what to do with the admirable human capital with which it had thus been so well provided . . . Classical education provided the *materia prima* for a higher human type than had hitherto been known, a type capable of anything — if only it could have found something, or someone, to devote itself to. When it failed to do this . . . classical humanism turned inwards in search of an immanent perfection and became absorbed in egoistic, aesthetic contemplation, which may well seem frivolous and futile to people who belong to a more severe or more ambitious culture . . .[5]

An introverted concern with conventional educational resourcing and method in schools and institutions of higher education has often blinded educators to the essential aim of providing that something or someone to whom the educated young can devote themselves. Consequently, adolescent energies become channelled into political, physical, or elementally destructive allegiances which can be opposite to the prescribed values of education. Indeed, education can even feel obliged to alter its values in recognition of these allegiances rather than to alter its structure and philosophy to minimize their basically anarchical motivation. Music is just one of many potent activities which can help to accommodate over-abundant emotional energy deriving from the discord between educational and real-life perceptions. Whenever institutional educators become over-absorbed in the definition and justification of their role, and whenever 'arts educators' become over-absorbed in 'egoistic aesthetic contemplation' — as is so often the case today — they become blinkered to the resource requirements of life outside, to which their institutions should fundamentally be aimed. Tempered by modern culture, the humanist ideal of the well-rounded citizen is as important as it ever was. But unless we structure purposeful 'extra-curricular' and 'extra-institutional' activity as an essential objective within an overall humanist aim, the arts in schools could well appear frivolous and futile to the legislators of our more severe and ambitious culture.

2

The Christian Legacy

The noble art of music is, as God declares, the highest of earthly treasures. It rules all thoughts and senses, the heart and the temperament. Do you want to comfort the troubled, to tame the impudent and wild into mildness; to soften the arrogant and so on? What could be better for such purposes than this high, dear, worthy, noble art?[1]

Martin Luther

The fundamental change in education resulting from the spread of Christianity in the third and fourth centuries and the subsequent onslaught of 'Barbarianism' was the linking of *moral* with *technical* education. The Greeks of the Hellenistic period had separated moral education from the largely utilitarian education provided by schools, thus establishing 'collective' education as a necessary but lightweight aspect of their culture. The Christians were to link Greek *ēthos* with *technē* and thus make 'collective' education a very touchstone of their culture. As, however, Christian expansion depended upon absorbing the Judaeo-Greek tradition, early adherents used the established form of education to answer only their immediate needs. The blending of their doctrinaire beliefs with the more open-minded philosophy of their pagan inheritance was a gradual process.

We should be as grateful to the harp-playing King David for the preservation of music within the education of early Christian culture as we should be to the music-loving Dionysus for the preservation of music in the education of antiquity. Dionysus had been representative of the triumph of patriarchal over matriarchal society for, as the sacred consort-King, he had avoided ritual death through the assertive power of Zeus, in whose thigh he had been sown to await rebirth. King David's birth was rather less romantic, but his prowess in war was no less supernaturally guided; and his life and personality fitted well with the Greek notion of beautiful

11

hero. More importantly, as bard of the Psalter, his music was endowed with divine powers, to the extent of 'freeing Saul from the unclean spirit by the discipline of the most wholesome melody'. The Christian bard could not, however, be so easily adapted to Roman culture. A severely practical people for whom education ('moral' family education as much as 'technical' school education) was a means of imposing unquestioning obedience to the state, the Romans considered music and dance unbecoming for future senators, allowing it only in small measure for women. Even Brutus' mother was accused of playing the lyre 'rather better than one would expect for a decent woman'.[2] We should therefore show some gratitude to the Christians for absorbing the Greek ethical and cosmic view of music, whereby it could 'make men out of stone and out of wild beasts' and revive those 'who were otherwise dead, having no share in the real and true life'.[3]

The Emperor Constantine's adoption of Christianity in 310 and his subsequent transformation of Byzantium into Constantinople caused a political split between the Christians of the East and West. Henceforth, the Roman Empire would be Christian and Constantinople would be its base. The Byzantines, under Emperors whose will was easily equated with that of God's and whose equality with God was made apparent to all in mosaic murals, were highly selective in what they took from Classical culture. They retained the existing school education for the training of bureaucrats, but for training in Christianity they established monastic schools which were ascetic in outlook and essentially for biblical study.

By contrast, in the western part of the Empire, the increasingly chaotic Roman administration and the constant threat of Barbarian attack caused Christian doctrine to become integrated with Classical education. As living became more difficult and unpleasant, a religion aimed at subordinating this life to some supernatural intent made more and more sense — religions are seldom adopted without cause. As Christianity increasingly immersed itself in philosophical speculation, it provoked the need for a rationale — a theology. In the process of acquiring one, it absorbed a surprising amount of pagan belief. This coalition through education of Christian and pagan interests survived until the fifth century, when 'Barbarianism' effectively destroyed Classical education. Only then did it become necessary for Christians to establish schools to meet specifically Christian needs.

Christianity needed priests who were literate and who could sing; and literacy meant knowledge of Latin, for the Christians of the West adopted the language of their imperial past, right through to the Reformation. It also needed articulate apologists. The sack of Rome in 410 had shaken the confidence of Christianity in the West. It was gradually rekindled by such works as St Augustine of Hippo's *The City of God*. This treatise, which was to become the favourite of the first Holy Roman Emperor, Charlemagne, was one of the many tracts suggesting means by which the ills of this life might be tolerated in justification for the next — the kind of thinking that naturally encouraged aestheticism and monasticism. The monastic tradition, started by St Benedict in Italy, enabled the Christian-Classical tradition to survive the Dark Ages. As the focus of monastic life was the reading and singing of scripture and the Holy Office, the teaching of literacy (Latin grammar) — and singing — became the fundamental aim of monastic schooling.

This type of education gradually spread from the monasteries to secular life. In 529 the Second Council of Vaison required 'all parish priests to gather some boys round them as *lectors*, so that they might give them a Christian upbringing, teach them the psalms and lessons of scripture and so prepare worthy successors to themselves'.[4] Episcopal schools, attached to a cathedral, began to apprentice young boys to the clerical life as *lectors* under a *magister*, while even in the humbler parishes, young *lectors* were recruited for singing and subsequently for the priesthood. Music therefore survived at the centre of Christian culture, although stripped of any vigorous flamboyance. The arcane associations given to music by Pythagorus were also kept alive, largely due to two Romans in the service of Theodoric, King of the Ostragoths in the early sixth century. Boethius expounded the Greek point of view, that 'music is related to us by nature and can ennoble or corrupt the character',[5] whereas Cassiodorus expounded the Christian point of view, that 'if we live virtuously, we are constantly proved to be under music's discipline, whereas if we commit injustice we are without music'.[6] Cassiodorus also described the Platonic modes, though in terms of numerical ratios rather than ethnic associations, paving the way for Pope Gregory's classification of the modes of Christian chant for use by the Church International. Boethius, however, took the Greek view further, and classified three types of music: *musica mundana* for the ordering of the cosmos, *musica humana* for a healthy body and soul, and *musica instrumentalis* for music that is actually audible. Importantly, he distinguished between art and handicraft, ascribing to art the more honourable role.

The writings of Cassiodorus and Boethius are important because they survived through the Middle Ages into the Renaissance. Boethius actually became the standard text for university reading until the beginning of the seventeenth century. Cassiodorus, however, has a further significance, because he instituted a monastery dedicated to the integration of humanism with biblical study. This created a type of synthesis that would provide a basis for early medieval scientific rationalizing of the relationship between spirituality and beauty. This, in turn, would eventually enable the Church to develop a new style of musical virtuosity which, during the fourteenth century, circumstances would oblige it to pass on to the new *secular* courts.

The twelfth century saw a renaissance of intellectual activity all over Europe. This was the result of Christian conquests over Arabs in Northern Spain which made a wealth of Greek and Arab learning newly available. Classical authors provided a basis and new importance for canon and civil law. In particular, the metaphysical and cosmological works of Aristotle, hitherto known only through the works of Boethius, stimulated a vast structure of scholastic and theological thought and created a definitive synthesis between Classical concepts and Christian precepts. As with the Greeks, God became synonymous with beauty, and it was argued that this type of beauty could only be achieved if the senses were touched by beautiful and precious things. 'The dull mind rises to truth through that which is beautiful',[7] wrote the great Abbot Suger of Saint Denis, inventor of the pointed arches and high windows that were to become the glory of Gothic architecture. This worship of beauty was to provide justification for the wholesale looting of precious objects by the West, from the military acquisitions of the Crusades, to the later archaeological acquisition of the Parthenon marbles.

The frenetic creation and appropriation of artefacts was the result of a fundamental concern for theory. So was the evolution of musical counterpoint. Theory came before fact. Greek science had been based upon observation. Medieval Christians, tied to their belief in a single perfect Godhead, appreciated none of the lively curiosity that had been the genius of Greece. The art of music was considerably elaborated but it was theoretically inspired — and justified. There was endless debate over the merits of perfect and imperfect numbers — the metaphysical superiority of three over two in relation to the Trinity. New complexities in ecclesiastical music resulted more from accurate systems of notation than from delight in the actual sound. Only in the last third of the thirteenth century did Franco of Cologne's *Ars cantus mensurabilis* attempt to reconcile a fully rational theory with current practice so that, by the fourteenth century, what was *sung* could actually influence what was *written*.

The new, disputatious form of ecclesiastical scholarship was hardly suited to the quiet life of Benedictine monasteries. Famous teachers, therefore, became itinerant, settling upon lively cathedrals and making these, rather than the monasteries, the centres for advanced learning. The episcopal centres of Paris and Bologna created the first self-governing universities. In England, Oxford and Cambridge developed schools of higher learning. Although the statutes of these two universities encouraged the practice of music in order to keep up a flow of religious services, musical study remained essentially scientific — based on arithmetic and astronomy — and degrees in music were not established until the mid-fifteenth century.

Following the Norman Conquest, some English cathedrals were reconstituted with chapters of secular canons, among which a *scholasticus* was responsible for running a school. These became the prototypes of future grammar schools for, in 1179, Episcopal responsibility for education was passed to the secular chapters and subsequently to every parish church of adequate means, in order to provide a schoolmaster to teach 'the clerks of that church and poor scholars freely'.[8] Naturally, the basis of such teaching was Latin grammar and singing. Any other form of education was only available privately and it existed not for any *ethical* value but to provide scribes for the court. Latin was the common bond of literacy, French the vernacular of the aristocracy. The Black Death of 1348–9 encouraged a growth in grammar schools to provide a regular supply of trained priests. William of Wykeham inaugurated the notion of educational philanthropy by founding a College and grammar school in his cathedral town of Winchester in 1382. This was followed later with Henry VI's foundation of Eton in 1440. Thereafter, philanthropic support for grammar schools became common among the merchant guilds of the late fifteenth century.

and formal gesture rather than with arithmetical proportion and symmetry. Musical astronomy was replaced by musical aesthetics. Music as an art developed *outside* the church and therefore outside institutions of education, for the musical needs of art and the musical needs of a church turned Puritan were to prove very different indeed. In Britain at least, musical art became *for* rather than *of* the gentry and communal performance a matter for 'hoi-polloi'.

'Hoi-polloi' were just what the Nonconformist movement was all about. The Puritan metrical psalters of the seventeenth century had already carried prefaces inducting the common folk into the mysteries of musical notation. The Nonconformists went a great deal further. Emanating from the sleepy torpor of Oxford, John and Charles Wesley with George Whitefield rode their fiery brand of evangelism — methodism was the sarcastic name applied to it — into the fields of the countryside, where they roused the masses of English and Welsh workers to a concern with heaven and hell worthy of the most potent medieval doctrine. Their means of arousing corporate enthusiasm was the hymn, and it was sung to stirring, easily memorable tunes. The rationalization and subordination of this dreadful life to some supernatural purpose rang the same kinds of resonance to the workers of industrial Britain as it had done to the victims of Roman degeneration and as it is doing in some viciously-exploited societies of today.

Corporate education arrived in the late eighteenth century, at least as a socialist concept, on a wave of Christian evangelism. Music arrived with it, not as a moral force in its own right but as a satellite to the religious 'cleansing' of the poor. At the start of the Methodist movement, Isaac Watts had suggested in his 'Divine and Moral Songs in Easy Language for Little Children':

> Tis dangerous to provoke a God!
> His pow'r and vengeance none can tell;
> One stroke of his almighty rod
> Shall send young sinners quick to Hell.[13]

Hannah More, a great pioneer of the Sunday School movement at the end of the eighteenth century, had her children repeat such songs weekly, in order to 'train up the lower classes in habits of industry and piety'.[14] And still, at Christmas, children throughout the land sing: 'Christian children all must be mild, obedient, good as He' — apparently without blinking an eyelid.

The question that vexed the antagonists of corporate state education was the one that had vexed the aristocrats of fourth-century Greece and that has vexed many a government or caste since: does education of the lower orders prejudice the privileged position of the well-to-do? (The events of the French Revolution had stirred particularly uneasy thoughts on the matter.) If such privileges were actually to include the right to salvation, the evangelical Christians could provide an uneasy answer: 'the meek shall inherit the earth.' Christian hypocrisy was hoist with its own petard. The populace had to be educated.

Whatever the poor inherited, they certainly did not inherit the music of the Western post-Renaissance tradition; nor, for that matter, the Classical-Christian tradition upon which it was based. Music might have been, as Martin Luther declared, 'the highest of earthly treasures' but, in the form in which it entered corporate, Christian education, it was considerably less than 'noble'. Music had become 'moral' by association, and its genuinely artistic qualities now lay largely outside the province of church and education. Music would subsequently have the utmost difficulty in establishing its presence in education as an art.

3

The Social Legacy

Those mighty workmen of our later age,
Who, with a broad highway, have overbridged
The forward chaos of futurity,
Tamed to their bidding; they who have the art
to manage books, and things, and make them work
Gently on infant minds, as does the sun
Upon a flower; the tutors of our youth . . .
Sages who in their prescience would control
All accidents, and to the very road
Which they have fashioned would confine us down,
Like engines; when will they be taught
That in the unreasoning progress of the world
A wiser spirit is at work for us,
A better eye than theirs, most prodigal
Of blessings, and most studious of our good,
Even in what seem our most unfruitful hours?

William Wordsworth,
The Prelude, Book V, 370–88 (1805–6)

In 1833, the British Government voted a sum of £20,000 for
education. This slender gratuity was made not for the founding of a
state system of education, nor even out of any great desire to create
a literate nation. It was a minimal response to the success of
voluntary efforts at educating the poor, first by the Nonconformists and then, of necessity, by the Church of England. The
'National Society for Promoting the Education of the Poor in the
Principles of the Established Church', founded in 1811, was a self-
defensive reaction by the Church of England to the remarkable
success of a Quaker, Joseph Lancaster, in attempting to make
'arrangements for the education of every poor child in the kingdom
at a very trifling expense to the public'.[1] The non-denominational
response to the Church of England's 'National Society' was to set
up its own 'British and Foreign Schools Society' in 1814. Both

20

societies operated the 'monitorial' system whereby children aged ten or eleven acted like drill sergeants to groups of ten or twenty other children, under the stern gaze of a single schoolmaster. Neither Society had ambitions to upset or even improve the palpably unjust social order. Each was concerned to teach working people, through its respective brand of devotion and piety, to accept the humble station which God had provided for them — to 'train them to the habits of virtue and industry', as the St Marylebone Day School of Industry expressed it. The first government grant to education was distributed through these two societies.

The needs of the poor were almost beyond description. The population of the industrial towns had more than doubled during the last half of the eighteenth century. Canals, cotton mills, iron foundries, and, later, coal mines and railways, caused new social groupings, destroying the traditional, rural way of life, characterized by the local squire, parson, poor law overseer, and schoolmaster. Exploitation of child labour — even the 'child market' — was commonplace; so, inevitably, was child crime. Poverty was rampant. Education — Christian education — was seen as a means of reducing crime while retaining work pressure. Education then became a national issue. In the process, it took to itself social and political criteria that had never before been its concern. Education's social brief continues to cloud a whole range of curricular issues. The historical fact of ruthless class exploitation in nineteenth-century Britain digs deep into our social fabric and presents us with educational problems, born of tradition, that are largely unknown in North America. As education has become a prime social factor in the politics of post-war Britain, the Greek legacy, the Christian legacy, and the social legacy have often become locked in seemingly irreconcilable conflict.

The situation in the first half of the nineteenth century was complicated by the fact that Dr James Kay, Secretary to the Government's 1839 Committee to supervise national education and the leading protagonist of educational reform, was made to appear to act for the wrong reasons. Having recommended the appointment of School Inspectors, he was obliged, in deference to the apprehension of the Church of England, to concede that their appointment should be subject to the approval of the Archbishops. For the same reason, his proposal to start a Training College for

teachers was turned down, and the first such college was inaugurated, not by the state, but by virtue of Kay's own philanthropy.
Singing in schools had to be justified for its 'civilizing' influence
and for its indispensability to public worship, rather than for any
intrinsic artistic merit. The prescribed syllabus for state schools had
to be fundamentally utilitarian, whereas the grammar schools were
actually encouraged to 'teach grammatically the learned languages'
as Dr Johnson had put it. Against such a background, it is little
wonder that music — on the one hand a complex museum culture
of a past (and largely foreign) élite, on the other hand a recondite
vehicle for working class relaxation, and on neither hand a dialectical living art — should have experienced such difficulty in finding a
consistent and purposeful role within education.

Nevertheless, music was to become a major activity in state
education by the latter half of the nineteenth century. Thanks again
to the unsparing efforts of Dr Kay, this time in promulgating
singing teaching methods culminating in the sanctioning of John
Curwen's Tonic Sol-fa method, singing became a 'mania' in state
schools. And not just in schools: vast choral festivals were held at
Crystal Palace and St Pauls' Cathedral, involving up to 4,000
people singing hymns and excerpts from favourite oratorios. In the
days before radio and the phonograph, singing provided healthy,
even cathartic, relaxation for manual labourers. Mini-Eisteddfodau
would be held during lunch breaks in the depths of the Welsh slate
mines to force the numbed brains of the face-workers into activity.
The mixed choirs of the Nonconformist churches joined together
in vast choral societies for block-busting performances of well-
loved and remembered classics. What the Germans called 'Das
Land ohne Musik' became a land with a great deal of music —
music, that is, of a certain kind, more social than artistic in content.
It would take well over a century for Britain to become an international *artistic* force in the world of music.

The nineteenth-century singing movement succeeded because it
presented, in an unsubtle, heavily directed, musical format, seemingly relevant themes that positively encouraged the cathartic side
of singing. Much has been made of the relative value of the Tonic
Sol-fa systems that were used, but it would seem likely that, then as
now, people worked largely from memory. If they succeeded at
singing it was because they wanted to. (I have personally worked
with Yorkshire singers who knew their complete vocal line of

Messiah from memory yet could not read a note of music.) Communal singing can provoke, in an almost supernatural way, a sense of community spirit and unity — a fact of which the evangelical reformers were well aware. The prerequisites for this are words apposite to the *sentiment* of the singers, simple and strong tunes, direct and emotional harmonies — and a compulsive desire to sing. In the last century, this combination of circumstances could be found in a variety of physical and social surrounds, from state schools to work-sites and from chapels to public schools to outdoor revivalist meetings. (It was to be found less in the Established Church, which still retained a certain kind of faded 'artistic' decorum.) The appetite for singing in state schools remained alive long after the awesome moral songs of Dr Watts were replaced by songs of gentler innocence. (When the 1870 Education Act, which made elementary education *possible* for all, omitted to ensure a place for singing on the syllabus, there was sufficient public outcry to get the omission rectified at once.) But as the socio-religious factors that provoked 'singing mania' began to alter towards the end of the century, the actual appetite for singing began to dwindle. It still survives in pockets, particularly in the mining valleys of Wales, where village work and domestic life have, until recently, been relatively unsusceptible to change and where, against a tough and ungrateful industrial background, pride in local traditions and a chapel-going community still exist.

For not dissimilar reasons, but at the other end of the social spectrum, communal singing was (and often still is) strong in the private schools we call 'public'. The kind of *esprit de corps* encouraged by 'inter-house' and 'inter-school' sports matches could be endorsed by the lusty singing of spiritual songs in Chapel or chauvinistic songs in competitive vocal events. (As in ancient Greece, these took their place beside competitive sporting events, but lacked the presumed subtlety and artistry that Greek music's endemic link with dance must have provoked.) Again, largely for the same reasons, the community singing tradition can still be encountered at football matches, at boy scout camp-fires, and on buses, the latter usually on the return from some team event and endorsing a kind of chauvinistic cohesion among a social unit about to be dispersed.

One place where the tradition does *not* still linger is the modern secondary classroom, for here the necessary prerequisites do not

obtain. Words that would be appropriate to any *communal* senti-
ments of the pupils would be at curious odds with the Greek,
Christian, and social influences on which educational principles
have come to be formed, and simple tunes and strong harmonies
would need propelling by electronic equipment not usually available or associated with *communal* singing. In other words the
combination of circumstances that made singing such a vital element of nineteenth-century England are as far removed from the
typical modern school classroom as can be. This is not to suggest
that group singing should not or cannot be encouraged and turned
to effect. It is simply to underline the fact that the social causes that
made it possible in the nineteenth century have largely — and
thankfully — disappeared, and that very different forms of motivation and very different objectives will be necessary today. When
'music educators' blame instrumental work for the demise of choral
singing, they blame the wrong thing.

Nineteenth-century schools proved useful *agents* in the promotion of the choral movement, but they were not the actual cause
of it. Rather, the choral movement was expressive of the whole
social movement that brought the notion of state-operated schools
slowly, haltingly into existence. State schools were constantly
opposed by those who were fearful of an educated populace: even
the 1870 Education Act was an open-ended compromise. Paradoxically, it was singing, linked so closely to a religion tuned to the
notion of keeping the poor in their industrial place, that helped to
perpetuate the concept of a working class, so very necessary for the
continuance of British industry, wealth, and empire.

Singing virtually excluded instrumental work of any kind: the
tyrannical modulator was hardly suited to teaching the manipulat-
ive skills of instruments. Indeed, there is little evidence of actual
voice training; the Lord must have been loved with a good deal of
vocal roughness. But outside school, the invention of the cornet
and other keyed brass instruments led to the phenomenon of brass
bands, the first of which appeared in England at Blane Ironworks in
1832. The brass band movement spread quickly and for precisely
the same reasons as the singing movement: they were relatively
easy to set up and proved useful adjuncts for industry, creating and
proving a healthy team spirit — just as chauvinistic singing and the
playing of rugby football created and proved team spirit among the
sons of the gentry. As organizations like the Salvation Army and

the Temperance Society came to be heralded by brass bands, the bands themselves became symbols of Christian virtue and philanthropy — to say nothing of competitive Christian industry. The Black Dyke Mills Band was formed in 1855 and the first competitive National Brass Band Festival took place at Crystal Palace in 1860. By the beginning of the twentieth century there were over 20,000 brass bands in England.

There are still over 3,000. The reason for the greater survival of the brass band over the singing movement is that instruments do not sing words. Industrial bands have therefore been able to lose their Christian trappings, whilst retaining their social functions. Their musical sights have been set much higher in recent years since orchestral brass players and composers have devoted time to them, but their *raison d'être* is still basically competitive. Most of their music bears all the hallmarks that characterized the old choral music: simple and strong tunes and direct and emotional harmonies — more social than artistic in content. There is also the same compulsive need to participate.

It is ironic, yet characteristic of a 'civilization' that created the artificiality of a special art form, that the above characteristics are ones that artists tend to dislike. Art is essentially about the purposeful and controlled expression of emotion, whereas communal singing and brass band playing — both the act of performing and the music that inspires it — is a release of unbridled emotion. In terms of the sensitive and cultured artist, the difference is between beauty and vulgarity. I shall return to this theme in Part Two; it is mentioned here simply to point to the fact that there can be an enormous gap between musical activity and artistic, or even aesthetic, perception. The nineteenth century working-class movement in music, which formed the musical legacy for the start of regular publicly-funded education in 1870, had very little to do with 'art'.

If the word 'music' is to be interpreted in the way that it would have been in France, Germany, Austria, Italy, Poland, Czechoslovakia, or Russia at the end of the nineteenth century — as an indigenous art form — England was still *Das Land ohne Musik*. As a nation, Britain was rich, materialistic, exploitive, and bigoted: it was not artistic. Its imperial ambition and moral hypocrisy were reflected in its indifference to Continental educational advances and in its musical decadence. For two centuries, its art music had been largely imported from the Continent. Outside London, its musical life centred on cathedral and parish church organists, who were immersed in a type of music emanating from the characteristics of the evangelical hymn and who, like the vast majority of the British, were ignorant of the vortex of musical change sweeping Europe. Such international musical knowledge as existed was the preserve of the privileged minority. As was the case with education, this minority generally preferred to keep it that way. When, in 1869, the small 'Philharmonic Society' (founded in 1813) was able to move its concerts from the limited accommodation in the Hanover Square Rooms to the 2,000-seat St James's Hall, a leading critic reported that, 'In losing their exclusiveness, the Philharmonic Concerts have lost their distinctive charm and the Society its only *raison d'être*'.[2]

Nevertheless, in London and in the larger cities, attempts were made to bring European music to wider and socially less exclusive audiences, even if some of the methods used were distinctly open to question. In 1839, a series of Promenade Concerts, modelled on a French precedent, opened at the Drury Lane Theatre. The programmes consisted of overtures, waltzes, quadrilles, and wind solos. When the Frenchman, Louis Jullien, took over these concerts two years later, his flamboyant manner created a devoted audience and encouraged others to imitate his ventures. At the climax of a musical work, Jullien would seize a violin or piccolo and play with the orchestra, and then sink into a gilt armchair after acknowledging the applause. He would even don a pair of white gloves, brought to him on a silver salver, and conduct with a jewelled baton, to point to the special importance of Beethoven's music.[3] The positive result of such charlatanistic methods was the gradual creation of a socially-mixed audience for concert music.

The New Philharmonic Society, founded in London in 1852, provided a less chauvinistic approach to the dissemination of orchestral music, engaging no less a person than Berlioz to conduct its first season. It offered cheap subscription series in the 3,000-seat Exeter Hall but, in doing so, evidently contravened the Hall's designation 'for religious meetings and the activities of charitable organizations'. Thus the large Exeter Hall played host to 'unartistic' musical activities involving thousands of hymn-singing industrial children and singing masters, while the 'artistic' concert music of the New Philharmonic Society was expelled to more exclusive venues until, eventually, the Crystal Palace Concerts took over its function.

In Liverpool, the history of concert-giving was rather less magnanimous. Following the success of a series of 'Gentlemen's Concerts' (no less attuned to popular taste on account of their exclusive designation), the 2,000-seat Concert Hall was opened in 1849 and for the next half-century its principal concern was to retain its social exclusiveness.

Manchester was the city that was to create the shining light of musical democracy. Charles Hallé, fortunately driven to England from France by the Revolution in 1848, had little understanding of the industrial class system of England when he took over the conductorship of Manchester's 'Gentlemen's Concerts'. From the start, Hallé insisted on setting his own standards, both of musical performance and of the music performed. He also insisted on the availability of seats for the lowest paid members of the community. As a result he created 'a large audience of working men who, standing packed together in great discomfort, yet listened for hours, and evidently with much appreciation, to much intricate and delicate music . . .'.[4] The significance of this achievement has been aptly summarized by Henry Raynor:

He did not, as Henry Wood was to do after 1895 . . . educate the musically illiterate in his audience by leading it through shoals of light music to easy classics and from them to the profundities of Bach, Haydn, Mozart and Beethoven. The Hallé policy was simply to play great music as well as his orchestra could play it, and his audience . . . accepted his offerings enthusiastically.[5]

Although the establishment of concert societies in the larger cities in the nineteenth century was essentially an educational achievement, ironically, it had virtually nothing to do with school education. 'Intricate and delicate music' had not yet entered school. When it did, it was often compromised by socially-orientated educational objectives.

Music has never proved easily adaptable to educational notions. When the Child Study Society was created in London in 1884, largely as a result of the spread of the child-centred educational advances pioneered by Friedrich Froebel and, later, by John Dewey, the old scheme of 'payment by results' was only just being undermined by the newly formed National Union of Teachers.

The famous Revised Code of 1882, aimed at reducing the strangle-hold of this scheme, actually applied it specifically to music: sixpence per head for the rote learning of a certain number of songs and a shilling a head for the ability to sing by sight.[6] However, the real problem lay in the fundamental notion of elementary schools and, later, 'Technical' and 'Central' schools, as being working–class institutions. At the time of the 1870 Education Act, the elementary schools were seen as catering for that class of children ranging from 'street Arabs' to the 'respectable working class'.[7] Early in the twentieth century, the NUT issued a pamphlet stating: 'Six million children are in the Public Elementary Schools of England and Wales. They are the children of the workers, to be themselves England's workers a few year's hence.' At that time, 'art' and the working classes were not generally considered to be even poten-tially compatible.

There are two polarized reactions of the working class when confronted by bourgeois society: one is to castigate it by creating or revivifying its own set of cultural and moral values; the other is to aspire to it. There are two polarized reactions of the bourgeoisie when confronted with working–class culture: one is to offer a simplified version of bourgeois culture (thus effectively maintain-ing the class structure); the other is to make available opportunities to enter into the more beneficial cultural pursuits of the bourg-eoisie. The latter of these viewpoints in each case largely converge; the former do not. Bourgeois society feels threatened by new cultural and moral standards; working class society is offended by bourgeois patronization. The solution is not as simple as attempt-ing to provide equality of opportunity through education; indeed, the belief that education *can* atone for inequalities of financial and cultural backgrounds has acted as a curse upon its curricular think-ing. At the time of writing, the world still needs hewers of wood and drawers of water; manual work is still, to a large extent, a hereditary occupation. So long as there is a wide disparity of wealth, these problems will remain: equality of opportunity has been taken as a matter for *educational* prescription, whereas *social* prescription should enable education to accept equality of oppor-tunity as an elemental birthright.

It is hardly surprising that music, of all the arts, has been a particular victim of these conflicting pressures. At the point of convergence of bourgeois and working–class inter-reaction, the issues are fairly clear. This is where the poor are able and willing to aspire to the cultural pursuits of the bourgeoisie. In music, this represents in-depth involvement in art music, which means making available skilled tuition on sophisticated instruments. The point of divergence is where the popular, the literal 'vulgar' is made respectable, or where the artistic is watered down or expressed as popular. It is here that the offerings of 'music education' have so often presented an affront to the natural musical intelligence and perception of the privileged and underprivileged alike. They still continue to do so.

The history of the social and curricular ideals and reforms in education of this century is familiar enough: so familiar in fact that the social influence on curricular thinking is often overlooked. Motivation becomes the touchstone of curricular content: an inevitable yet often disastrous overloading of the educational function. A very brief survey of the innovations in music education of the first half of this century is sufficient to make the point.

During the 1900s, Christian songs were joined by newlycollected folk-songs, in the meretricious belief that children represented the ideal means of preserving them; yet they were offered with the expurgation of those very 'vulgarities' that were, and are, so inimical to working-class culture. Later, the *National Song Book*, showing distinct traces of ancestry from *Hymns Ancient and Modern*, offered a carefully contrived mixture of pure and composed 'folk', with a few 'art' songs thrown in for good measure, stressing the themes of patriotism, virtue, and godly retribution. Percussion bands, intended to interpret rhythmic movements in dance, consisted of small, cheap, non-pitched instruments which were, in practice, used to accompany — or rather, debauch — pianistic renderings of the classics. In the 1920s, cheaply-produced recorders, whose sound bore — and still bears — little relation to the original of this fine Renaissance and baroque instrument, were introduced as an easy means of reproducing the music of the masters. At the same time, there was a short-lived vogue for the Pipers' Guild, which encouraged children to make and play bamboo pipes to no great musical or artistic purpose. None of these innovations was related to the living world of music outside school.

Other innovations were occasioned by external factors. Emile Jaques-Dalcroze developed his 'eurhythmics', which were introduced to English schools in the 1920s, in order to assist the development of inner hearing. From his analysis of the process of 'motor-tactile' faculties, Dalcroze deduced that the natural response to rhythm must be through muscular and nervous bodily reaction. (Interestingly, this represented a very different musical response from that of the Manchester audiences for Charles Hallé's concerts.) During the 1920s, the development of the gramophone encouraged the teaching of 'Music Appreciation'. After that, as late as 1927, the Board of Education suggested that the subject title 'The Teaching of Singing' should be replaced by the subject title 'Music'. By 1933 the Board could announce that a school lacking a gramophone and a stock of records was under-provided.

Of more intrinsic and lasting importance were the innovations of external *agencies*. The first concerts for children were organized in 1911 by Gwynne Kimpton; they were followed by the Robert Mayer concerts in 1924. These however were aimed at a bourgeois, conditioned audience. Serious attempts at introducing orchestral concerts in a manner relevant to socially-mixed school audiences were not made until well after the 1944 Education Act. Another outside agency, the BBC, started its Schools Broadcasts Service in 1934. Although, from the start, it tended to reflect the education-based musical activities common in schools, it brought first-class, musicianly minds to the task of producing well-prepared proto-types. In fact, the *real* educational content of the BBC's offerings has always lain right outside the Schools Broadcasts Service — and this is true not just of music.[8]

However well-intentioned, none of these early experiments in school music had much to do with the living world of music; nor, for that matter, did they have much to do with the grammar schools or the public schools. For despite attempts during the 1920s and 1930s to bring elementary and secondary education into a more organic relationship, the grammar schools, now offering an increasing number of free places, remained wedded to the Classical tradition. Free school education, established in 1870 to serve the utilitarian needs of the state, in fact only mirrored a culture in decline. Because of the class layers in English society, this was equally true of the state, grammar, and public schools. It would be well into the 1960s before some of the grammar schools would be offering, with substantial LEA support, a form of musical instruction and involvement that has seldom been matched by individual schools since.

The reasons for this brief musical ascendancy were more curricular than social. In general, the grammar schools never felt burdened by the specifically social responsibility of comprehensive schools, even though by the 1960s they were recruiting over a wide social spectrum. They were in fact free to perceive curricular issues simply as curricular issues. Many of them, of course, were unimaginative in approach and remained wedded to a Classical education aimed at university entrance requirements. Nevertheless the more liberal grammar schools structured music in an intelligent way that provided and encouraged skilled instrumental instruction and purposeful musical performance, along with some general introductory work in the classroom, unencumbered by fashionable theories about aesthetic education.

That so many of the comprehensive schools failed to maintain the musical traditions of the more enlightened grammar schools was due less to the fact that children of varied backgrounds and abilities were grouped together, than to the social role that comprehensive schools felt obliged to accept. Music's essential irrationality ensured that it would be used as a focal point of social integration. In the course of its history, music has acquired, throughout the cultures of the world — and now in our global village — a wide range of sometimes incompatible social, political, and arcane functions. To talk about the 'joys of music' is to beg a thousand questions. To talk about 'bringing the joys of music to everyone', without a detailed rationalization of what, in practical terms, that can mean, is quite likely to ensure that the 'joys of music' will be brought to no one — no one, that is, in schools.

William Wordsworth, in the lines with which this chapter was prefaced, viewed with some trepidation the new 'tutors of our youth . . . Sages who in their prescience would control All accidents . . . confine us down, Like engines'. Wordsworth was no guardian of aristocratic privilege: he was in deep sympathy with the French revolutionaries. What he foresaw, with some perturbation, was the inevitable underpinning of spurious theories that would result in emotionally-enervating systemization: that education, by very reason of its socially-enabling function, could actually become a vehicle of *limitation*.

'Those mighty workmen of our later age, Who with a broad highway, have overbridged The forward chaos of futurity' may learn 'That in the unreasoning progress of the world A wiser spirit *is* at work for us . . .' That spirit is contained in art — not just the modish, dreary process of educational induction and indoctrination, but face to face encounter with the real, living world of art; art of any culture in which traditions born of spiritual idealism have caused 'the dull mind to rise to truth through that which is beautiful', as Abbot Suger expressed it in the twelfth century, or 'by which men have transmuted their world from brutishness to civilization', as Professor Aspin put it eight centuries later.[9] If we are genuinely to aspire to 'develop and improve the knowledge and understanding of the arts'[10] in our society, we will need to plan beyond the dogma-laden capabilities of school curricula in order to syncretize art, education, and the community.

4

Post-War Developments: Art and Aesthetics

> Even today, true creativity in art takes place only when there is emotion without ego. Emotion is the *sine qua non* of art; art without emotion is craft.[1]

M. R. Gautam *The Musical Heritage of India*

The most significant musical advance in post-war education in this country has been the widespread appointment of instrumental teachers by Local Education Authorities, along with the rapid growth in youth orchestras, bands, and ensembles of every variety which their teaching contribution has made possible. The *acceleration* of instrumental activity over the past quarter-century was caused by the realization that there existed a vast, untapped potential among the mass of children for acquiring skill on instruments. It was also realized that there existed an exceptional educational value in providing for youth orchestras and bands, through which physical, mental, and emotional energies could be exercised within a purposeful and disciplined social environment — or, to quote again the 1980 Government paper *A Framework for the Curriculum*, to provide for the 'development of mind, body and spirit' incorporating the 'acquisition of knowledge, skills and understanding'.

It is therefore a particular irony that these very musical achievements should have caused dissent among some educators who view any activity involving selection with distaste, and for whom egalitarianism has become a *mot juste* conditioning all pedagogical theory. For them, the instrumental movement is seen as a hindrance to the establishment of an effective classroom curriculum — as an élitist activity which militates against the inculcation of musical understanding among the majority of children. As a result, school music has often become based upon socially-orientated theory, while the emotional, cathartic, and even technical aspects of music have tended to take place *outside the school curriculum*. This, it

33

may be remembered, was the situation in Hellenistic Greece, where schooling was essentially utilitarian, allowing the essential features of Greek culture — athletics and *mousikē* — to have a life of their own, unencumbered by educational theory.

Modern education, however, is not like Greek education: it has subsumed important aspects of general culture and acquired social and artistic responsibilities. It continues the Christian tradition of combining the *technical* with the *moral* and purports to offer a 'whole' education. Encumbered by its extended brief and constrained by its more recent social obligations, it still operates largely through the traditional pedagogical format of the classroom, which inevitably conditions its theory. If any activity or experience fails to accommodate itself purposefully within the classroom format it is in danger of being considered unnecessary and expendable. Music has therefore been forced into this format, although it is largely unsuited to it. The human, physical, and material constraints of the classroom have distilled music's emotional, artistic essence. Instead, they have invoked its 'humanizing influence' (which, it will be remembered, was rooted in musical theory rather than practice) in order to elicit unrealistically egalitarian theories based on concepts of 'creativity', themselves largely alien to the nature of the medium. As, for many educators, creative music in particular and classroom music in general have become the touchstone for enlightened educational thinking, they deserve some detailed scrutiny.

The first impetus in this country for creativity, in the sense of children improvising and composing in class, came from Carl Orff's *Schulwerk*. Orff effectively took Dalcroze a few steps further forward, by linking movement with *improvised* music. The musical approach itself was somewhat formal, based largely on the creation of pentatonic ostinatos, with the teacher or an advanced student improvising over them. The British, with typical pragmatism, adapted the system on a rather freer basis to meet their more child-centred ideas. As a means for discovery-based exploration of musical materials and elements, this Orff-influenced approach, making substantial use of the increasingly widespread pitched percussion instruments, had (and certainly still has) a considerable usefulness in primary schools. However, the rather basic structuring of the music and the severe limitations of 'Orff' instruments had (and still have) very much less appeal to self-conscious secondary children.

When the music department at York University became fully fledged in 1965, its new Professor, Wilfrid Mellers, was interested in the cyclical cultural process evident in the evolution of the 'new primitivism' (expounded in *Caliban Reborn*[2]). At the same time, he perceptively linked the self-consciousness of Western art music with the growing self-consciousness of post-puberty adolescents, while linking 'primitive' musics with the essential 'primitivism' of pre-puberty children. There was much in children's art and behaviour to support the point, though obviously the strong influence of cultural conditioning prevented any too literal application of the theory. However, it was this kind of thinking that established 'music in education' as an important elective element in the York syllabus. Professor Mellers and some of his team initiated experiments involving children and teachers in group improvisation, often involving 'life-enhancing' ostinatos, but incorporating a new awareness of the sound world of composers like Varèse and Penderecki. Improvisations would be based on emotional or elemental themes and could elicit quite remarkable responses. These ideas were, however, slow to catch on, partly because useful response to such methods required a sustaining of activity and level of involvement difficult to create in a classroom, partly because of the inhibiting factor of class control and partly because few teachers, left on their own, had sufficient confidence to handle the musical and social consequences. This approach had (and still has) a value, but it is limited by the fact that any real follow-through requires substantially more skill than can be acquired within a class situation.

Meanwhile a new approach to solving the classroom problem was being pioneered by George Self at Holloway School. Self had hit upon the idea of using a simplified version of Penderecki's musical notation, along with such musical or non-musical sounds as came easily to hand — milk bottles being one of them — to provide compositions that could be performed in class with a minimum of skill and a maximum of (short-lived) enjoyment. Brian Dennis followed up this approach in Shoreditch with greater sophistication, by rationalizing methods of class improvisation with textural sounds, and by finding ingenious ways of enabling children to perform his compositions without recourse to complex music-reading or instrumental skills. The charge has been levelled at both approaches that they are teacher-directed and therefore not 'creative', but this seems rather beside the point. These approaches had limited objectives — eliciting an aural awareness of the simple parameters of musical sounds — and as such they still retain a limited use.

Other initiatives were influenced by the unprecendented explosion of pop music in the late 1960s, with its attendant notion of pre-composed rock-orchestral fusions. A few enterprising schools started producing their own rock-operas, often composed largely by the pupils. Ten years later — and ten years too late — schools up and down the country were performing rock operas, as often as not composed by the teachers. This proved yet another method of occupying children in a music class with an apparent purposefulness.

The common factor among all these innovations of the past twenty years has been, quite literally, their limited usefulness. They reflect, equally literally, the limited usefulness for music of the secondary classroom. The unfortunate result of these innovations, however, has been to create a belief in the unlimited usefulness of the classroom. This has resulted in two major Schools Council projects: 'The Arts and the Adolescent' under Malcolm Ross at Exeter, and 'Music in the Secondary School Curriculum' under John Paynter at York.

The problem with 'The Arts and the Adolescent' project, so far as music is concerned, is that it dealt with the arts as an entity, seeking common denominators in terms of creative components. And here music presented it with a problem: for the truth is that music is basically a recreative art. The report showed a reluctant awareness of this problem: 'Perhaps music is, as so very many musicians have insisted to us, rather a special case after all'.[33] 'The creative use of sound as a medium of self expression does not come easily', it continues. An understatement for all time, Bach, Beethoven, Wagner and a host of others would have had little difficulty in agreeing with this. Indeed, musicians often use the word 'facile' to describe music that appears to have been composed too easily and hastily and that lacks emotional depth. It is sometimes assumed that it is only in the west that performers have been constrained by the requirements of composed music and that in eastern and tribal cultures the role of the performer has been that of improviser. I know of no musical culture in which the performer has been allowed greater freedom, relatively, than, say, the continuo player and 'divisioner' of baroque music, except perhaps in some forms of jazz. It is true that many oriental and tribal musics attach greater importance to the *manner* of playing than to the content, but this is merely a difference of kind. Tribal musics were invariably related to the supernatural and were consequently controlled by strict formulae and subject to strong, superstitious taboos.

Indian music is often thought to allow the performer a degree of freedom not encountered in the West. In fact, the Indians invented a form of notation long before the Europeans, even though they did not use it in performance. Their music has the oldest known ancestry of any in the world and is subject to very strict laws. The *Hindustani* music of the north allows greater interpretative licence than the *karnatac* music of the south, but because of the importance attached to ornamentation — the manner of performance — it subjects the performer to even greater technical precision than the more exactly delineated music of the south.

In Bali, musicians were also subject to strict procedures. As Balinese instruments are the prototypes for the instruments commonly served up in this country for 'creative' purposes, it is worth quoting that great observer and collector of Balinese music, Colin McPhee, on the Balinese approach to performance;

Without the drudgery of having to learn a notation, a musical *sophistication* is experienced from the very beginning. From the outset, musicians can concentrate on complex rhythms, changes of dynamics and precision of ensemble. While one club plays with brilliant intensity, allowing the swiftly moving music to rise and fall with dramatic turbulence, a club two villages away will perform *the same music* with cold precision and even indifference. Much depends on local or regional styles, on the enthusiasm of two or three leading spirits of the club, and above all the two drummers who animate the entire orchestra.[5] [My italics.]

This indicates a very different approach to musical style and performance from that which is common in the West and, indeed, a glory of musical texture that would be unthinkable in terms of the cheap imitation instruments we use in school. But it does *not* indicate any absence of technique or pre-composition. You do not concentrate on 'complex rhythms, changes of dynamics and precision of ensemble' unless you have already learnt to play your part. The Balinese musician, playing from memory skilled music of considerable complexity and antiquity, was not so very different from our solo musical performer, with his pieces known from memory, approaching his task with a joy born of confidence, his interpretation depending, to some extent, on the actual mood of the moment.

The *The Arts and the Adolescent* report accused music of 'lagging behind art and drama in several respects'.[6] This, again, is precisely what the known facts of history should lead us to expect. Music lagged behind the other arts quite substantially in all the major artistic developments of the West. In some other cultures, traditions of performance have remained largely unchanged over hundreds and even thousands of years. (Only in recent years has the lure of Western materialism — the present curse of art — affected these proud traditions.) Culturally, music has been an agent of tradition as much as a focus of polemical change. It may be remembered that Damon of Athens suggested that changes in musical style were always accompanied by changes in the laws of the state. The Athenian state was prepared to be ruled by music; later states have used music to endorse their rule. In India, the finest proponents of classical music have been afforded the status of saints: Indian musicians are *proud* of their ancient ancestry. Yes, music may be a special case after all.

The *The Arts and the Adolescent* project involved the sciences of sociology and psychology in formulating a new epistemology for predicating 'aesthetic' response. The danger inherent in this kind of approach is that the fine but immensely important distinction between 'art' and 'aesthetics' is easily overlooked: the essential value of *art* lies in the uniquely personal nature of the individual response. Analyses of feelings and responses tend to bypass the essential mystery of *art* experience and, in the particular case of Robert Witkin's *The Intelligence of Feeling*,[7] (which provided the basis for the *The Arts and the Adolescent* enquiry and is now required reading for many B.Ed and M.Ed. students) predicates 'creative' activity, seemingly in justification of its conclusions.

'Aesthetics' was a product of the Enlightenment and was an attempt to rationalize the concept of Art at a time when it was becoming embarrassingly clear that Art was indeed an élite activity, largely denied to the poorer classes. Like most aspects of philosophy, it was concerned to disentangle the intellectual and the sensual components in perceptive cognition. One of the problems inherent in any study of aesthetics — and one that applies fully to attempts at justifying art in egalitarian (classroom) terms — is that the concepts and arguments are likely to be unintelligible to all but an élite of intellectuals. Even Beethoven, who took a keen interest in the philosophies and politics of his day, took a distinctly simplistic view of Kant (whose philosophies of freedom and beauty were being discussed in German coffee-houses while similar philosophies were being fought out in the streets of France): 'The moral law in us, the starry sky above us — Kant!!!', he noted in his conversation book in 1820. Thus it is difficult to see how, for example, the metaphysical 'theory' section of Witkin's book can do a great deal for the cause of art, civilization, adolescents, or egalitarianism, except lead to some doubtful conclusions. However, in the more easily digestible 'Praxis' section of his book, Witkin painted an all too familiar picture of the music teacher in the classroom. As I write, some years later, his words can still ring painfully true:

The music teacher is often condemned to work out his existence in the secondary school as the martinet on the other side of the music stand, hiding his own sensitivity to protect it from further abuse and thrusting the rudiments down reluctant throats. He does his duty grimly like a soldier in an unpopular war, 'the unwilling doing the unnecessary for the ungrateful'. Often he likes music too much to be happy about it.[8]

Following this most understanding description of the problems faced by so many music teachers, it comes as a surprise to find these problems blamed upon the *instrumental* training of the teacher, in that it is concerned with the 'enactment' rather than the 'making' of 'idea'. It is even suggested that it would be better if the teacher were *not* an instrumentalist, so that pupils 'can realize themselves in idea'. And how is this to be achieved? 'The existence of the 'Orff'-type toned [sic] percussion instruments makes possible a whole world of experiment for relating sound to impulse and producing musical idea.'[9]

This castigation of performing skills — the very stuff of which musicians of any sort are made — is a natural though regrettable consequence of the subsuming of music by education. Few musicians would consider that 'Orff' instruments offer a 'whole world of experiment', useful though they might find them. Indeed, few thinking musicians would ever have suggested that conscripting groups of thirty children on no other criterion than similarity of age, and placing them in a restricted space in an authoritarian institution for two prescribed periods of forty minutes every week, was an ideal or even feasible way of developing musical under-standing and activity. It is only because of the fact that musicians have had to brace themselves to this seemingly inevitable task that the sorts of noises that commonly emanate from music classrooms are considered to have anything to do with music at all. They very rarely appear on public show. They exist purely because schools send classes of children at regular intervals to be educated in the mysteries of music. The more recent creation of 'faculties' encour-aging integration and flexibility of grouping has not atoned for the fundamental falseness of the approach.

Nevertheless, over the past quarter-decade, musicians have been remarkably resourceful in finding ways of turning necessity to advantage. Given a good school atmosphere, appropriate physical and material resources, and a supportive service of instrumental teaching to provide the vital means of follow-through, many teachers have proved that the classroom *can* elicit vital musical experiences. Successful class music teachers have usually turned instinctively to discovery-based and subject-integrated methods, for successful class music teaching calls for creative minds, and creative minds turn to creative methods.

The Schools Council's *Music in the Secondary School Curriculum* project provided a useful service in citing and developing many of these methods.[10] Again, however, educational rather than musical theory and practice was allowed to dominate its thinking. The virtues of the classroom were extolled on the very unlikely assump-tion that schools would all have the human and physical resources needed to copy the methods described, while those who would attach too great an importance to 'extra-curricular' activities were berated, though not without equivocation, on the grounds that such activities tend to be exclusively for the talented. The report's honourable intention was to provide an egalitarian basis for music. Unfortunately it appeared unwilling to recognize the difference between equal ability and equal opportunity. The report seemed to be based on the socially admirable but musically unacceptable theory that music, properly presented, can affect everybody equally. The pragmatic effect would have been to *deny* any pupil who could not acquire satisfactory music lessons *outside* school the opportunity to shine positively at music — or, in the report's own words, 'maintain self-respect through self-realization'. This is, of course, precisely what the acquisition of assured musical skill provides. The report's failure to accept the *fundamental* importance of a pyramidal structure involving class and instrumental teachers effectively denied opportunity to shine in music to the mass of people whose interests it was at such pains to protect. The overridingly important issue is not whether curricular or extra-curricular activities should predominate, but *whether far-sighted musical opportunities are put in front of our children in sufficient quantity and whether our children are appropriately motivated to know whether or not they wish to accept them.* (It is in this latter capacity that the main value of the classroom lies.)

I have frequently referred to the subsuming of music's essence by education and to the arcane musical theorizing to which this situation has led. One of the principal causes of this has been the equating of music with painting and the notion that it can be moulded creatively in the same way. The analogy is useful in order to stimulate simple, *introductory*, child-centred music teaching. But it is not sufficiently apt to justify making 'group composition' a progressive course throughout the secondary school. As I have already demonstrated, music is not — so far as history informs us — essentially a 'creative' art. The common analogy with the other arts has led to a great deal of confusion. One has only to observe a typical adult education centre. The painters will be creating their own works (though possibly according to predefined principles), the actors will most probably be playing parts written by others (though they may be given considerable interpretative licence) and the musicians will be performing a set work with as much exactitude as possible. As we have seen, this last — and it applies with equal force to the others — has been common to artistic cultures throughout the world. Why, therefore, it is attested that children should be fundamentally preoccupied with composing, is particularly hard to fathom. Very few adolescents follow through a desire to compose, once they have found out just how difficult a task this is. Indeed, composing is one of the most difficult things it is possible to undertake: there have been less than thirty composers over the past two hundred and fifty years in Europe who are generally remembered with any deep sense of gratitude now. Genuine creativity is given to very few: and that, too, goes for all cultures of the world.

Creativity has acquired a meaning that far outreaches the original concept, when the word first became fashionable nearly twenty years ago. My own simple definition of creativity has not changed since I wrote it on an overhead projector slide in 1967, to preface all practical sessions and discussions on the subject:

CREATIVITY is a *METHOD*
> for achieving our objectives,
> defined in the light of:

Children's educational needs
Children's musical needs
Our awareness of historical tradition
Our present cultural ambience

The fact that creativity — spontaneous, largely unskilled group composition — has since been seen as an end in itself, as a means of artistic awareness and encounter, and as a means of turning skill into artistry, is a typical instance of the arcane theorizing to which the social-educational pressures on school music have led. Creativity is still entirely appropriate and apposite in its original conception: providing a practical, discovery-based introduction to musical materials and elements, intended to motivate subsequently, for those who would respond to it, a deeper pursuance of musical skill. But to conclude from this that there can be artistry without skill, that artistry can *precede* skill or, indeed, be detached from it, is really quite preposterous. Genuine musicality is invariably linked to sensitivity. Musically sensitive performers know that their hard-earned skill was a necessary pre-condition for turning their musicality into artistry, and that it was their compulsive need for music that motivated their perseverance in acquiring the skill. What was of fundamental importance for many such people — professionals and amateurs alike — was that *they were provided with the opportunities for developing their musicality in this way*.

Given all these considerations, it is clear that any rationale for music in education must allow for distinctions between two quite different sets of concepts: egalitarianism and élitism, aesthetics and art. I have already pointed to the danger of applying psychological analysis to aesthetic response because it usually bypasses the essential mystery of art. In the case of music, such analysis is always confounded by music's irrational pre-verbal essence. Responses can be analysed in terms of social-association and aural-familiarity (in the sense of familiarity with a musical culture), for these can have a profound effect on the listener's *attitude*. But attempts to anticipate or prescribe for individual response are usually distorted by the very nature of self-expressive art. Music is particularly resistant to de-mystification of its intrinsic exclusiveness: concepts of musical beauty are defied by the irrational behaviour of musical elements.

It might, for example, be thought useful to make an aesthetic judgement on the sensations derived from different combinations of tempo and density. It could be said that a slow motor speed, together with absence of contrapuntal movement, leads to a feeling of enervation. In general, this would be true. The 'Pilgrim's March' from Mendelssohn's 'Italian' Symphony answers to this description and I personally find it distinctly enervating. But take the *Molto Adagio* movement from Beethoven's Quartet in A minor Op. 132 which, prior to the music of Messiaen has, for the first thirty bars, as slow a motor speed and as little contrapuntal movement as any piece I can think of: I personally find this piece not enervating but *elating*. So, presumably, did Beethoven. He called it 'Hymn of thanksgiving to God of an invalid on his convalescence'. The problem here is in the use of the words 'enervating' and 'elating'. There is no single *word* that will encompass my very different sensate reactions to these two pieces. The common denominator is a purely musical element — motor speed. The difference between my sense of *enervation* in response to the Mendelssohn and my sense of *elation* in response to the Beethoven is the difference between aesthetics and art. Both pieces could be said to be beautiful: I can certainly recognize beauty in both in the sense that both have efficacy in terms of the styles of their time — but the former usually moves me to boredom whereas the latter moves me on to a new emotional plane. I can only explain this by analysing the music (rather than myself) in relation to certain musical norms.

To describe what it is in the Beethoven that moves me emotionally (and it is to do with harmonic progression and chord spacing) would be well outside the scope of this essay and would be by no means easygoing for music degree students. In other words, long experience of a cultural, musical norm enables *me personally* to recognize, in sensate terms, the overriding greatness of this particular piece of Beethoven. Even so, the final mystery of artistic profundity will elude my analysis: for the greatest aspect of art music is the ability of its supremest composers to create constantly varying worlds of emotion, irrespective of motor speed, contrapuntal movement, and so on. Nevertheless, my ability to analyse my response in musical terms, which requires both professionalism and intuition, *heightens* for me personally the emotional experience. Because of my heightened emotional experience through the Beethoven, I am less tolerant of what I (professionally) discern as the mediocrity of the Mendelssohn. I would also be intolerant of an inadequate performance of the Beethoven because it would lower my emotional plane. *Through skill and accumulated knowledge I have moved from aesthetic to artistic experience.* This is the crux of the whole matter.

I have used the first person *singular* deliberately: too many essays on art and aesthetics use the first person plural. Art is a singular experience. The degree of general receptivity to it and the enrichment derived from any example of it will vary from individual to individual. The degree of *critical* receptivity to it will depend also upon experience, knowledge, and artistic perception. The critically aware artist may hate a musical performance or work of art that an 'art lover' enjoys — and he may love another with an intensity that the latter has never experienced in regard to art.

The difference between aesthetics and art is that mysterious something we know to be irrational. For example, a visit to a nudist camp could be said to be a study in aesthetics, but a visit to a Picasso exhibition could turn out to be something quite different. The pleasurable contemplation of light on water is an aesthetic act, but the contemplation of Turner's paintings should provoke in us very different responses. We cannot prescribe for preferences: Picasso to a nudist camp, Turner to a sunset, *St Matthew Passion* to *Jesus Christ Superstar*. What we *can* do is establish potential values: for art occupies that essential middle ground between indulgent sensuality and intellectual reason. We must hope that all adolescents, at some point in their lives, will feel moved by an experience in one or other of the arts. For this the classroom can provide only a preparation: pupils soon need confronting with potential art experience in as meaningful a way as possible. Art experience in music can best be achieved through participation in high-level, skilled performance. It can also be achieved through attendance at live performances. I do not believe it can be achieved, initially at least, through group or individual composition. I, for one, have never received an art experience from any form of practical music-making I have heard going on in a classroom.

There is a further danger in placing too great a reliance upon attempting to explain art in terms of preconceived aesthetic principles. If it is true that the first stirring — or sudden — recognition of greatness in art is, for all the cultural pre-conditioning, intuitive, then this intuitive recognition will come about precisely because the 'art object' does *not* make sense in terms that are familiar. It may be necessary to establish some familiar patterns before an art experience can occur — the cultural environment sees to that anyway — but the actual art experience must happen before it can be analysed. This point is well made by Professor David Aspin:

It is . . . a fundamental 'truth' in and about Art that in any art work there will be whole layers and kinds of meaning, embodied in it and so inextricably intertwined and connected that they all fuse into one complete organic unity. The various kinds and intensities of meaning of *Guernica*, for example, like that of Blake's *Sick Rose* or Brahms' *3rd Symphony*, can only be fully understood and savoured by attending to the totality of the work and 'letting it be'. The activity of 'stripping away the layers' of meaning brings about effects in the perceiver that illuminates and transforms his vision of the truths about the world he sees about him as a result of the disclosures that his receptivity to the work precipitates . . . In this respect the Arts can act as powerful agents of a real integration, in the sense that wide varieties of meaning and value are brought together and reconciled, presented for understanding and appreciation, in one harmonious manifestation.[11]

Musically, these 'varieties of meaning and value' may eventually be assimilated passively — the degree of artistic receptivity depending upon the experience and natural musical intuition of the listener — or they may be absorbed through active participation in performance.

'Even today, true creativity in art takes place only when there is emotion without ego. Emotion is the *sine qua non* of art; art without emotion is craft.' These words come from a leading Hindustani musician. 'Beauty', he says, 'begins by gratifying the senses and ends by exalting the spirit.'[12] The self-consciousness of Western art has not encouraged the elimination of the ego. Yet there is a sense in which the greatest Western music achieves this transcendental plane: when the composer has put every particle of his being into a work, with a conviction that transcends his own ego; when, as Sir Michael Tippett has put it, 'the discovery of suitable material is involuntary';[13] when the blues singer or jazz player transcends 'self' in the beauty and subtlety of his treatment of established formulae. This is the point at which the music of East and West meet. It cannot be reached without the highest technical mastery and the highest musical imagination. In the end, art is a calling, and it is the duty of education, among all its many other pressing responsibilities, to ensure that that calling can be obeyed.

Throughout history, man has shown a desire to transcend his mundane pre-occupation with economic survival by turning to activities involving his spirit and imagination, by finding means to beautify and sometimes aggrandize his surroundings with painting, sculpture, and architecture, as well as through the spiritual catharsis and renewal that music can provide. According to his cultural mores, man has either shown reverence for his art or taken pride in it: sometimes both but very seldom neither. Irreverence for art has usually only occurred when invading cultures, ignorant of the meaning of the art they have found, have supplanted it with forms and processes that attest more accurately to their own cultural mores.

The new cultural invader is technology which, through its transformation of communication, information, and behavioural patterns, is not only endorsing an inartistic approach to art, but is upsetting artistic forms and balances on a global scale. As the machine is taking over from the book — the mind — it is also upsetting the social and reasoning habits that made European and many Eastern art forms possible. It is also undermining the idealism that informed works of the human spirit. Modern education has a prime responsibility to preserve knowledge and understanding of our cultural and artistic pasts, because only in this way can any cultural future contain the roots that are essential for meaningful artistic growth. To do this it must fire people with art's intoxication, purvey its essence and legislate for vital art experiences. The danger is that, having subsumed artistic disciplines in relentless pursuit of its egalitarian, social ideals, education will succeed only in denying art's essential emotional spirit.

Perikles, the great statesman and architect of Athenian culture, is quoted by Thucydides as saying: 'Our system is called "democracy" because the city is controlled not by a small class but by the majority. The law gives everyone equal rights . . . some people are respected more; and whenever they are known to be good at something it does not matter what section of the population they come from; they gain advancement in public life according to their quality.'[14]

This high idealism ignores, of course, the importance of slaves to the success of Ancient Greek culture. Nevertheless, if modern education could provide a milieu that could give honest substance to these words, a milieu in which our younger generation could find that 'something, or someone, to devote itself to' (see earlier, page 9), in order to shine and profit therefrom, we should have less to fear for our future. At least this could be our aim.

5

Criteria for Aims

`I have already suggested that aims for music education are very difficult to define, that it is easier to assess the usefulness of active ability in music than of passive appreciation, and that it is particularly difficult to account for the wide disparity in personal reactions to specific musical types and styles. Music is such a vast and varied phenomenon that any set of overall aims must of necessity be highly generalized. The main purpose of this chapter is to draw together some of the concepts and dilemmas encountered in the previous chapters and to establish criteria by which educators may test and assess their musical philosophies and provisions.

The co-ordination of mind, body, and spirit

It has been noted that the importance attached by the ancient Greeks to the linking of physical prowess and beauty with moral intelligence and sensibility finds strong resonances in the reference in a recent DES document on curriculum to the need for 'the development of body, mind and spirit, and to 'the acquisition of knowledge, skills and understanding'. Similar resonances have been noted in connection with the outlet provided by modern youth orchestras and bands for the exercise of physical, mental, and emotional energies within purposeful and disciplined social environments. The development of body, mind, and spirit has characterized Greek, Christian, and modern education, in all of which music has served some kind of moral as well as social cause.

The extent to which the development of 'lively, enquiring minds' (to quote the DES document again) has affected the freedom of spirit essential to the creation and personal appreciation of Western art has depended upon the extent to which reason has been guided by observation rather than by divine revelation. The Greeks of the fifth century BC encouraged lively curiosity and generated a great flowering of music and art. Christian culture, based upon revelatory doctrine, retained for music a fundamental role in education as a spiritual adjunct. This was in contrast to Roman culture, whose severely practical and autocratic philosophy had found little use for creating 'lively, enquiring minds' — or for music. Similar limitations were evident in the culture of nineteenth-century England, where corporate state education was also severely utilitarian. Education in the nineteenth century found little place for music as an art but only for music as a satellite to a religion intended to 'train up the poor in the habits of industry and piety'. Throughout the nineteenth century, music touched the spirit only in so far as it related to religious spirit or to a communal spirit aroused by industrial hardship. The aesthetic and artistic appreciation of music could be found only *outside* school in such enlightened enterprises as Sir Charles Hallé's public concerts in Manchester.

In the first half of the twentieth century, attempts to inculcate a wider musical appreciation through school education resulted only in a distilling of the emotional aspect of music. Music provided co-ordination of mind and body but largely failed to incorporate that further touching of the spirit, unique to the media of art. In the second half of the twentieth century, education has, on the one hand, provided unprecedented opportunities for children from all types of background to acquire instrumental skills, whether or not they rise from the level of craft to art; on the other hand, it has developed techniques of a very different sort, deliberately tailored to the constraints of the conventional classroom, in an attempt to create a sense of aesthetic awareness through music among all children. Socially-orientated arguments have tended to exaggerate the usefulness of these classroom developments by failing to recognize the fine but important distinction between aesthetics and art and the fact that not everyone is equally susceptible to aesthetic or artistic experience. This has led to an underestimation of the necessity for some children of achieving that very special sense of fulfilment accruing from the emotional and technical disciplines combined in musical performance. It is only in this sense that music fulfils its time-honoured function of co-ordinating, completely and genuinely, the attributes of mind, body, and spirit.

In the light of these considerations, I suggest the following criterion as one which could reasonably be upheld:

Provision of music in education should reflect art's essential and unique ability to co-ordinate the attributes of mind, body and spirit and should reflect the fact that children respond to music at different levels of aesthetic and emotional intensity, and that they have different degrees of need for active participation in it.

Music as a humanizing influence

Since the time of Homer, music has been regarded as a comfort to the soul. For this reason Damon of Athens in the fifth century BC considered it an art worthy of freeborn ('liberal') men and ascribed to it political connotations. The humanist view of music, which was to influence the music of the Middle Ages and Renaissance, arose from the Ancient Greek belief that musical modes, conditioned by the words attached to them, could create 'moral' states of mind and define character. This kind of belief has, however, nearly always been rooted in musical theory, and such theory has usually been shattered by performing virtuosity. The instrumental techniques pioneered by Timotheous of Miletus at the end of the fifth century BC created a musical élite that challenged the role of music as an essential core of education. The early Christians actually discouraged virtuosity so that concentration should be on the words rather than the beauty of the singing. Further, the *musica humana* which Boethius considered the key to a healthy body and soul was — in contrast to *musica instrumentalis* — not actually audible. When, however, the Church began, like the Greeks, to equate beauty with godliness, it opened the way to a form of musical virtuosity that, once again, became the preserve of a professional élite.

The European Renaissance led to the re-introduction of the Aristotelian view of music as a tasteful leisure pursuit. Operatic composers of the early seventeenth century then resuscitated the ancient humanist ideal by again focusing attention on the words rather than the singing. Although this was to lead to yet another new style of virtuosity in the eighteenth century, the social effect of the lingering humanist approach to music was — in England at least — to discourage the practice of music among the gentry. Nineteenth-century educators in England were forced to justify music in schools on the grounds of its 'civilizing' influence: school music became detached from the wider world of art music. More recently, The Schools' Council's *Music in the Secondary School Curriculum* project referred to music's humanizing influence in theory but concerned itself with activities that were largely opposite to those appropriate for training in musical performance.

The fact that notions of music's 'humanizing influence' have been rooted in theory rather than practice indicates that they have usually contained strong elements of wishful thinking and that they have represented a confused reaction to music's irrational but powerful essence. From this it is reasonable to propose the following criterion:

> Music should not *generally* be regarded as having any direct (rather than associative) humanizing or civilizing influence because any such influence is dependent upon exceptional musical insight which can only result from a high level of skill acquisition and sustained musical experience.

The functional use of music

Education, in common with most social institutions, has usually regarded music as an important adjunct to ceremonial occasions, a fact that has often helped music to retain a secure place within it. Similarly, music has also been seen as an indispensable adjunct to religion, a fact that is largely responsible for music's traditional place in the curriculum. The ceremonial and religious attributes of music also secured its place in European aristocratic society, leading to the development of music as a personalized art. This, in turn, has led to much cultural confusion and, recently, cultural antithesis, as art music has been steadily democratized since the French Revolution. This matter will be treated fully in Part Two, but enough has already been said to propose the following criterion:

> Provision of musical resources in education should be geared to the known needs of children and students rather than to the ability of music to enhance public and religious occasions.

Élitism and egalitarianism

The history of education attests to the danger of its enabling function acting as a source of limitation. The enabling function, rightly and inevitably, places emphasis on a common core, yet the pursuit of excellence and virtuosity in any subject tends to threaten the core's mean level. This is particularly true of musical art. The problem was experienced by the Greeks, the beginnings of whose artistic decline coincided with Aristotle's influential declaration that schools should not attempt to inculcate professional technique, but should provide only as much technique as is needed to develop taste. The problem was also experienced, though from a religious more than a musical standpoint, by the Christians of the later Middle Ages, as the new musical virtuosity began to detract from the central liturgy. The Aristotelian standpoint was also experienced during the sixteenth to eighteenth centuries, during which period it proved necessary to create 'academies' for the teaching of technical skills. During the nineteenth century in England, music remained at the core of state education for associative reasons, but education itself was not concerned with musical excellence or virtuosity. However, in the private 'public' schools, where musical skills gradually came to be encouraged as 'extras', music had little place in the core, even though it was used largely in connection with religion or local chauvinism. Attempts by state schools in the first half of the twentieth century to establish music as a core subject in its own right resulted in the distillation of its artistic essence. The post-war years have seen enormous advances in the provision of opportunity for children to acquire musical excellence and virtuosity. However, the creation of a skilled musical élite among school children has been seen by some as a threat to the efficacy of music as a core subject. It has led to feverish research into methodology justifying the importance of the core, often at the expense of developing expertise and based on some spurious musical reasoning. Many of these problems have resulted from a failure to reconcile two disparate concerns: that a too broadly-based education could lead to dilettantism; and that over-specialization might create single-minded, selfish citizens.

The social criteria that have been foisted on education — providing it with an 'all-embracing' role — were properly responsible for the encouragement of provision of instrumental teaching in the post-war years. These same criteria, however, have also led to some 'anti-élitist' reaction to the natural and laudable results of that provision. This reaction has, in some cases, led to a distillation of art's essentially cathartic essence, resulting from social dogma rather than any desire to deny artistic experience.

This discussion leads me to suggest that the following criterion should apply:

> Musical provision in education should reflect a balance between the need to offer artistic experience and opportunity for all and the need to establish teaching resources for the acquisition of varying degrees of musical excellence and virtuosity — both aspects also reflecting the fundamental importance of the *artistic* element in musical experience.

Curricular or extra-curricular

With the development of musical virtuosity in the fifth century BC, Hellenistic education became literary and intellectual leaving technical skills to be taught outside schools. Christian culture, because music was necessary to its doctrine, linked such musical skills as were necessary for its ritual with its provision of education — a link that has been retained through some grammar schools to this very day. Musical skills were not taught in Britain as an educational benefit in their own right (apart from their association with religion) until the private 'public' schools started to appoint Directors of Music from the mid-nineteenth century onwards. Since that time the public schools have tended to place emphasis on instrumental teaching and choral and orchestral activity (made possible largely because, of their mainly boarding status) whereas state schools, for all the advances that have been made in instrumental provision, have tended to place priority on music in the classroom. Some grammar schools during the 1960s and 1970s provided a rational balance between musical induction and follow-up opportunity, because their curriculum thinking was not specifically influenced by social 'egalitarian' criteria.

Provision of humanistic education (aimed at producing well-rounded citizens) requires further provision of outlets for intellectual, emotional, and physical energies — and it requires 'causes'. Failure to make this provision can cause art and athletic subjects to seem frivolous and peripheral to utilitarian-minded legislators of any ambitious culture. Whatever advances may have been made in classroom music, it is high-level musical performance that demonstrates the importance of music to those taking part in it. One purpose of classroom teaching is to provide motivation towards such activity, because young people need to discover, through empirical experience, where their own personal interests and potential abilities lie. Provision of subsequent choral and orchestral opportunity is a natural requisite of music education. This demands extra-curricular activity which, in many cases, is best provided on an area rather than school basis. The cathartic essence of music can often be better expressed outside the confines of the secondary school, where the generally formal atmosphere can prove inhibiting to emotional expression. Structured in this way, music, like activities in theatre, dance, sport, and other outdoor pursuits, can provide 'that something' for our 'admirable human capital . . . to devote itself to'. Equally, when the musical role is passive, artistic experience can normally only be provided in an extra-curricular capacity, whether it be inside or outside schools. Visits to or by professional musicians form a necessary corollary to classroom music if genuine musical awareness is to be elicited.

The following criterion seems to me to be indispensable to any legitimate musical aims:

> Schools should recognize the indispensability of musical activity outside the classroom for the inculcation of lasting musical skills and responses, by providing and encouraging extra-curricular provision on a local, regional or national basis.

Environmental factors

The question as to how far education should enable those of the lower orders to aspire to the knowledge and skills of those of the higher orders is one that has vexed all political legislators of education. It affected the vested interests of the aristocrats of fifth-century BC Greece as much as those of the Anglican Christians of the nineteenth century; and it affects the ambitions of all governments, particularly at times of cultural and technological change, when education can be seen as a means of indoctrinating new mental habits and work priorities. The selection of controllers and doers is still, effectively, conditioned largely by heredity and environment. A strain has been placed on education by the belief that it can subsume financial and cultural disparities in children's backgrounds. Although education has made considerable advances in this direction it cannot, of itself, entirely subsume environmental disparities.

In addition to its social role, education has rightly assumed the role of 'cultural provider', a role that is made particularly difficult by disparities in cultural background. The question as to how far, in general, children from poorer backgrounds should be *expected* to adopt the artistic values of the bougeoisie and how far they should be encouraged to preserve their own cultural values (or establish new ones) is a particularly difficult one. However, it is a unique feature of art that it has the power to *transcend* differences in cultural attitudes and it is clear, without equivocation, that *all* children, if they are susceptible to musical art, are able to attain musical excellence and virtuosity and a resulting sense of fulfilment. They can attain this regardless of cultural and financial background, so long as education provides appropriate small group and individual instrumental instruction as an integral part of its provision and provides, where necessary, financial assistance with purchase of instruments and courses of further study.

In view of education's social and cultural responsibilities, I propose a last and most important criterion:

> State education should ensure that all children have the opportunity to determine their level of interest and ability in practical music and that, by making suitable local and regional provision for instrumental instruction as an integral part of its general provision, no child should be debarred from attaining his or her fullest potential in music on account of a financially poor or socially deprived background.

Aims

The following general aims, taken in conjunction with the above criteria are, I suggest, appropriate for musical instruction and activity within school education:

1. To create an awareness of the power of music as a resource for the emotions.
2. To encourage the practice of the art of music.
3. To enable children from all backgrounds to be able to discover talent and interest in music and to provide means of enabling them to reach their fullest potential in the subject.

PART TWO

OBJECTIVES — The Musical Background

6

The Genius of Western Music

I am overwhelmed with work and in poor health, so people must be a little patient with me . . . Apollo and the Muses will not yet allow me to be handed over to the bony Reaper, for I am still so much in their debt, and before I depart to the Elysian Fields I must leave behind me what the spirit has endowed me with and ordered me to complete . . . I wish you all success in your efforts on behalf of the arts; it is these, together with science, that give us inclines of a higher existence and the hope of attaining it . . .[1]

Ludwig Van Beethoven (1824)

When people talk about education in the arts today they are generally more explicit about the nature of education than art. They usually assume that education in the arts will lead people to increased artistic sensibility, and that for them to develop judgements and preferences according to generally accepted terms of aesthetic criticism is, *de facto*, in everyone's best interests. In fact the extent to which those educated will acquire increased artistic sensibility — let alone artistic perception and insight — will depend upon their former experience of art, their degree of receptivity to art, and the extent to which they are confronted by works that are not merely decorative but have intrinsic artistic purport. As I hope to show in this and the next chapter, art — and that includes musical art — is not necessarily synonymous with beauty. Musical art communicates essentially through the emotions and therefore has the power to be deeply disturbing.

Western music, like the whole of Western art, acquired a dialectical element that enabled it to disturb the very mores of its culture. It could do this, however, only when its various elements were moulded in perfect balance by composers of exceptional genius. When its elements were moulded with deliberate imbalance, it also acquired the power, through association, to enhance extra-musical causes. Since the time of the French Revolution — the first substantial political erosion of the aristocratic base upon which Western music was nurtured — there has been an increasingly confused interaction between the various forms that composers have foisted on music and the various functions which music has been expected to fulfill. If Western art is to continue to have genuine meaning in our present multi-racial society, it is important to attempt to distinguish between the social and artistic attributes that music has acquired. It is also important to attempt to distinguish between music that is genuinely artistic in communicative terms and that which is largely decorative, as well as to examine the extent to which these factors have been perceived and appreciated by listeners.

Western music is unique in the extent to which it allows the silent act of composition to be considered as an entity in itself, separate from the art of performance. While most cultures of the world are based upon pre-determined compositions, they usually depend upon the exercise of interpretative *manner* for their effect. In no musical culture outside the West is composition notated with such complexity and precision as to make the performer the servant of the *composer*: the performer usually is the servant of *music*. It is this that gives Western music its special distinction.

The extent to which this distinction has confused musical responses may be highlighted by a brief comparison between Western music and that of India, where music is often still regarded idealistically as an élite art form — even more so than in the West. In India, musical composition — a combination of a specific *rag* (a form for a melodic pattern) and *tal* (rhythmic cycle) — exists only as *theory* until a musical artist brings it to life through his own, unique personality. The performer is in no sense a 'free' composer: his task is to re-interpret the *rag* according to elaborate and time-honoured principles. In this sense, the spirit and letter of Indian music are inseparable: the spirit of the performance is enhanced by the degree of virtuosity with which the performer adheres to the letter of the prescribed manner. Bodily gestures contribute to the total artistic effect. The *rag* is chosen to suit the time and mood of the day. As these times of day have spiritual significance, distracting, external musical associations are largely eliminated: the music's spiritual ambience helps to relate the artistic performance to the listener's mood.

Some of this is also true of Western music. The finest artistic experience usually occurs when the performer dedicates his virtuosity to the presentation of a piece of music exactly as the composer prescribed it; the charisma of the performer is an important element and the style of the stage manner can affect the sincerity of the performance. The fundamental difference between Western and Indian music lies in the fact that, in the West, these various elements of artistic creation are not *essentially* integrated.

It is not possible — nor has it usually been considered desirable — to relate the mood of a composition to the predicted mood of an audience. Furthermore, the importance attached to the act of composition creates a situation of potential conflict — rather than union — between the composer and performer, for it can lead to a degree of arrogance on the part of the performer that can make him a rather less than humble servant of the composer. While these are aspects of the intrinsic tension with which Western music is able to achieve a unique personalization of expression, they also cause a host of non-musical associations to detract from the immediacy of the audience response.

Historically, the paramountcy attached to composition in Western music sprang from the medieval penchant for theorizing and the consequent establishing of a form of musical notation that was to become a *determining* factor of composition. Only when individual human aspirations began to question and bypass such theorizing did creative musicians begin to *adapt* theory to their own sense of musical expression. This pull between prevailing theory and the composer's inclination to adapt or disregard it, eventually enabled composers not just to enhance emotional states but actually to *condition* them. It also caused change to become a fundamental factor in Western musical evolution. The combination of words and music enabled composers to copy their colleagues in symbolic art forms and illuminate aspects of life and human feelings. Eventually — by the end of the baroque period — musical composition had harnessed such a complex musical theory with such clearly recognizable *associative* symbolism that it became possible for composers of exceptional sensibility to create such illumination in purely *musical* terms, without the need for the association of words.

The personalized nature of musical composition made possible the incorporation of polemic with emotion and psychological perception with expression. Composers could now express their insights and ritualize their emotions with such acuity that they could affect the mores of their culture. This situation could exist, *providing* — and the proviso is highly pertinent to our present 'global' culture — *the musical conventions from which this ability stemmed were fully understood and accepted by the receivers as well as the creators of this emotionally dialectical process.*

To sustain such an arrogant stance, it was necessary that music's irrational essence and the rational means of moulding it should be held in perfect equilibrium. Where this equilibrium was not in balance, music lost not only its dialectical function but also its power to enhance the emotional state: it became purely decorative — beautiful by association. Where, however, this equilibrium was ideally balanced — through the kind of superbeing we now refer to as 'genius' — music bore the stamp of a universal validity and veracity, an expression of some deep psychological truth, defying and denying all period values.

The *classical* concept of genius had belonged to the world of the spirit: each individual household had possessed its own special genius to preside over its destiny and protect it from harm. With the cult of individualism in the West, the concept of genius was reserved for human beings whose exceptional ability and aspiration appeared to be the result of some special, supernatural providence. Thus genius was transferred from the individual household to become the guiding spirit of art and culture: the ultimate expression of élitism.

Western art music became essentially idealistic. It also became intrinsically implosive. The psychological manipulation of an aesthetic, which became the composer's means of communication, proved too deep and too personal a process for universal understanding. The total ascendancy of the composer caused his creativeness to turn inwards, towards a visionary, prophetic, and exclusive condition, distancing itself from the musical condition of its general audience. Unlike Indian music, where the fundamental absence of ego enables listeners to welcome musical performance uninhibitedly into their private emotional worlds, Western music has the effect of *discouraging* its listeners from actually trusting their own emotions. Where Indian music encourages *artistic* humility from the start, Western music, with its insistence on the genius of the composer, can only achieve humility from a starting-point of total arrogance.

Not surprisingly, the number of geniuses thrown up by Western civilization has been remarkably small. It is for this reason that so much of our present concert life concerns itself with music of very slender artistic merit. Some of this music is aimiably decorative; some of it emanates a turgid, superficial emotionalism. Much of it is concerned with challenging the virtuosity of the performer. For, ironically, the cultural importance placed by Western music on the genius of the *composer* causes a disproportionate amount of attention to be devoted to the individual *performer*: the composer's wilful and indispensable servant. As a result, the performer (and his PR man) can have a no less disproportionate effect on the extent to which composers of all periods do or do not receive public hearing.

Although the performer is, by Western definition, a second-class musical citizen, the degree of technical virtuosity of which he is capable has made him susceptible to 'stardom'. With its many unartistic accoutrements and its intrinsic subsuming of artistic principle on account of deference to market forces, 'stardom' has posed a threat to genuine musical artistry in the West since the international trafficking in castrati during the first half of the eighteenth century. Indeed, such was the interest in instrumental virtuosity at that time that German cities used actually to feature instrumental virtuosi and child prodigies alongside itinerant jugglers and rope-walkers — an interesting hark back to the ambience of the skilled medieval troubadour. At least, in the eighteenth century, performing stars were content merely to add graces and cadenzas to the compositions of established composers. But the 'stars' of the nineteenth century tended to make extra-musical demands of composers (it is well known that Paganini was insulted by the rather modest part composed for him by Berlioz in his symphony *Harold in Italy*) and even set about composing their own pieces in order to exhibit their virtuosity. These pieces, of themselves, did no great harm: we all enjoy circus tricks at times. Their significance lay in the extent to which virtuosity came to shape the musical culture of the nineteenth century. This detracted from the importance attached to the composer, even though the composer's work still represented the essence of musical culture. Performing virtuosity has played an increasingly important part in shaping the musical culture of the twentieth century and its effect has been the more disastrous as our concert life has come to emphasize past rather than present composers. Today's globe-trotting superstars have turned market forces in favour of the performer rather than the composer to such an extent as to mock the very nature of musical art.

The artistic component in musical appreciation is probably at its lowest ebb since the actual concept of art music burgeoned in the Middle Ages. As a result, musical responses have become fundamentally ritualized. Only last night, my transistor radio, tuned into that vast ritual, the Henry Wood Proms, strained to the thunder of cheering applause that would not have been out of place at a Roman gladiatorial fight, or, at least, a 'full effects' performance of Tchaikovsky's '1812 Overture'. (Mounting volume seems to have a substantial effect upon audience stimulation.) This applause was, in fact, for forty-five minutes of instrumental music by Rameau, performed with great precision and style by a baroque chamber ensemble. The music itself was excellently and predictably wrought in the best French manner, with as little emotional content as the *Tafelmusik* of Telemann, Vivaldi, and countless other baroque composers, whose talent enabled them to produce music to a prescribed order that was neither disturbing nor demanding, but was nevertheless well-ordered and, at times, entertaining. Why then such thunderous applause, which is normally engendered by fortissimo heroics and stirringly emotional tunes and harmonies? Whatever the reason, I suggest the music was extrinsic to it. Such applause symbolizes a ritualized response to music.

This ritualization of response to art music has been the inevitable consequence of a basic contradiction within the Western cultural ethos; for the cultural development that made possible the notion of artistic genius ensured, as it were by definition, that such genius would distance itself from its audience, causing a degree of emotional inhibition in the response. As an aspect of culture in general, this problem is not unique to art. The human response to any phenomenon that is not fully understood will contain a mixture of direct emotion, sensory intuition, and personal contrivance. As long as education is concerned more with stimulation than indoctrination of mind and spirit, responses to any partially understood phenomenon — whether it be natural, scientific, artistic or political — must contain a healthy element of cynical inquisitiveness. We in the West are naturally resistant to educational indoctrination; yet education is now an intrinsic aspect of our culture, whose very existence presupposes a degree of indoctrination — as an inevitable corollary to the whole process of responding to the prevailing culture. *Acceptance* of Western artistic norms results from acceptance of this cultural ambience, a process to which school education is *necessarily* a contributor or adjustor. By accepting this cultural ambience, it is possible for people to enjoy art without necessarily understanding it. Through indoctrination, it is possible for artists to understand all the norms of their art without necessarily accepting their validity. Unfortunately, if inevitably, a vast number of people have rejected both artistic norms and artistic indoctrination.

Despite all this, the power of art is such that it *can* appeal to emotional people at a level that *transcends* knowledge and acceptance. (This is particularly true of musical art, because of its essential lack of direct symbolism.) Yet the full emotionalism of musical artistic experience can only take place when all its components — composition, performance, style of presentation, mood, place — exceptionally coalesce to produce that form of worldly sublimation that is the essential mystery of art. Such a complete response also demands a rare combination of knowledge, understanding, and emotional susceptibility on the part of the listener. When listeners lack these attributes, as is generally the case with the majority in any audience, they tend to respond ritually — though sincerely — with instantaneous, uncritical applause. Their response is essentially conditioned: their lack of professional knowledge discourages them from questioning the accepted veracity of the composition and their true feelings about the performance. (When, as sometimes happens, applause turns to booing, this is because *aesthetic* rather than artistic sensibilities have been shocked.) Instantaneous applause often only indicates that the essence of the performance has been lost, for it is a response to the performance more than the music. Any one who can, for example, 'Bravo' Isolde within three minutes of a really powerful performance of the *Liebestod* has almost certainly failed to catch the emotional essence of the music. For Wagner's *Tristan and Isolde* retains its emotional charge because it is a work of supreme genius: eternally sage, eternally youthful, and eternally *modern*. And this is the point: popular sensibility to art is *not* modern — it is not in tune with the mores of modern culture. This is why it so largely fails to recognize the difference between performing excellence and performing charlatanism and between artistic composition and aesthetic shibolleths to which the creative artist reacts.

This alienation of society from the essential modernity of all real musical art has been an inevitable consequence of the exclusive, aristocratic base from which post-Renaissance art was conditioned. When that base had been *theocratic* — as it had been in the early Middle Ages and in most cultures of the world — music had retained a functional *universality*, endorsing a doctrinaire understanding of life. When that base began to crumble, due to the imperial ambitions of secular princelings, the unifying function of musical art (like the religion it served) changed to that of aristocratic service, involving mutual exploitation between servant and served. Music became individualistic and utilitarian, a political accoutrement rather than an empirical medium, tied to a contemporary aesthetic. To rise above this level of pleasurable aimiability to the status of art it required the application of exceptional genius.

Musical art is characterized by its capacity to ritualize emotion. It must therefore be capable of reflecting the *infinite variety* of mood to which emotions give rise. The few composers of outstanding genius succeeded in doing this in purely musical terms through their ability to integrate the musical elements of melody, rhythm, harmony, counterpoint, motor speed, thematic development, dynamics, timbre, and words — *independently* of the mood created. This flexibility of operation alone can lead to complete emotional variety in purely musical terms. With it a composer of genius can dare and succeed: creating the ideal equilibrium between music's irrational essence and his own rational means of moulding it.

If an artist is to combine the intuition and experience necessary for his greatest work to retain its sense of eternal youth, wisdom, and modernity, his work is bound to evolve from three essential processes. These processes may overlap and vary in length, but all three are essential to supreme genius. Firstly, the artist must battle with the past: not to reject it, but to manipulate it into a form appropriate to the present. Secondly, having formulated a uniquely relevant style, he must use and develop it with sufficient confidence to reflect and expose the mores of his culture. Finally — and this is the stage that most of the 'great' composers fail to reach — the accumulated experience and confidence must drive the artist into his own exclusive, visionary world, to create works of such depth that they deny the past, the present, and the future. That is what I mean when I say that the greatest works of art remain eternally youthful and eternally modern. And that is why a *sense of modernity* is so essential for understanding Western art.

A comparison between Bach and Handel may help to illustrate the point. In fact, it was not until the end of the baroque period that musical art had acquired sufficient emotional power to contain the individual and dialectical expression of this type of genius. Its ability to do so was due partly to the tensions and releases of harmonic discord and concord in relation to those of melody and rhythm — already powerfully exploited by Monteverdi and Schutz. More importantly, it was due to the establishment of a system of key relationships capable of sustaining thematic development and — subsequently — thematic opposition. Bach's unique genius lay in his ability to *sustain* musical argument, anticipating the symphonic development of thematic motives in a way that completely transcended current conventions. Far from being the 'summative' composer he is so often held to be, Bach was one of the most modern composers of all time. That was one reason why his music (like the late quartets of Beethoven) had to wait so long for recognition of its true worth. The scale of its recognition later (and it was never entirely lost: Beethoven was profoundly aware of Bach's example) was due to the extent to which Bach's modernity was rooted in the past. In his late compositions, Bach became obsessed with counterpoint and canonic symmetry in relation to the new style of rococo. In *The Musical Offering* he imbued a rococo theme with the sturdiness of baroque conventions, while in the Goldberg Variations he took a baroque theme and treated it with variegated rococo expression.

By contrast, Handel lacked that forward-looking modernity of the very greatest genius. The extraordinary popularity of *Messiah* indicates that musical popularity and supreme artistic precocity are not necessarily synonymous. *Messiah* is, of course, a great work and Handel a great composer. Handel acquired the ability to integrate musical elements independently of the mood created (the setting of 'He was despised' in a *major* key is an instance). When the words demanded it (i.e., in *vocal* music only) Handel extracted the maximum degree of emotional variety and contrast from baroque manner; and the libretto of *Messiah* provided stimulus to his imagination at a more sustained level than any other libretto he set.

Messiah is one of the most extrovert works of great musical art in existence: for the non-professional listener it appeals directly to the emotions and makes few immediate demands on the intellect. This is both a strength and a weakness: it is certainly one cause of its popularity. Yet in none of Handel's *instrumental* works did he outshine any of his contemporaries. He did not learn to sustain a purely musical argument, nor did he ever attain that combination of conviction and introspection that would cause him to try. Handel was essentially a child of his time, reacting with musical emotion and ingenuity to the many literary themes he tackled. That he avoided artistic vulgarity was due — fortunately for him and for us — to the formal constraints of his day. Where Bach, with the precocity of absolute genius, made the decisive leap into the unknown, confident of his *own* self-control, Handel became the darling of his age, occasionally shocking aesthetic sensibilities but never overturning aesthetic principles. It was Handel, not Bach, who was the 'summative' composer of the baroque.

In the eighteenth century, instrumental styles developed, as they have always done, from the process of setting words to music. Baroque instrumental forms were a direct offspring of the operatic and sacred concerto styles of the seventeenth century. Classical instrumental style owed more to Gluck than the composers of Mannheim or Potsdam; and the miracle of mature classical symphonic form, with its drama sustained by key relationships, sprang directly from the musical-theatrical problems which Mozart solved so magnificiently in the ensemble writing in *The Marriage of Figaro*.

Beethoven, whose revolutionary style was to provide a catalyst for the middle fifty years of the nineteenth century, equally formulated his instrumental styles through the setting of words. Where, however, Mozart had contained the political polemic of his operatic libretti within the basic musical conventions of his day (only in the last act of *Don Giovanni* did he anticipate the gestural largeness of Beethoven's style), Beethoven allowed the *political* sentiment of his libretti to condition the dramatic nature of his whole musical style. Beethoven's originality and conviction were such that he enabled musical art itself to become political. The censors of Metternich's secret police, who left Beethoven in relative peace because they regarded him and his art as half-crazed, little knew what *supra*-political artistic forces were being unleashed. The early and little

known *Funeral Cantata on the death of Joseph II* (the last liberal
monarch of the Austrian Empire) provided suitable provocation for
Beethoven to rationalize musically some of his most impulsive
instincts, prior to composing the early symphonies, concertos, and
chamber music. Similarly, the composition of *Fidelio* (particularly
Florestan's wonderful oration at the start of Act II) provided the
technique for containing exceedingly contrasting moods within a
single movement and motor speed — so characteristic of the Fourth
to Sixth Symphonies and Fourth and Fifth Piano Concertos which
immediately followed *Fidelio*. It can also be seen that the means for
evolving the formal synthesis of the late style was provided by the
vocal element of the *Missa Solemnis*. This was clearly understood by
Wagner, whose whole symphonic revolution was created almost
exclusively in conjunction with the verbal language of theatre.
Little of it however was understood by nineteenth-century instrumental composers, who tended to favour the element of melody at
the expense of all others. Even less of it was understood by the
majority of Beethoven's contemporaries, who ascribed to him such
popularity in his day. This popularity sprang not from his great
symphonies and concertos but from his 'Wellington' Symphony
and a host of other nationalistic works of almost unbelievable
banality which he churned out in the aftermath of 1812, during a
troubled, non-creative period brought on by approaching deafness.
That Beethoven's music could have sunk to this overt level of
jingoism (the 'Wellington' Symphony is no more than a robust
orchestration of 'For he's a jolly good fellow' and other militarily
associative tunes, interspersed by march-type flourishes for side
drum and trumpet) is an indication of the sheer effort that had been
required to sustain a revolutionary artistic stance against a hostile
musical and political background. It also indicates the knife-edge
between artistic precocity and vulgarity that Beethoven's emotionally violent style had constantly, and with enormous effort, to
negotiate. More importantly, it indicated the extent to which
political fervour could be aroused by a new type of musical vulgarity: usually a result of neglecting to balance and integrate the
various musical elements — often with an obviously emotional
melodiousness, containing strongly emotional, *extra-musical*
associations.

Of all composers of the Western world, Beethoven held music's

irrational essence in the most *daring* balance with his manipulation
of it. No composer relied more on the vision and impulse of his
genius and, inevitably, no composer more nearly or more frequently got it wrong. Nowhere is the knife-edge between artistic
precocity and artistic vulgarity more keenly felt than in the last
movement of Beethoven's Ninth Symphony. Where most composers exercised too great a restraint on music's irrational essence
(particularly after the nineteenth century removed the restraint of
formal style conditioned by the manners of the eighteenth century)
Beethoven's impulsiveness frequently led to too little. The 'Hymn
of Joy' is a potentially dangerous work — politically, because it
contains explosive musical fervour yet fails to speak in purely
musical terms (quite apart from its literary associations). Its musical
style, reminiscent at times of the parade ground, has strongly
political and patriotic connotations. I have personally witnessed the
'Hymn of Joy' arouse a German audience to a state of frighteningly
uncontrollable, neurotic, jingoistic adulation.

Where, in the eighteenth century, music had served as a political
accoutrement whose only overt form of political rebellion could be in
the subject matter of opera, the nineteenth century — largely as a
result of Beethoven or, at least, his occasional artistic miscalcu-
lations — enabled music to be a *political force* in its own right.
Words, rather than 'affected' moods, came to *adopt* associative
musical gestures, creating — again by association — a specific type
of musical sentiment with which to enhance their own, often extra-
musical purposes. This was due to the *lack* of formal restraint
which eventually undermined the eighteenth century's 'enabling'
integration of musical elements.

Lesser composers of the nineteenth century, rather than integrating musical elements, tended actually to *use* individual elements to
create a mood, causing their music to lack that sense of spontaneous
inevitability that characterizes the greatest musical art. In doing so,
they dredged from these individual musical elements a limiting,
chauvinistic attractiveness, ignoring the wider truths to which
musical art should have been contributing. This was also a problem
in most of the 'nationalistic' music of eastern Europe. It was also a
problem in the music of the post-Wagnerian romantics, Mahler and
Strauss, whose music can radiate an expressive, heart-warming
sensuousness, but whose musical emotionalism was never, ulti-

mately, in totally balanced control. A similarly limiting framework
of composition was to be forced upon composers even more
pungently by the social and political forces of the twentieth
century.

In the nineteenth century, the characteristics thus used were,
generally, melody and harmony. Compared with the formally
mannered harmony of the eighteenth century, itself a springboard
for rhythm, the cloying, chromatic twists of nineteenth-century
harmony generally led to rhythmic stagnation. Even with a composer of such emotional radiance as Brahms, excessive restraints on
the rational means allowed chromatic harmony and overt melodiousness to limit rhythmic stimulation. As rhythm is the primordial basis of music's irrational power, music in the nineteenth
century tended to exercise its irrationality essentially through extra-
musical associations. These new associations were not just verbal:
art music had increasingly come to absorb influences from popular
sources. Melody began to acquire associative connotations in relation to social and political institutions, from the church, court,
and militia to the ballroom, salon, and the peasantry — for the
increasing use of folk-inspired melody in art music also had social
and political connotations.

The nationalistic fervour endemic by association to Beethoven's
'Choral' Symphony became even more endemic to the operas of
Verdi, due again as much to *musical* associations as to verbal
content. It was of course the resemblance between the story line of
Nabucco to the oppressed plight of the Italians that, ostensibly at
least, cast Verdi in the role of national hero. It is, however, most
unlikely that this would have happened without Verdi's unique
melodic strength, achieved partly by the retention of a simple but
overt form of *harmonic rhythm*. With this underlying rhythmic
excitement, Verdi strengthened immensely the melodic gestures
that, in a stereotyped manner and closely allied to harmonic clichés,
had come to be associated with particular moods and themes.
Thus, whatever the dramatic mood, Verdi could usually find a
means of enabling the music itself to exude the dramatic sentiment.
Like Beethoven, he constantly walked a tightrope of emotional
excess and was saved from falling into vulgarity only by the
strength of his innate rhythmic vitality. Unlike Beethoven, however, he did not overturn the aesthetic principles of his day. He

simply discovered in these aesthetic principles a powerful political weapon and one of his unique accomplishments was to be both political and artistic simultaneously.

By contrast, Wagner, perhaps more than any composer who ever lived, succeeded in appealing to the subconscious in purely musical terms. He achieved this by freeing music from external associative symbolism and associating it instead with symbolism of the music's own making. And although (from *Rhinegold* onwards) the music was at all times conditioned by theatre, it never subjected itself to the plot. Rather the plot provided the formal means for the music to be perpetually self-renewing. The genius of the *Ring* cycle is that the leitmotives were completely disassociated from the musical associations of political and social institutions, all deriving by stages from the initial arpeggio 'nature' motive. The distance Wagner had had to travel to achieve this unique state may be measured by comparing this psychological symbolism with the overt associative symbolism of his early opera *Rienzi*. In *Rienzi* the music derives its descriptive symbolism entirely from external associations, particularly those of the parade ground. As a result, such appeal as the music of *Rienzi* has is at a directly conscious level. The *losing* of consciousness — the moment of supreme truth in art music — can only be achieved when music has a life entirely of its own, expressing that which can *only* be expressed in music. This is the condition of ultimate genius. By the time Wagner used direct Christian quotation in his final opera *Parsifal*, it became indistinguishable from his own musical style, causing the association to be subconscious to the listener.

Where eighteenth-century music, with its formal integration of musical elements, had been characteristically unsusceptible to emotional content, requiring manipulation by composers of supreme genius to provide it, nineteenth-century music with its tendency to overt melodiousness and chromatic harmony, *was* susceptible to emotion, but often of a type that was artistically superficial. I referred in Chapter 3 to the fact that the musical characteristics which made possible the great popularity of nine-teenth-century singing and brass band playing were, and are, ones that artists tend to dislike: that they contribute to an unbridled release of emotion rather than a controlled expression of emotion which, to cultured artists, represents the difference between vulgarity and beauty. The writers of evangelical hymn tunes made no attempt to hold the various elements of music in rational balance. Rather, their music had a specifically social function and the musical elements of melody and harmony were used quite deliberately towards an extra-musical end. This applied to composers of music for all popular causes — the dance hall, the brass band, and the operetta. (It still applies with no less force to — among others — modern writers of 'jazz cantatas' and other 'educational' music for schools.)

The nineteenth century made possible the writing of music aimed at deliberate popular appeal in specific types of social ambience, essentially unartistic in style and function but based on the styles and formulae of art music. Thus art music, which had taken so long to find an exclusive dialectical function, lost its exclusiveness almost as soon as it had found it. It began to share a greatly enlarged arena with music whose intent (in varying degree) was more popular than artistic. It took then — as it takes now — a high degree of musical sensibility and cultural awareness to see the artistic wood for the trees.

This, ultimately, is the central point at issue. Genuine appreciation of art, in tune with modern cultural mores, depends upon knowledge and understanding of cultural norms *throughout history*. As life proceeds, this is a gradually deepening process. To take, for example, only the popular norms of the nineteenth century as a basis for musical awareness is to miss most of the essential background for a real understanding of Western music. It should be a function of musical education to explore and experiment with the basic elements of music in order to understand more deeply how they have been used by the great artists of Western culture. This, however, can only be fulfilled by teachers who have themselves a sense of the universality of Western culture.

That this is not always the case is not entirely the fault of education. Musical art itself has been subject, culturally, to the same dilemmas of criteria as has education. The cultural forces of the nineteenth century demanded, rightly and inevitably, a democratization of art music, just as they demanded a democratization of education. Like education, music gradually acquired extrinsic criteria that confused the central issues. Unlike education, however, art music still has a directly *active* rather than an *enabling* function. Although modern cultural forces have precipitated drastic changes in the *modes* of artistic activation, art continues to be produced

because artists believe that there are still things that can only
be said, attitudes that can only be shaped, feelings that can only be
delineated through art. Artists also know that if there is any relief to
be found from the brutal, exploitive history of man — and not just
of Western man — it is to be found in art: that the germinating
force of the art of genius is a profound sense of humanity, a
visionary intuition that speaks — often laughs — beyond the frail
turrets of human pretension.

To the sensitive, cultured artist, it would seem that this humanizing influence is constantly being undermined because people
appear to find it *objets d'art* or pieces of music that are not, by
Western standards, intrinsically artistic. This is the paradox of
Western culture. However, because the idealism and philosophical
vision of Western civilization was epitomized in its art, artists
inevitably see their function as continuing this dialectical process —
in ways that will perhaps shock, perhaps offend, perhaps make
people think again. The tendency for modern man to find in his so-
called 'artistic heritage' a nostalgic reminder of a better, bygone
age, its atrocities blunted by the passage of time, only forces the
creative artist into more radical gestures of protest. Whatever the
failures of modern musical art — and they are legion — there are at
least partical successes which start from an overwhelming belief in
the *necessity* of artistic statement for the humanity of man.

The intrinsic problem remains: popular sensibility to art is not
modern. This is particularly true of *musical* art, due to the implosive
imbalance between the status of the composer and the performer.
Audiences turn to adulation of the performer, partly because he is
actually still alive and partly because his role appears so much easier
to assess than that of the composer. Thus the notion of the musical
performer as the perpetuator of musical art is endorsed: a fallacy at
the heart of the modern decay of musical artistry. Because it is not
modern, popular sensibility frequently *abuses* musical art. Art can
be an important catalyst in society or, through association, it can be
a dangerously implosive agent; it can provoke a valuable source of
questioning and learning or it can create a dilettante and foppish
form of entertainment; it can add apparent dignity to lofty occasions or it can mock the cause it appears to serve. The fundamental need is to restore art to its essential function as a major cultural
force: a cultural force *for* our own time, just as and because Bach,

Beethoven, *et al.* were cultural forces *for* their time. The artistic challenge to education is to make popular sensibility to art *modern*.

As the passage of time blunts the daring precocity of the artist, so the line between illumination and entertainment becomes blurred. Understandably, audiences find it difficult to define the nature of their adulation: it is usually a mixture of extrinsic association, music's irrational power, and an arcane belief in the 'civilizing' power of music. The artist of genius illuminates. Can he alone be illuminated? Not if he has the vision to disturb the mores of his society. For then, in a truly arcane way, he will contribute to the evolution of civilization. And so-called 'civilized' people will live with this phenomenon, without necessarily being aware of it.

7

The Problems of
Twentieth-Century Music

Nothing is so dangerous as being modern.
One is apt to grow old-fashioned quite suddenly.
> Oscar Wilde *An Ideal Husband*, Act 2

It is an inevitable paradox of our time that the more modern music is generally disliked, the more its propagation becomes an educational fetish. As modern music provides an essential link between the musical past and a presumed musical future, failure to recognize the importance of the musical present would suggest that the musical past is no longer relevant. The 'moral' myth of music must therefore be perpetuated: whether or not modern music exudes its own dialectic, modern man must be educated to *like* it.

Modern man, however, is presented with a bewildering array of musical forms and styles all claiming to represent modern music. His musical ambience lacks cultural and artistic norms on a scale unprecedented in history. Because of this, modern music itself is in danger of losing art music's traditional, dialectical function. Many composers are now adopting a style of easy familiarity, a cosmetic sheen with which to win back the hearts and minds of that majority of people to whom the avant-garde developments of the past half century have clearly been anathema. Throughout the twentieth century, art (and particularly music) has experienced a period of unprecedented instability. This has led to many spurious ideals and has created many blind alleys. The result has been a greater confusion of audience response than at any other point in the history of Western music. It is therefore of considerable importance, educationally, to establish some sort of perspective on the music of this century, with the hope of identifying cultural and musical norms which may help to distinguish between that which is potentially lasting and that which is seemingly ephemeral.

When did modern music begin? Had that question been asked in fourteenth-century Paris, no educated person would have answered anything other than 'now, all around us' — and the answer would probably have been given with enthusiasm. Had the question been asked in parts of early seventeenth-century Italy, the answer would probably have been 'now', though not everyone would have accepted the *stile moderna* as an improvement. Had the question been asked in 1820, the answer would have been 'now', with all fingers pointing at Beethoven. Had the question been asked in 1876, the answer would have ben 'now', with enough people pointing the finger at Wagner to say 'right here, in Bayreuth'. Had the question been asked in 1925, forty-two years after Wagner's death, eleven years after *The Rite of Spring* and four years after Schoenberg had published his principles of atonality, the answer would probably still have been 'with Wagner': few would have cited even Debussy. When the question is asked now, it can only be answered with prevarication: 'It depends what you mean; perhaps with Boulez and Stockhausen.' Within the context of this book I want to ask the question with a very specific meaning: when did modern music first break deliberately and totally with the cultural mores of the past? I will answer it no less specifically: with the music of Charles Edward Ives.

Born in 1875 in America, Ives was in a place and a position to *see through* the aura of pretentiousness and bombast that surrounded European musical culture. For Ives, that meant *German* musical culture: the droppings lay around him in America — thus disposed of by European émigrés, or Americans who had been to Europe to absorb its culture — 'to be finished'. Of course, Europeans had also seen through this bombast, particularly in France, which had traditionally stood in opposition to Italian and then German culture. But the French could do little more than offer ridicule: Satie's delightful reproach was fundamentally antithetic to the concept of musical art, while his followers were never really free from art's beauteous seductiveness. Ives, however, *was* free from the lot. He was not just born in America; he was fastened there, inspired — thanks partly to the influence of an unusually free-thinking musical father — with a conviction about American independence and American music. 'You'll not get a wild, heroic ride to Heaven on pretty little sounds', his father had told him.[1]

From across the Atlantic, Ives could hardly appreciate the great affirmation of German musical culture contained in Wagnerian opera. (As a student, he had been to a performance of *Götterdämmer-*

ung and found it 'a great deal of work over nothing'.) What he *could* see, with an acuity denied to Europeans, was the irrelevance of the whole German tradition of musical art to the social, political, and cultural mores of his time. While Europe, at the turn of the nineteenth century, was feeling its way backwards out of its musical impasse, towards a form of musical rhetoric that would hold to ransom the notion of 'artistic beauty', Charles Ives was, in the words of the *New York Times*, exercising a 'gumption . . . not derived from a *Rite of Spring* or even from anything but the conviction of a composer who has not the slightest idea of self-ridicule and who dares jump with feet and hands in a reckless somersault or two on the way to his destination'.[2] That was in 1927, eleven years after the composition of the work in question. Even then an Ives performance was of itself a rarity, with or without the attendance of a perceptive critic. Most of Ives's music had to wait over thirty years for public performance, let alone public recognition.

Much has been made of Ives's technical innovations. The fact that he used polyrhythms, polytonalities, polytextures, serial procedures, clusters, microtones, spacial separations, *sprechgesang*, and parody before anyone else, is characteristic but scarcely important; for all this was simply an inevitable part of his *style*. Ives had a profound contempt for the 'manner' of music; it was the 'manner' of German music that he recognized as being so restrictive. Indeed, his deliberate propensity for breaking the rules — inserting wrong notes and rhythmic distortions in the traditional music he incorporated — became a predominant characteristic of his own 'manner'. This 'manner' was a direct consequence of the 'substance'; because for Ives, musical 'substance' was fundamentally germane to the process of artistic creativity. Ives, uniquely, saw that the 'substance' of German music was conditioned by its limiting 'manner'. The problem with this 'manner' was that it could not contain representation of life as a whole, but only one tiny part of it. *That tiny part conditioned the whole appearance of musical culture.* If the 'substance' of art was to be so unrepresentative of *life as a whole*, then the fault must lie with the 'manner' — with the very concept of 'art'. Ives's pertinent obsession with 'substance' overruled any concern for stylistic consistency. His artistic integrity lay in his uncompromising absorption *into his musical language* of every aspect of his contemporary musical ambience: revolutionary war songs, sentimental civil war songs, music of marching bands, spirituals, hymns, anthems, minstrel songs, ragtime, and vaudeville — even Beethoven gets a miniscule 'wrapped-up' quote in the Fourth Symphony. In this process, Ives stumbled upon virtually every musical 'manner' into which European music would eventually rationalize itself. Because of his compulsive need to present the past, the present, the sacred, the secular, the light, the contrived, all living together as legitimate raw material for musical art, Ives allowed the resulting technical procedures to jostle together, gloriously consistent in their inconsistency. This was the essence of his anarchic originality. In challenging the comfortable notion that art involved some kind of 'superior' sense of beauty (one that appeared to rest largely with the ruling establishment, even though it *was* susceptible to being passed 'downwards') Ives's music represented a strong political statement. It was, however, political by association; and it was the last such political statement in music to have been born of political *confidence*.

This political confidence was more imagined than real. The revolutionary 'manner' of Ives's music concealed a basic nostalgia in its 'substance'. Although the integrity of the artistic intent was unshakeable, the political irrelevance of the musical 'substance' was revealed painfully in 1917, when Ives was asked hurriedly to set a war poem called 'On Flanders Field'. Associative tunes like 'Columbia, Gem of the Ocean' and 'Battle Cry of Freedom' which had served Ives so admirably in his modern-sounding, nostalgic collages, were hardly appropriate to the living horror of the 1917 trenches — of 'In Flanders Field the poppies blow between the crosses, row on row . . .'. In any case, the 'crosses, row on row' were not even American. Thus, ironically, the *cultural* importance of Ives's music in fact consisted in his 'manner' — his *anarchic* treatment of his 'substance'. For the 'substance' itself was intensely national at a time when the world was becoming increasingly international. Three years after *Flanders Field*, the political ousting of Woodrow Wilson destroyed the ideal of a 'League of Nations' as surely as it destroyed the political confidence that had fired Ives's creativity. A tub-thumping piece of doggerel, *An Election: Nov. 2nd, 1920*, for chorus and orchestra was virtually the end of Ives's creative output. Modern music had been born and the modern world was doing its worst. If modern music was to continue to have dialectical meaning it would have to adjust to a world gone sour, a Western world at least whose confidence has been totally, finally shattered.

The importance of Ives to this study is that his mixture of musical genius, naïvety and artistic-political conviction enabled him to anticipate and, to an astonishing extent, overcome virtually every musical problem that would beset composers of this century. He understood the way in which commercialism would strike at the spiritual roots of art and refused to compose for a living. ('Bach, Beethoven, Brahms, etc . . . they couldn't exactly help it . . . they had to live at least part of the time by the ladies smiles . . . or die'.[3]) He recognized the need for a completely new language, one that would counter the nineteenth-century tendency to regard beauty as an end in itself. He recognized that complacent acquiescence in the traditional stemmed from over-familiarity with melodic and harmonic conventions; doubtless he also recognized that this had been severely detrimental to rhythmic vitality. He recognized the need to incorporate *familiar* elements within his new language and he understood that this would have to be in the form of quotation. He recognized a new social need for musical art to incorporate a universality of musical sentiment, and he understood the need for this to be a part of his actual musical language, rather than to be treated bit by bit. Above all, his approach to art was positive and affirmative. The spirit of man should not acquiesce in the mundane but should conspire to eternal questioning. For Ives, art was essentially about asking questions that had never been answered. Maybe they never would be, but the questions still needed asking.

Such questions were entirely appropriate. The European culture to which Ives had been so averse had nurtured a 'love of art' as a testament to its apparent superiority, achieved as a result of ruthless acquisitiveness and exploitation. This culture was, like that of Ives, rooted in Christianity, with its doctrine of self-denial and its symbol of the Cross. Unlike that of Ives, this culture had had eight centuries for its art to be conditioned by this doctrine and symbolism. Many of the problems of modern music are rooted in this history.

The very nature of Christianity caused martyrdom to be seen as the supreme symbol of faith. The reward for this faith and for abiding by ascetic Christian doctrine was the surety of a beauteous after-life in heaven — in contrast to the ghastly torment of hell. As visual art had provided the fundamental means of instructing a largely illiterate population, there was nothing illogical, extrinsically, about the fact that a great deal of Christian art concerned itself with the depiction of crucifixion, torture, and the torments of hell. What *was* illogical, *intrinsically*, was the coalescence of this subject matter with the medieval love of beauty: with Abbot Suger's declaration that 'the dull mind rises to truth through that which is beautiful'. While many artists had tried hard to depict some inkling of the joys of heaven, the subject proved very much further from their immediate experience than the atrocities of hell. Thus, from the time of the artistic awakening of the Middle Ages to the beginnings of modern art, art itself embodied the fundamental paradox that it actually beautified torture and other forms of inhumanity, in justification of a higher purpose. This paradox is contained within *Messiah*, the *Matthew Passion*, the *Missa Solemnis*, and countless other musical masterpieces of Western art: *Laus Deo*.

The renewed interest in Greek culture at the time of the Renaissance lent further justification to the depiction in art of cruel and bellicose themes, for the essence of Greek culture had lain in heroism and valour. The unique Greek synthesis of strength and beauty as 'morality' proved extremely attractive as justification for the more bellicose pursuits of the princely patrons of Renaissance and baroque art and it enabled the artists themselves to continue to extract beauty and nobility from themes far removed from the Christian 'peace that passeth all understanding'. During the seventeenth and eighteenth centuries, aristocratic love of art became essentially narcissistic.

It was to take the combined efforts of geniuses such as Mozart, Rousseau, Kant and, ultimately, Napoleon to reverse this process. Following the French Revolution, the politics of the nineteenth century compromised the 'morality' that had justified and sustained patronage of artificially affected — 'mannered' — art. The nineteenth century bereaved the artist of his traditional, courtly role. It forced him to confront nature and its process alone in a new, unequal, and heroic partnership. As a result, art became larger than life, as a comparison of eighteenth and nineteenth century operatic subject matter will show. Art, for the ruling classes, became the touchstone of aristocratic tradition. (Along with its spurious connotation of 'morality', it also became a necessary commodity to share with the less privileged classes, to whom it was so obviously denied.) Art aggrandized, *confirmed* the 'morality' of a love of beauty. During the nineteenth century, beauty became loved in the *name* of art. This placed upon art a need for pretentiousness and upon musical artists an unprecedented challenge: to evolve, within accepted musical traditions, forms that could satisfactorily contain art's dialectical function along with its enlarged aesthetic image. It was one that few composers could meet — Wagner and Verdi alone did so satisfactorily — and it led to a great deal of 'beautiful' musical moonshine.

The general falsity of this love of *beauty* (as opposed to *art*) was to be made manifest in the twentieth century. Hitherto, inhumanity and deceit had been justified as subject-matter for art — or so art lovers had been conditioned to believe — providing it was contained within an overall context of apparent nobility. Although theatre had made this particular style of nobility open to question since the middle years of the eighteenth century, it was to take the unprecedented atrocities of the First World War to destroy it completely and, with it, the ambience of political optimism which had nurtured art for so long. For the musical artist this produced a crisis in what, for want of external associations implicit in the essence of music, I shall have to call, with Ives, 'substance': what playwrights and painters would call 'subject-matter'. And perhaps I can illustrate this best by looking at the 'subject-matter' of relevant musical theatre.

In 1918, the Hungarian composer, Béla Bartók started work on what was to prove one of his greatest works: the score for the ballet *The Miraculous Mandarin*. The subject-matter was lurid — sufficiently so that it was rejected alternately by the socialist and the bourgeois societies of his time. The work was first performed as a concert piece in 1926. The story tells of how three destitute thugs persuade a prostitute to tempt men into their room for the purpose of robbing them. Two decoy games outside the house produce a destitute cavalier and a shy boy respectively, each of whom is thrown out after a dance with the prostitute. The third very elaborate and demonic decoy game produces a Mandarin who confronts the girl with determined, lifeless eyes. Indescribably lonely and 'other-worldly', the Mandarin knows only two degrees of emotion: total coldness and devouring passion. These extremes are manifest in his 'non-waltz' with the prostitute and his subsequent lustful chase. The thugs attempt to kill the Mandarin, first by hanging, then by suffocation, and finally by a sword — but all these attempts fail. The Mandarin can only die when the girl has found the compassion to allow him one moment of ecstatic love.

It will be instructive to compare this plot with that of Wagner's *Parsifal*. Although the subject-matter of *Parsifal*, along with that of the *Ring* cycle epitomizes the most polemical vote of political 'no confidence' in the history of opera, it is cast in a setting particularly suited to traditional ideas of nobility, significantly incorporating elements of Christianity. In essence, however, the plot is no less lurid than that of *The Miraculous Mandarin*. A wicked magician seizes from a noble company a spear with which he inflicts a wound on its leader and from which the leader can neither be healed nor die, except by a touch from that same spear. All attempts to retrieve the spear are foiled by an ugly but purposefully enchanted seductress who lures assailants fatally from their mission. Only an ignorant fool can recognize the compassion that alone can foil the seductress, win the spear, heal the leader, and allow him to die in peace.

The themes of these two stage works are strikingly similar. Both contain magical symbolism, both analyse the destructive and healing powers of love and both point to compassion as the sole entry to the latter. Only the settings and metaphors are different: one being the ambience of the Holy Grail, the other a brothel; one Christianity, the other larceny. Adultery and salvation are intrinsic to both. Wagner's prophetically spurious, didactic Eden belongs to the *Fin de la Belle Époque*. Bartók's dialectical hell followed the atrocious butcheries of Paschendale and the Somme. Who could be innocent after civilization became barbarous? The Mandarin personified untouchable sorrow: the 'primitive' outsider, seeking and necessitating conciliation through love. Both plots confirm universal truths, in ways appropriate to their very different cultural ambiences. Wagner sought them on the path to heaven where, in the 1880s, people might still have thought to look for them. Bartók sought them in the gutter. Berg too, would seek them in the gutter, as would countless artists prior to the Second World War.

This was not what lovers of art had been led to expect. Henceforth they would look for *their* universal truths in the nostalgic dreamland of romanticism, careless of any distinction between art and mere decoration. Consequently, such truths became lies, because decorative romantic art works, along with their associative 'moral' values, were transposed out of a culture to which such associations were intrinsic into a culture in which they could only be hypocritical. Man's natural love of beauty makes it very difficult for him now to distinguish between that and any intrinsic love of art.

The politics of the twentieth century have created cultural problems of such magnitude that they have virtually overreached the capacity of art to contain them. Art must coexist with the experience of two horrific World Wars, which have resulted in continuing torture, butchery, and every known form of human exploitation and injustice. The present, relative detachment of the Western world from these atrocities can appear to make a lie of the art that has apparently reflected its culture. On the one hand, it is quite apposite to dredge such humanity as we can from the art works of Western genius, for there alone we seem able to find it. On the other hand, it is equally apposite to examine George Steiner's thesis, that the paradox of this superior 'humanity', rooted in Christianity (whose art was so often about the beautification of torture and of Hell) was that it did not prevent intelligent Germans with aesthetic sensibility from administering the Final Solution; that the emotional tendencies that led to the Holocaust were to be found within the artistic traditions of Europe since the Middle Ages. To quote Steiner himself: 'To have neither Heaven nor Hell is to be intolerably deprived in a world gone flat. Of the two, Hell proved the easier to re-create. (The pictures had always been more detailed.)'[4] Art does not *necessarily* humanize.

The *technology* of the twentieth century has actually ridiculed traditional Western musical art, rooted as it is in the world of Newtonian physics. It has also vastly expanded our knowledge of this whole art process, while pitting it mercilessly against the art of quite different cultures — including Western pop culture. This has led to a culturally intrinsic yet musically implausible imperative: to treat of universally valid themes in a universally valid dialect. (Only Ives and Tippett, among internationally recognized composers, seem to have faced this problem with consistency.) Many of the 'new' musical cultures lack the poignant self-expression of Western art and can therefore seem more pertinent to our modern culture than the artistic tradition which has been its pride. Hence the intrinsic 'universal' imperative: for we cannot eradicate our past, even should we want to. If we could silence its music, we could not, short of widespread demolition, prevent our daily confrontation with the abundance of civic art and architecture testifying proudly to its supposed achievements. The personalized, self-expressive tradition of Western art exists in precarious relationship with modern cultural mores, rendering the kind of perfection sought and achieved by Bach, Mozart, Beethoven or Wagner a virtual impossibility. The unprecedented complexity of the modern artist's task has led to an ever-widening gap between his imagination and his achievement.

An examination of Igor Stravinsky's journey through the turmoils of the twentieth century will illustrate only too clearly the way in which genius can be compromised by cross-cultural, political forces, too great to meet head-on. Stravinsky's composing career has often been referred to as 'Protean'. The truth is, however, that it has been remarkably consistent. With hindsight, it can be seen that, musically, *The Rite of Spring* was not the 'primitive' assault on musical conventions it was generally taken to be. It clearly had roots in Mussorgsky, Rimsky-Korsakov, and Debussy. Formally, it owed everything to the symmetries of Western music while such melody as it contained was largely rooted in folk music: only in the use of polytonality was there any assault upon convention. Yet the original power of the work was such that, in the scuffle following the first performance in Paris, fifty people stripped themselves naked and finished up in the *Commissariat de Police*. It was inevitable that Stravinsky would then be seen as a champion of the onslaught against tradition. This was not, however, a role to which he was artistically or temperamentally suited. Stravinsky revered the past; he revered his teacher and mentor, Rimsky-Korsakov. An exile all his life, Stravinsky's greatest desire (eventually fulfilled) was to be recognized in his native Russia. From 1913 onwards, Stravinsky became victim to the cultural dichotomy between the present and the past. He was to produce the most convincing synthesis of present and past of the century — but at a price: the loss of consistent, sustained emotion and, in consequence, of true aspiration. Stravinsky increasingly took his manner from the past. His musical affirmation, even in his 'serial' period, was also of the past: he never quite affirmed the present.

Following the eccentric outburst of *The Rite of Spring*, Stravinsky's style quickly evolved and maintained an extraordinary degree of clarity, and it was achieved without any of the melodic and rhythmic sacrifices made so compulsively by Webern and his followers. It enabled Stravinsky to devote the most part of fifty years to presenting the past in terms of the present and to do so *with respect*. This, in turn, should represent our own respect for Stravinsky.

Stravinsky's self-imposed restraint was exemplified in his much quoted statement that 'Music is essentially powerless to *express* anything at all'. In one sense this was a form of escapism, but in another sense it provided a means of musical development. Stravinsky must have been developing this line of thought when working on *Les Noces*. In *Les Noces* Stravinsky's unique genius fashioned *folk style* into *art form*, the 'primitive' into the urbane. Although the work was completed in 1917, it took the composer a further five years to decide upon its scoring. This period must have represented a painful turning point for Stravinsky: a fundamental and final turn-about in aesthetic belief. For it was, I suggest, during this period that Stravinsky accepted the limits to which folk music could be utilized as the basic substance of art music. *Les Noces*, largely because of its pulsating folk rhythm, lacks true emotional variety. Stravinsky could have atoned for this, at least partly, by scoring *Les Noces* in the manner of *The Rite of Spring*: after all, orchestral largesse was currently smothering a great deal of musical banality emanating from the so-called 'Late Romantics'. However, during those five years of deliberation, Stravinsky clearly settled for the abandonment of the folk-inspired, 'nationalist' path: the attempt to perpetuate the romantic image of art through exotic substance and extravagant orchestration. In specifying four pianos and percussion as the definitive orchestration of *Les Noces*, Stravinsky decided upon an aesthetic based on the integrity of the notes themselves — notes which, whether original or parody, would be presented with the utmost formal clarity. This aesthetic would involve emotional compromise that earlier composers of profound genius had not been compelled to make.

The future path started with the ballet *Pulcinella* (1920) in which Stravinsky proved his ability to make any material his own, conforming to the manner and substance of the past yet adding his own unique contribution in the style and density of harmony and orchestration. Some thirty years later, with the opera *The Rake's Progress*, Stravinsky had made *everything* his own: the musical substance was modern or, at least, uniquely Stravinskian, while the manner was entirely Mozartian, even in the kind of devices used for dramatic characterization. In combining first-rate classical crafts-manship with a unique twentieth-century sensibility, it achieved the goal of expressing 'nothing', for such erudite perfection could only be achieved at the expense of *intrinsic* musical emotion. The emotion to be found in some of Stravinsky's earlier music — *Oedipus Rex* for example — was largely a result of stylistic incon-gruity. In *Oedipus Rex* the emotion was strongest where the music smacked most of nineteenth-century Italian opera. Even in so powerful a work as *Symphony of Psalms*, the emotional impact springs essentially from the gestures of ritual. Stravinsky eventu-ally attained his 'powerlessness' to 'express anything', through slavish adherence to formal manner. That he was deeply aware of the paradox contained in his achievement is evident in the bitterness that rankles beneath the burning and humorous intelligence of his many recorded verbal utterances.

In his final serial phase, Stravinsky took a *modern* manner and made *that* his own. He brought to serial writing a characteristic clarity of texture. Far from being a volte-face, this development was entirely consistent with Stravinsky's musical aesthetic: it was not a change of direction but simply a change of manner. The music retains its inimitably Stravinskian sound — the hallmark of true musical genius, provided by the prodigiousness of its musical ear.

A touch of asperity marks almost the whole of Stravinsky's *oeuvre*. Having necessarily exiled himself from his own country, first artistically and then politically, his pungent musical response to this estrangement was the development of a metaphorical musi-cal style. With this he could further exile his art from his true emotions, thus protecting himself and his art from the dichotomy between his vision and reality. His confrontation with the cultural forces of his time was selective rather than total.

I suggested earlier that 'modern music' might commonly be thought to have begun with Boulez and Stockhausen, for the novelty of their music after the Second World War created their aura as leaders of the avante-garde. This novelty resulted from a total rejection of the past, a total disrespect for musical memory on a scale without former precedent. The aftermath of the Second World War absolutely demanded this rejection which was achieved, brilliantly, by Boulez. The subjection of all the par-

ameters of music — pitch, duration, density, timbre, and dynamics
— to mathematical processes, produced a kind of music that not
only rendered the composer a mere servant to a mechanical form of
composition but successfully eliminated any memory of such long-
standing musical elements as melody, rhythm, harmony, orchestration, and thematic development. It did not, however, eliminate
such memories from music's audiences.

Boulez suffered the misfortune that his first creative flush coincided with this culturally destructive imperative. With hindsight, this
problem can be seen to have affected most of the composers of his
generation. The composers who adhered, literally, to integral serialism can now be seen as 'historically important' composers, progenitors of a new musical language from which others may, if the
contradictory paths of twentieth-century culture permit, produce
lasting works of art. There was nothing essentially new in this
process: what *was* new was the thoroughness with which the
composers of integral serialism tried to eliminate musical memory.
Ironically, their courageous efforts successfully encouraged the
belief that modern artistic truth lies in that which is most destructive of the past.

In the aftermath of Hiroshima and the Holocaust, it would have
been unreasonable to expect art to retain, without equivocation, its
traditional self-belief. Nevertheless, even if we accept with George
Steiner that 'in locating Hell above ground, we have passed out of
the major order and symmetries of Western Civilisation',[5] music's
role must in the end be both positive and affirmative. It is for
politics to *confirm*; art's function, whether its aura be one of happiness or sorrow, beauty or despair, should be to *affirm*. Music that
simply derives its manner from political belief does no more than
confirm the transient. John Cage's search for 'nothing' and the
deliberate repetitiousness of the minimalists do not represent *art*:
quite intentionally so, for basically they are musical statements of
philosophical, political belief. But if art is to relate to humanity and
transcend the here and now, it must seek out universal truths for
affirmation. Too much of what passes as 'art music' in this century
has succeeded only in being negative.

Although it is inevitable and proper that the subject-matter of
contemporary art may be lurid, the problem with much contemporary art is that its subject-matter is lurid for the sake of being
lurid, merely reflecting the present — confirming the transient. The

musical representation of ugliness for its own sake or, at least, the creation of music that denied the motivic efficacy of melodic and rhythmic elements, may have been imperative and therefore essential to the development of musical techniques in this century, but it is not, ultimately, essential to musical *art*. For example, Penderecki's *Threnody to the Victims of Hiroshima* tells us as little about musical art as it does about the destruction of Hiroshima. At the time of its composition, its 'cluster' technique was novel. This particular technique has since been absorbed, where appropriate, as an element — and a small element — of contemporary musical style. Any stylistic element that contains no reference to the past cannot, of itself, have artistic integrity: it can be no more than a mere artistic gesture. This is the eternal misunderstanding of modern music and it is one that is new to our age. To continue to compose using only small elements of musical possibility — whether it be the 'textural' devices of Penderecki and Ligeti, or the more complex language derived from 'integral serialism' — can result only in artistic bombast. It can reflect only one small aspect of modern life, ignoring the wider truths to which it should contribute.

In retrospect, the mere attempt to confront Hiroshima in art, however sincere or inevitable in its motivation, can only be an affront to the atrocious reality of the subject. This kind of lone confrontation with nature and its process was appropriate only to the artist in confident, post-revolutionary nineteenth-century Europe; the explosive revelations the twentieth century has brought about in our understanding of the human psyche, coupled with the awareness of human atrocity that technology has imposed on our senses, has made its continuation into modern times as false as the patronizing 'love of art' that has sustained it. The only possible role for the twentieth-century artist is that of psychological investigation: a search for what is *not* self-evident.

No composer has confronted this task more vigorously and openly than Michael Tippett, born nearly a quarter of a century after Stravinsky. Once imprisoned for his pacifism, strongly influenced by North America, Tippett nevertheless had the advantage over Stravinsky that he was able to mature his talent in his own country. Like Ives, he has intuitively understood the need for musical art to portray a universal humanity and to embody a musical vernacular. Both composers also developed a musical language that could contain direct quotation, not only in opposition to that language, but also in coalescence. Unlike Stravinsky, both composers also developed sufficient inner warmth and confidence to allow their musical intuition to condition their musical manner. Unlike Ives, however, Tippett's style has developed profoundly, consistently, and purposefully throughout nearly half a century of public composition. And in total contrast to Stravinsky, it has acquired a degree of complexity that has estranged it from a large part of its potential audience.

From *A Child of Our Time*, (1941) — the work with which Tippett first won international acclaim — to *The Icebreak* (1976) — the last opera to date — Tippett's literary themes have all been concerned, in one way or another, with means of reconciliation between the human psyche and the cultural forces to which it is subject. Musically, each opera has marked a new stage of technical development, usually in terms of the facility to juxtapose, superimpose and, where appropriate, reconcile different types of musical 'substance'. Tippett has developed the capacity to make every aspect of this constantly variegated substance — which includes much quotation — essentially his own. This ability springs partly from the originality and haunting beauty of his own musical substance; more importantly, it also springs from an unfailing sense of 'rightness' of the *vertical* effects of the stylistic and tonal coalescence. It is this that gives to his music such an unusual breadth of emotional content.

Ever since the death of Wagner, the ability to cope rationally with this vertical musical element — what we now call harmony — so that listeners familiar with European precedent can perceive in its use an obvious rightness and inevitability, has proved a particularly besetting problem. Schoenberg's 'serialism' was essentially a process of rationalizing music *out of* its dependence upon tonal harmonic progression. The 'integral serialism' of the 1950s aimed at obliterating harmonic progression entirely, in order that the appreciation of contemporary musical procedures should not be conditioned by familiarity. One of the least attractive aspects of much Western music of the past few decades has been the fortuitousness with which it has treated the vertical aspect of musical construction. (It has also been the false starting-point for much of what passes as 'creativity' in musical education.)

The particular genius of Tippett is that he has managed to develop an individual and purposeful harmonic style that is neither

fortuitous nor gratuitous and that enables him not only to juxtapose, superimpose, and reconcile different musical materials, but
also to *develop* them. This intuitive sense of harmony and thematic
development has enabled Tippett to acquire a style of enormous
complexity over which, unlike the complexity of 'integral serialism', he the composer has total control. This complexity has, of
course, created problems of assimilation for the listener. But it
would seem to be an inevitable result of Tippett's courageous
confrontation with the psychological pressures of the twentieth
century, embracing in an often electrifying way quotations from
the past — from Beethoven to the Blues — yet always working
them into a style that is intrinsic to his own. No better example of
this stylistic subsumation can be found than the last movement of
the Fourth String Quartet (1978), where the basic material is no less
a work than Beethoven's *Grosse Fuge* and is made quintessentially
Tippett. Where, for example, *The Rake's Progress* could be called
'Eighteenth-century opera à la Stravinsky', this quartet movement
could be called 'Tippett à la Beethoven'. There is no other composer of the twentieth century to whom such a compliment could
be paid.

Tippett did not stumble upon contemporary methods as a result
of any compulsive leap into an unknown future: modern culture
and politics do not radiate that kind of confidence. Rather, Tippett
started from a thorough rooting in traditional musical styles, particularly counterpoint, and gradually absorbed elements of contemporary method as a part of his style. *The Knot Garden* (1970) shows
an obvious indebtedness to serial language (though not to serial
procedure): the disjunct angularity of Thea's music is no doubt a
cunning relating of her contrived, hierarchical character with that
of integral serialism.

The variety of style and technique that Tippett has made his own
is epitomized in the latest orchestral works. Similar contrasts of
form, style and mood are to be found in the late quartets of
Beethoven. The strength and uniqueness of Tippett's *oeuvre* lies in
the very laboriousness with which it grew from the past, absorbed
the present, and has attained a visionary quality: 'An acute sense',
to quote Meirion Bowen, 'of the independence of the creative
faculty from the external and even internal ferment: a wilful concentration of psychic energy towards specific and extraordinary
goals.'[6]

Xenakis has said something rather similar:

Art, and above all, music has a fundamental function, which is to catalyse the sublimation that it can bring about through all means of expression. It must aim, through fixations which are landmarks, to draw towards a total exultation in which the individual mingles, losing his consciousness in a truth immediate, rare and perfect. If a work of art succeeds in this undertaking, even for a single moment, it attains its goal. This tremendous truth is not made of objects, emotions, or sensations; it is beyond these, as Beethoven's 7th Symphony is beyond music. This is why art can lead to realms that religion still occupies for some people.[7]

I have suggested earlier in this book that 'losing of consciousness' is not only an essential mark of genius in the West, but the point at which the best in Western and Oriental traditions merge. Xenakis was one of the few composers of his generation to stand apart from integral serialism: his concern was to search for new beginnings rather than for ways to destroy the past. This was intrinsically physical rather than musical; it was based, initially, on statistical laws of probability which subsumed Western and Eastern concepts of musical time. It seems to be necessary that every modern musical achievement must be at the expense of some other. Ives's achievement was at the expense of political reality; Stravinsky's was at the expense of intrinsic emotion and universality; Tippett's has been at the expense of clarity. Xenakis's achievement has been at the expense of performability, for his music creates a dichotomy between the actual composition and the possibility of properly performing it. Yet in that very dichotomy lies much of the music's strength. It creates a sound world of strained activity; a kind of desperate bid for a supreme goal that remains elusive. In this latter aspect, it has much in common with Indian music. Rationally approached, much of Xenakis's music is literally unplayable. Yet the unique power of music itself is essentially irrational; the dynamism of Xenakis's music resides in the desperate attempt at the impossible. The key to much of it lies in the varying degree of order and disorder created within the musical textures and their superimpositions. This respects the listener's musical memory; and it is this essential pre-condition of musical form that imbues Xenakis's music with a bewitching quality, frequently lacking in the music of 'textural' composers.

Emotion in music does not *necessarily* have to exist through the traditional parameters of melody and rhythm, though it does require some sort of reference to previous musical norms. I am not suggesting that Xenakis, with his esoteric use of advanced mathematical calculus and behavioural physics, holds any essential key to the future of musical art. It is way beyond the scope of this book or, indeed, of education to do that — for it is beyond the scope of man himself. It is only possible to point to aspects of musical form and function that have been validated by long tradition in an attempt to distinguish what is likely to prove long-lasting, from what appears trivial and ephemeral. There do seem to have been, at least up to this point in history, certain recurrent themes in artistic behaviour — of which transcendence has been the most universal. If I state that Beethoven, Xenakis, and Tippett each aspired to a form of transcendence, I am simply stating what is known. If I state that they *achieved* their aspirations, I am entering that mysterious territory of emotional subjectivity peculiar to art. As to whether a composer achieves these aspirations or not is ultimately for posterity to judge.

The question that faces us now is whether posterity will get the chance. With world culture projected at us daily in our living rooms, cultural norms — let alone artistic norms — are extremely hard to establish. Musical fashions, like any other fashions, erupt and disrupt within a vortex of psychological confusion. I have tried to define for musical art a continuing purpose and I have tried to separate aspects of musical stability from those of ephemeral fashion and to point to aspects of lineage that contribute to civilization. In this age of instant communications, news is novelty and novelty is news. If the artist has a function left at all, it is surely to penetrate this aura of ephemeralism. It is precisely here that education has such a vital role to play, for it can help to steer society towards the positive, affirmative aspects of contemporary musical art. If education can lose its subsuming stranglehold on artistic validation, in order to become an 'enabler' of artistic tradition, old and new, it could steer society to encounter art's essence rather than its periphery. In so doing, it could prevent art itself from 'growing old-fashioned'.

8

Music in a Multi-Cultural Society

How partial, like mutilated eunuchs, the musical
artists appear to me in society! Politics, bank-
ruptcy, famine, war — nothing concerns them but
a scraping on a catgut or tooting on a bass French
horn. The crickets in the grass chirp their national
song at all hours, quite heedless who conquers . . .

R. W. Emerson, Journal for September 1862.[1]

There are word complexes that appear to fade in and out of the
English language according to political and social needs. Multi-
culturalism is one of them. There is of course nothing new about
multi-culturalism in Britain or any 'developed' country. The culture of the aristocrat, the burgher, and the workman have been
dissimilar, even antithetic, since the agrarian revolution turned
communal hunting societies into structured urban groupings
requiring controllers and doers — since, within a single society,
one set of people has been exploited by another. Multi-culturalism
has become a current burning issue due less to artistic perspi-
caciousness than to enforced realization that recent exploitation of
community groupings in Britain has been connected with race and,
in effect, with Britain's colonial misdeeds of the past. There has
also been an enforced realization that the West Indians who were
encouraged to come to this country to do work that the indigenous
population preferred not to do have been left largely in socially
deprived ghettos; and that the Indians who arrived in this country
did so for a variety of causes all stemming from British colonization
and subjugation of India.

Multi-culturalism is often thought of as implying cultural integration. In fact, it should provoke hard thought as to how far and
in what areas of social activity integration is possible or even
desirable. To attempt to integrate the *arts* of different cultures is
usually to weaken them. The real necessity is to transplant and
strengthen forms of art that represent cultures different from our
own.

94

As has so often been the case in times of political-social need, education — and through it, art — has been expected to carry a large part of the responsibility for effecting change. And education, with its pressing social responsibilities, has inevitably tended to see this task — artistically as much as socially — as one of providing means of integration. This has meant working from common points of contact. Yet artistically, common points of contact can be extremely hard to find and, when found, can turn out to be very slender. For some years now, many schools have been paying lip service to the cultures of their ethnic minority groups: mainly of Afro-Caribbean and Indian stock. Many schools with sizeable West Indian populations have adopted steel band teaching: indeed they can take such pride in these bands that one could be forgiven for believing that they were the very invention of British educa-tion. Yet how conscious are these schools that the comparatively unsophisticated form of the steel band arose in the face of British repression? How conscious are these schools that reggae and Rasta-farianism are the result of a desperate search for roots which could bypass the colonially exploited West Indies en route to a suppo-sedly beautiful Africa? How conscious are they of the cultural desperation that leads expert steel bands to adapt Western music to their own cultural sound world, when the heart of West Indian culture is in its folk and dance traditions? For school music simply to turn a large part of its attention to steel bands is insufficient, for, within education at least, they have become a multi-cultural con-venience rather than a vehicle for genuine cultural growth.

The ethnic groups of Indian stock have been no less patronized by education. Their artistic culture is as genuinely old as that of the West Indies is new. It dates back at least to the Vedas of the third Century BC, through the Upanishads to the Ramayana and Mahab-harata; through the practical arts of music and dance, first codified by Bharata (probably contemporary with Pythagoras) and per-fected by the medieval Moghul emperors. It survived the years of British subjugation to burst anew in the writings and activities of such men as Bhatkhande, Tagore, and Nehru. Education has made a number of polite gestures to this culture, such as the inclusion of tablas, temple bells, and the like, into the classroom orchestra and of some rhythmically diluted folk music into the song repertoire. Indians in Britain have generally tolerated such gestures politely while practising the essence of their culture within their own religious communities. For the most part, school education has been no more successful at propagating the essence of its ethnic cultures than of its own inherited culture.

Three questions, as important to art generally as to education specifically, need addressing in detail:

1. To what extent is it possible and desirable to enable members of ethnic minority groups to gain skill and understanding in their own cultural practice and history?
2. To what extent is it possible and desirable to incite members of one ethnic group to participate in the cultural pursuits and acquire the artistic skills of another?
3. To what extent is it possible or desirable to create a fusion between different ethnic cultures?

The answers to these questions are not as simple as might at first sight appear. I shall deal with the first two only in terms of the largest minority groups in Britain, the Indian and the Afro-Caribbean.

The answer to the first question would appear to be unequivocally affirmative until the all-important corollary is faced: what does the ethnic group, with its possibly limited first-hand experience of its own culture, actually see as being its culture? Once this somewhat testy question has been posed, the popular verdict will not of itself suffice.

Indians in this country are exposed largely to popular film music: usually a fusion of Indian vocal, sitar, and tabla sounds, with Western orchestral instruments. Some of this music is not without merit and is, moreover, based on traditional ragas. Nevertheless, it is a far cry from the classical music of Indian tradition. Although most Indians in this country are acquainted with simpler forms of sacred and folk music, comparatively few have had exposure to the brilliant tradition of their classical music.

The case with the Afro-Caribbean population is similar though more complicated. The Afro-Caribbeans have no direct living line with their original cultural roots. Culturally, they were dominated by their various European masters until the abolition of slavery and such musical forms and styles as were to emerge in the following hundred and fifty years were inevitably Western influenced. Thus, in purely musical terms, Caribbeans of African descent have no indigenous traditions: as a downcast people, their forms have been largely cult-orientated. It is therefore hardly surprising that it has taken the extreme movement of Rastafarianism to give identity to an ethnic group that still feels, and to a large extent still is, exploited in this country. If multi-culturalism is to have anything to do with art and if art still has anything to do with cultural identity, it is important to establish real and meaningful artistic roots in order to create an appropriate milieu for the propogation and advancement of ethnic arts. Merely to accept Trinidadian steel bands, Jamaican folk music, Indian popular folk dances, film music, and Western-influenced 'Ghuzals' as components of educational activity is insufficient.

If it is accepted that there is a need to propogate and provide instruction in the musics of ethnic minority groups there will be a number of practical and cultural difficulties to overcome. With regard to Indian music, performing talent on the level of the best performing talent of Western music is virtually non-existent in this country. Indians who had some performing ability when they entered this country have had little opportunity to use it outside their religious activities and, as a result, their skills have tended to lapse. This vacuum has opened the way to a considerable amount of musical charlatanism, which, coupled with the general lack of expertise on Indian music among musicians in this country, has created severe obstacles to the promotion of the real tradition.

Further complications arise from the way in which Indian music is woven into that country's social fabric. The *Guru-Shishya-Parampara* (Master-Disciple-Tradition), though not entirely different from our own, has considerably greater cultural significance. While, in the West, we have, for example, many distinguished 'schools' of violin-playing, and famous performer-teachers can attract pupils from far and wide, in India the *Guru-Shishya* arrangement is far from being a commercial transaction involving a weekly one- or two-hour lesson. The Shish (Disciple), once accepted by the Guru, shows his 'respect' for his spiritual mentor by unquestioning obedience to his tenets. He lives with his Guru, practises up to eight or ten hours a day, is under constant supervision and rewards his Guru by his constant 'respect', which can include servial as well as musical obligations.

The greatest problem in adapting this cultural phenomenon to Western culture lies with the element of *parampara* — the tradition. Indian composition is not usually notated, though numerous compositions based on various ragas have been handed down from Guru to Shish over at least some five centuries, very often from father to son. (The caste system arose and was practised in a way that delineated family occupation and it is therefore very much in keeping with the culture that music should be seen as a family tradition.) From the time of the Mogul Emperors, different Gurus established different *Gharanas* — special styles of playing that might be called musical 'dialects'. Again, it is not difficult to discern parallels in Western music. The real problem lies in the element of secrecy. The ability to perform the composition of a particular *Gharana* is a secret that a Shish will not pass on until he himself becomes a Guru, demanding respect, obedience, and secrecy in turn from his disciple. A true disciple could be reluctant or even unwilling to learn anything from a Guru representing a different *Gharana*. And a Guru might be reluctant to pass on his knowledge unless his pupils accept discipleship within his *Gharana*. Indian musicians still show a reluctance to codify their music, even though the recording industry and jet travel has tended, in practice, to eliminate differences between *Gharanas*. Knowledge of Indian music in India is passed on not through schools but at the feet of Gurus. Moreover, it is an entirely oral tradition, learned as a mother tongue and lacking a codified grammar or methodology. The problems that this poses for teaching Indian music within British education will be discussed in Part Three. It is, however, worth pointing at this juncture to some of the characteristics of classical Indian music that make it virtually irreconcilable with our own.

It is commonly held that Indian music is improvised on the basis of different scale patterns and time cycles (*ragas* and *talas*). This is such a vast oversimplification that it distorts the very essence of the music. The scales of Indian music are known as *thata* or *mela*. The concept of *Thata* is that from which *raga* derives: i.e. it is not an active musical element but is a lifeless melodic formula. There are seven notes in North Indian music which, in their pure form, correspond to the Western major scale. Of these, what we would call the second, third, sixth, and seventh notes may be flattened by approximately a semi-tone. What we would call the perfect fourth may be sharpened by approximately a semi-tone. Interestingly, what we would call the tonic and dominant are unchangeable. The basic scalic ingredient of Indian music, therefore, is based on the perfect fifth with the major third playing a decisive role. Microtonal differences in the intonation of notes of different *ragas* have much to do with problems of 'temperament' — familiar enough to Westerners.

There have been many attempts to codify Indian music on the basis of scalic and melodic patterns. No such classification can be all-embracing, but Bhatkande's publication of his *raga* classification based on ten heptatonic scales, in the early twentieth century, has provided a convenient but inadequate basis for *institutionalized* instruction ever since.

The concept of *raga* is both creative and technical. It is a musical entity which defines the literal *intonation* of notes used, the *order* in which they are used, and the relative *duration* with which they are used. The notes used form a scale which may be different in ascending and descending order. More importantly, each note has a limited possibility of duration depending upon the raga and phrase in which it occurs. *Ragas* are recognized not by tempo, key, or scale pattern as in Western music, but by phrase structures, specific notes of stasis and also forms of ornamentation. The most important aspect of a *raga* is its general melodic movement, wherein certain phrases are linked to each other and notes have their proper relative duration. These are fixed, however, only within a context. A raga cannot, therefore, be defined simply by the ascending-descending order and the *pakada* (catch-phrases) which Bhatkande defined.

Raga can be rendered in four ways: *Alāpā* (considered the finest as it makes no use of rhythmic cycles and allows the artist to employ the notes for durations that suit the *raga* and thus to present the intricate essence of the *raga* in detail), *Bandish* (a form of fixed composition which links words, rhythm, and melody in a logical flow to express the essentials of the *raga* as well as the structure of the *tala*), *Layakari* (the deliberate creation of unexpected rhythmic shapes by varying the duration of syllables of words — a type of rhythmic excitement that lends energy to the piece), and *Tāna* (the virtuotic rendering of fast runs consisting of constant variation and extension of very little material).

Although *raga* can exist independently of rhythm (as in *Alāpā*) it is generally associated with and controlled by the concept of *tala*: the immutable division of time. A *tala* consists of a fixed number of beats performed in a cyclical manner. The *tala* defines the number of beats in a cycle as well as the number and incidents of points of stress within it. Intricate rhythms are defined by a time-honoured system of syllabic mnemonics (*bols*), forming a logical whole, centred around the first beat. The integration of *raga* with *tala* is further conditioned by the concept of *laya*: basically equal to our word tempo. At particular points an artist will increase the speed, sometimes slightly and sometimes to exactly double. Following this he may increase the speed to four times and even eight times, leading to a concluding display of virtuosity, the increasingly histrionic nature of which has more to do with modern media presentation than to the traditions of Indian art. Nevertheless, this element of virtuosity, coupled with the freedom to interpret *raga* in different ways according to its own laws, has characterized the 'Hindustani' music of the north from the 'Karnatac' music of the south. Much of the inspiration of Hindustani music derives from the contrast of virtuoso and expressive elements: artistic aspects and contrasts that are particularly evident in the Kathak dance of North India. Vocal music has always been the basis of Indian music — and although the traditional music of India includes (besides classical) semi-classical, folk, tribal, and religious forms, all these forms provided the roots of classical music. Hindustani music is an intricate and indivisible fusion of melodic and rhythmic elements for which there is no parallel in the West and which cannot be defined within Western categories of composition and improvisation.[2]

Because of all this, it is hardly surprising that music is the aspect of Indian culture that has proved least easy to recreate in Britain. It is perhaps significant that very few Indians, from Britain, India or elsewhere, have become accomplished in European music, particularly in comparison to the peoples of south-east Asia and Japan. The cultural and artistic temperaments of India and Europe are very different. The Indian community in this country needs our educational system in order to improve its job opportunities and living standards. It does not, however, have any inherent need for British or European music. It is important to make this point, for there are many who consider that it is for the Indians to appreciate our arts before we propagate theirs. Nothing could be further from the truth, historically, morally or pragmatically. Only when we have enabled Indians to establish their own musical heritage in this country can we begin to expect them to take any great interest in our own musical culture.

The minority groups of African and Caribbean descent have an even greater need to establish an artistic culture of their own as an aid to racial equality. For, throughout human history, art — that unique product of the merging of the imagination, intuition and rational intelligence — has proved the touchstone for the definition of a culture. Of all the minority groups in this country, the Afro-Caribbeans have least in their immediate tradition with which to identify *artistically*. Their real cultural roots lie not in the Caribbean but in Africa; and the cultures of Africa are rich in their heritage of art and artefacts and in their traditions of folk and classical musics. Because of the large gap in time from these roots and the lack of real knowledge and skill pertaining to them, attempts by Africans and Afro-Caribbeans to adapt this African heritage to their new cultural ambience can often appear self-conscious. There is therefore as much need for the teaching of traditional African musical skills as of Afro-Caribbean folk and dance traditions.

The Islands of the Caribbean contain a greater admixture and diversity of races than almost anywhere else in the world. Aboriginals, Spaniards, Portuguese, French, British, Dutch, Americans, Indians, Chinese, Jews, Syrians, and Lebanese have all left their mark. However, the predominant cultural mark was left by enforced slavery. The Africans who were dragged so unwillingly and in such inhuman conditions to be auctioned off to the British sugar plantation owners were discouraged from practising their own music. The new white settlers who owned these plantations were induced to the Caribbean essentially by the profit motive. Unlike their North American neighbours, they did not emigrate as the result of any religious scruples. Consequently, they were less concerned to establish a new culture than to exploit new-found resources. They were, and still are, a minority race. They did not establish a new folk culture or recreate classical European culture in their own vein. Nor did their African slaves have the inducement to wed their own musical sensibilities to a vital folk tradition. (The emergence of some *black* slave owners in parts of the Caribbean doubtless further discouraged any such fusion.) Instead, Africans under British colonial rule were actively encouraged to play European dances on European instruments. By the beginning of the nineteenth century they were playing quadrilles, Scottish reels, waltzes, polkas, and mazurkas to entertain their masters: a less sophisticated version of some of the fare shortly to be offered by Louis Jullien in his Promenade Concerts at the Drury Lane Theatre in London (see Chapter 3).

Against the background of this strong European influence, the slaves of the Caribbean did not produce a new form of musical fusion as did their North American counterparts with jazz. (Historically, the fact that they were released from slavery some thirty years earlier created a quite separate set of cultural circumstances.) Rather, music became a tool with which they could fuse their own animistic religious traditions with Christianity — from the 'Revival Zion' movement of the 1860s (in which biblical Saints and Evangelists share with God and Jesus Christ a polytheistic pantheon of spirits capable of 'possessing' the living) to the more modern Rastafarian movement. Early cult musics mainly derived from an Africanizing of Christian hymns and choruses.

Afro-Caribbean folk music has been similarly influenced by non-African musical traditions: not just by that of the British Evangelical Church but also by Spanish folk music (itself influenced by the Orient through the Muslim connection) and by the music of the Indian sub-continent — for thousands of Indians emigrated to the British West Indies to work the sugar plantations vacated by the freed African slaves. Characteristically, Indian music has had the least influence and, as Indians intermarried with Africans, this influence was largely distilled into the Spanish-Muslim elements. As with folk music the world over, the words provide the soul — and the soul in Caribbean folk music is essentially sad, bowed, yet resilient and hopeful and surprisingly unreproachful.

The steel pan music of Trinidad has shown aggression if not reproach in both its history and its style, though in essence it is a joyful music of celebration — in this case a Carnival on 'Mardi Gras' (Shrove Tuesday, the day before the beginning of Lent). Initially a high society affair of the colonial settlers, it became a street festival of African drumming after the abolition of slavery in 1833. When drums were banned by the authorities, African rhythm returned to the streets in the form of 'Tamboo Bamboo', wherein bamboos of different lengths and pitches were struck, notched, and scraped. As Bamboo Bands became associated with the traditional ritual stick fighting, they too were banned, only to be replaced in 1937 by Steel Bands, consisting of dustbins, buckets, car hubs, and any noise-making objects that could be found. Gradually it was discovered that different dents in metal lids could produce different types of pitches. It was, however, not until the Americans left behind large quantities of oil drums after the 1939–45 war (Trinidad prospered on oil during the mid-twentieth century) that the characteristic sound of the modern steel pan was born. Although at first these steel pans were feared by the authorities as much as their predecessors, they were eventually recognized for their worth and were encouraged by the Trinidad Government following Independence. In fact, there was no option but to encourage such folk music forms because Caribbeans — in stark contrast to Indians — were never able to develop a sophisticated, classical musical style of their own: their music has always been forced to reflect a subject rather than a ruling people. Moreover, the forced integration of musical styles has often resulted in acceptance of a common denominator that is, artistically, debilitatingly low.

Steel bands have also been encouraged by British education, to the extent that many West Indians in Britain (whether of Jamaican stock or not) have developed a remarkable expertise in playing them. Yet paradoxically, as steel-band players have increased in skill, their repertoire has moved from the Caribbean Calypso to the European Classic, doubtless representing a chronic desire and demand to be accepted equally in Western terms, while still retaining pride in their black identity.

I shall doubtless be accused of reading too much into all this, of making the theory fit the fact; and it will quickly be pointed out that not only black and white music but also black and white children appear side by side in steel-band music. And this is precisely the point: the propagation of steel bands in schools is often due to its cosmetic multi-culturalism, rather than to any rational artistic reasoning; and it has the further merit of being relatively easy to master in the early stages. And of course it is loud — very loud — far too loud for an average school to tolerate; yet its very volume contains its self-perpetuating multi-cultural advertisement. The uniform ring of steel bands is becoming as distinctive a school sound in its general mediocrity as the badly played upright piano, accompanying dreary, dispirited class singing. This is a criticism of education rather than of steel bands. Steel bands have become an exhilarating vehicle for a genuine folk music and they have provided purposeful activity for many bored and sometimes embittered children. Like folk musics the world over, they are unsophisticated and immediately representative of their ethnic culture. They do not however, of themselves, open the way to any classical form of culture; and it is not always realized that there are classical traditions from Africa as much as tribal-folk traditions. If black people in Britain are to establish an *artistic* musical culture of their own, it is more likely to spring from a fusion of *African* and Western forms than from the folk form of the steel band. There is already a growing black involvement in Western arts and it must be hoped that education will find a means of encouraging this process. It may yet be that the peoples of African lineage in Britain will find their own fusions with Western arts as did Afro-Americans in the first sixty years of this century.

I have written elsewhere of the rise of jazz in America.[3] In pointing to the exploitable element of jazz pursued by the whites and the essential racial element of jazz for ever being rescued and resuscitated by the blacks, I have been accused of being fashionable, modish, and making the theory fit the facts. Whether such an interpretation is modish I care not. But as to whether it is correct I do care. Everything I have heard, observed, discussed, and read about jazz in North America continues to convince me that the facts are correct. I rehearse and uphold the argument here only because I believe we could be witnessing a not dissimilar set of circumstances in Britain.

What I have not written before, because I was too close to it to perceive it, is that jazz ceased to be 'black' or 'white' in the seventies — Miles Davis's *Bitches Brew*, the herald of 'jazz-rock', was also the herald of black-white fusions in popular music. Musically, jazz entered the international market place: it opened its fundamental forms and clichés for universal indulgence. What it gained in universality, it lost in individual personality: an inevitable consequence of the American Civil Rights Movement and the gradual integration of black and white communities in America.

In his brilliant book *Aspects of Wagner*,[4] in a chapter called 'Jews — not least in music', Bryan McGee has propounded an original and convincing explanation for the Jewish Renaissance in the latter part of the last century. Heavily précised, the argument goes as follows: originality in fundamentals is inimical to any closed, authoritarian culture. The great flowering of European art and science began with the emancipation of these activities from the Church, taking two or three generations to reach full growth in the seventeenth century. The Jews, in reaction to their general ostracization, lived within a closed, authoritarian religious culture of their own. Within three generations of the ghettos being opened in the nineteenth century, they had produced three of the greatest men of their time — Marx, Freud, and Einstein — and had come to dominate much of European art and science. However, assuming this explanation to be right, the Jewish Renaissance could neither continue nor repeat itself because integration increased and the difference between Jew and non-Jew diminished.

McGee's observations could be applied analogously to the blacks of North America. Being a musically ebullient race, within three generations of emancipation the blacks had produced — and for a further three generations retained — a music that, in terms of soulfulness and originality, left the rest of North America standing. And it was precisely at the period of integration of whites and blacks, when blacks were beginning to assume some political power, that jazz ceased to belong distinctively to a black culture.

It is worth attempting to extend the analogy to Britain. Jazz never became a symbol of black power in Britain (as it did with John Coltrane in the sixties in North America) because the exodus from the West Indies and black disillusionment with Britain happened too late for that. And Britain has never *officially* ostracized the blacks any more than it has officially adopted slavery or a caste system. But it is all a matter of degree. It took the riots of 1981 to bring home to much of Britain the reality of its inner city poverty and the racial prejudice that still exists. Racial equality, in practice as well as theory, is now, at last, a burning issue — and it could well be that, free from authoritarianism and self-induced, quasi-religious attitudes and taboos, exemplified in Rastafarianism and the new wave of 'Gospel' singing, we shall shortly witness a great flowering of originality and creativity among the blacks in Britain. (Already, reggae has greatly increased in emotional range and variety as it has ceased to be regarded by blacks as a racially *exclusive* music.) If the black population in Britain is to achieve true equality of status, this will need to be manifest not just in politics but also in art: in music, theatre, literature, and dance, where African tradition and temperament wedded to personalized European sensibility could produce a much needed vitality and originality in the arts generally.

In terms of artistic interchange, the ideal needs of the ethnic minority groups of African and Indian lineage are different: the former can only benefit from involvement in Western arts at their highest level; the latter can only benefit from establishing their own traditional arts. The question of integration within multi-cultural-ism gives rise to fundamentally serious issues that threaten the very existence of individual cultures, as well as of overall cultural stability. These issues will not disappear through cosmetic lip service. They will not disappear by producing selections of tunes from the Masters, calypsos, pop songs, and *rags* for performance on glock-enspiels, xylophones or keyboard computers. Far less will they disappear through any distillation of the essential élitism of art. Multi-culturalism should be a call to strengthen *all* individual arts so that they can coexist and, if it seems natural, attempt some kind of temporary or permanent fusion.

The history of attempts to fuse the music of different cultures is not encouraging. If it is accepted that the aristocracy and the work-force have always represented two different cultures, it is no less true that aristocratic culture has absorbed a great deal from peasant culture. (The history of all classical musics is, to a large extent, that of the sophistication and adornment of the popular musical language.) But in no sense does this represent a *fusion* of cultures, however great the debt to peasant music may be, for aristocratic music remains supremely and deliberately apart from peasant culture, even though the roots may be of common stock.

The problem besetting more recent attempts to fuse popular and classical musical elements is that the roots are *not* of common stock. Where Mozart could merely note the Turkish influence in the eighteenth century and continue writing music that was quint-essentially European, eighteenth century, and Mozartian, com-posers such as Milhaud and Stravinsky, working at a time when European music seemed largely to have exhausted itself, attempted to absorb elements of Afro-American music, quite alien in style and function to that of their own tradition. To modern ears, the results of this short-lived collaboration seem at best light-weight and at worst — as in Milhaud's *Le jazz* — patronizing. Europeans have seldom understood the extent to which the tragic wail of the blues lay at the heart of all jazz improvisation until the mid-seventies. The European musical mind, to a very much greater extent than the American, has been nurtured on contrapuntal symmetry, and European jazz musicians have seldom been able to acquire the confidence to abandon entirely such inhibiting legacies to the sensory world of the blues.

Later attempts to fuse jazz or popular music with the symphonic tradition have often appeared gimmicky — for the same reason that the forms and functions have been virtually incompatible. In one sense, they fused most naturally in the 'Musical' — and it is doubtful if any composer has yet made this fusion more effective than Leonard Bernstein. In another sense they have fused only when Western musical conventions have been cheapened sufficiently to absorb the clichés of jazz and the popular musical styles that have emanated from it. At its worst, such music is to be seen littered all over the educational press: so called jazz and rock cantatas and operas whose musical and educational worth is virtually nil, but whose easy style is able to arouse some immediate enthusiasm among school children.

A number of established, contemporary composers have, however, addressed the problem with some success. I referred earlier to Sir Michael Tippett's ability to incorporate the blues into his style in such a personal manner as to make it seem an essential facet of his own musical language. Peter Maxwell Davies is another British composer who has demonstrated a remarkably eclectic approach to composition. Temperamentally, his sense of parody has tended to lead him most frequently to pre-Renaissance forms which, predating the dominance of treble and bass — of harmony — makes his music particularly difficult for the average listener to grasp. But Davies has also been fascinated by more modern popular forms. This was first evident — admittedly in a rather antithetic manner — in the piece for jazz band and orchestra *St Thomas Wake* (1969). More recently, however, as a result of his work with children in Orkney, Davies has fashioned a very personal form of 'Children's Opera'. Where at first he tended to juxtapose different elements of musical style somewhat uncomfortably, as in *The Two Fiddlers* (1978), in *Cinderella* (1980) he adopted just one aspect of our modern musical ambience — one could call it the 'popular' — and fashioned it with sufficient originality, both musically and dramatically, to make this style uniquely his own. As a result, it has that sense of spontaneity that is the stamp of great music. It is multi-cultural in the sense that it combines popular music (containing Afro-American and Caribbean elements) with classical convention. It is also socially conscious in the polemical twists effected on the traditional story. It is not 'multi-cultural' in the sense that it embraces or attempts to embrace simultaneously the music of different ethnic cultures: that is an altogether harder task and not one that is likely to be achieved within school education.

Most attempts to fuse elements of Oriental, Caribbean, Western, and Afro-American musics have been little more than acts of self-indulgence. However, Nigel Osborne, in his recent work, has incorporated elements of Caribbean music in a very unindulgent manner. The audience for his *Sinfonia No. 1*, was surprised to discover that, in a movement entitled 'Reggae', the references to that style were merely implicit. Yet why the surprise? What sensitive, thinking artist could *indulge* in a style that exists largely (as did the early blues) as an escape from human persecution? That a movement entitled 'Reggae' should contain no reggae at all is an act of courage and self-abnegation on the part of the composer. In his Sinfonia No. 2 Osborne attempted a wider cultural synthesis involving the abstraction and overloading of a Vietnamese melody, subdued treatment of elements of ska, reggae, steel band, and burra drumming ('melted down to reveal their basic musical resources') and a musical conflict between 'culture or what we learn to construct and nature'. (Culture, represented melodically, is constantly shattered by craggy, chaotic forms representing nature, implying an inevitable cycle of cultural rebirth and collision). Osborne uses quotation from Eastern and Caribbean musics to question the relationship of man to these cultures and of these cultures to each other, rather than as mere synthesis or integration for its own sake.

The West, in its usual acquisitive way, has generally absorbed what it has wanted of Eastern culture without in any way attempting to write Eastern music. Conversely, the East — with the exception of India — has tended to ape the West, and in terms of purely instrumental skill (perhaps subconsciously identified with technological skill) has often beaten the West at its own game. Extrovert gestures of fusion by Western musicians have, sadly, proved as futile as those with jazz and pop. Colin McPhee's understandable enthusiasm for Balinese music earlier in this century caused him to write a number of works in imitation of it for Western orchestras. To modern ears, however, the real Balinese sound is likely to be preferable. More recently, the 'Ling Ying' group from Hong Kong has concocted its own special fusion by performing music with Western harmonies on Chinese instruments. In the event, once the novelty has worn off, the results only prove how *un*suitable these instruments are for the performance of Western harmony. (The same could of course be said of 'Orff' instruments!) At the other end of the spectrum, a work like Ravi Shankar's Sitar Concerto does nothing more for musical art that introduce the sound of the sitar to European audiences. Indeed, Ravi Shankar's willingness to bend the principles of Indian music to popularize the sitar in the West has not found general favour with Indian musicians.

Despite fundamental differences in form and function, the music of the East, with its intrinsic lack of tension, continues to haunt a largely de-Christianized West. Douglas Young is a composer who has worked consistently to balance the dynamic thrust of Western music with the reflective stasis of Eastern music: to write, as it were, without beginning and end, yet still make something happen. *Virages: Region One* for cello and orchestra is essentially concerned with the converging and fusing of 'dynamic' and 'temporal' elements. The orchestra is divided into thirty-four chamber groups, each corresponding to melodic 'paths' initiated by the solo cello. Working with the Sri Lankan cellist, Rohan de Saram, has helped Young to absorb the spirit of the East. Young was attracted to de Saram's playing by his ability to sustain utter stillness, to maintain an inner calm even in the most frenetic passages. This ultimate and enduring sense of calm is the Oriental essence of much of Young's Western-styled orchestral music. *Third Night Journey under the Sea* divides the orchestra into seven groups, each concerned with one particular musical element and each containing its own dynamic thrust. These seven elements with their seven separate orchestras, are used simultaneously, and the constantly varying overlaps create a musical mobile, made intelligible by a clearly thought out 'harmonic' language, whereby, despite the fortuitous contrasts in the degree of musical activity, the overall effect is one of reflective stasis. This work is remarkably successful in fusing, in purely musical terms, the apparently contradictory essences of Oriental and Occidental music.

In a later work, *Lament on the Destruction of Forests*, for solo sitar and orchestra, Young has confronted the antithesis between the ancient, static world of a Punjabi folk melody (open, within its own performance traditions, to infinite subtleties of interpretation) and the modern, dynamic world of the Western orchestra.

Attempts by the orchestra to embellish the simplicity of the Punjabi melody only result in movement towards its annhilation, forcing the lone sitar to increasingly extreme attempts to retain its traditional role. The score reflects some lines of W. H. Auden which, although written nearly fifty years ago, still retain a modern relevance:

They are our past and our future; the place between which our desire unceasingly is discharged. A desire in which love and hatred so perfectly oppose themselves, that we cannot voluntarily move, but await the extraordinary compulsion of the deluge and the earthquake.[5]

I have cited three British composers who have instinctively attempted to fuse the music of different cultures within the ambience of Western art music — who have in fact, attempted 'multi-culturalism' long before the politicians. I do not mean to imply that there are no others. I have cited their work in order to demonstrate that the problem of cultural-stylistic musical integration is one of enormous complexity that can be solved, if at all, only by the finest and most acutely creative musical minds we have. It is unlikely to be solved at a popular level. Musical integration is not a task that necessarily *should* be accomplished and it is certainly not one to be left solely in the hands of school educators.

Nothing is to be gained by throwing the musical cultures of the world into the same melting pot. With tolerance and understanding, musical cultures of many sorts can coexist and ultimately enhance tolerance and understanding. They can do this only if they are nurtured and strengthened in their own right rather than diluted through inept, fashionable integration. True art of any culture contains a dialectical element. True art, the touchstone of cultural ascendance, can never be all things to all people.

9

Objectives

As with the final chapter of Part One, the main purpose of this chapter is to draw together some of the concepts and problems encountered in the previous pages. This will lead to the definition of certain objectives, consistent with the aims declared at the end of Part One and the criteria governing them.

As the purpose of this part of the book has been to give musical substance to the educational aims, the objectives that follow deal with the *nature* of music rather than the performance or composition of it. They will therefore be of a rather different kind from those commonly encountered in school syllabi: e.g., 'to improve the aural imagination', 'to learn to sing', etc. If musical art is to have more to offer than a mere decorative appendage to living, to detail such items as objectives is to beg a thousand and one questions about the nature, the purpose, and the usefulness of 'music'. Rather, these should be regarded as aspects of *method* and, as such, they will be considered in Part Three. The objectives listed here are not intended to be exclusive, nor to be taken straight into the classroom. Their function is to condition methodology in terms of content.

Musical style and content

As music is a pre-verbal medium, bypassing any direct form of symbolism, it is difficult to evaluate musical substance or content verbally in any but subjective terms. It is possible to discuss the literary content of musical word settings and the effect of the music on the words: indeed most radically new musical styles gained the confidence to become purely instrumental precisely because they evolved through the setting of words. Yet the fact that there is such a thing as a purely instrumental — wordless — style and that, to the initiated, such styles belong very clearly to their own cultural periods, indicates that musical content — or 'substance', as Ives called it — is identifiable and is fundamental to the art of composition.

In theocratic, authoritarian cultures, music has a functional universality, endorsing a doctrinaire understanding of life. However, in the early Middle Ages, European culture nurtured a 'love of art' on the basis that beauty leads to goodness and truth. Despite this, the music of the time was bound, impersonally, by theory. It was only by the time of the late Renaissance, when these theories had been fractured and re-structured in terms of what the ear heard (rather than what the eye saw) that the musical artist and his manner became more important than the artistic substance and its purpose.

Change in musical style usually occurs later than in other arts. It was therefore only by the baroque period that music fully absorbed the Classical Greek elements of the Renaissance. As opera, on 'moral' (if often brutal) themes became the fashionable entertainment of all Europe, the music itself acquired moral associations. Yet, because it was the manner rather than the substance that came to express the artistic idea, music acquired, by the eighteenth century, a large number of stylized mannerisms which became associated symbolically with particular moods and feelings. The sophistication of this aesthetic base enabled the prodigious genius of J. S. Bach to create music of such emotional power that it transcended those very 'period' aesthetic conventions. However, in most music the substance was essentially controlled by the manner. Thus it proved possible for a variety of pressure groups, from Princelings to Presbyterians, for a variety of causes, from self-enhancement to evangelism, to perpetuate the notion that musical art (soon to become synonymous with musical beauty) and morality are inseparably linked.

Beethoven's revolutionary balancing of musical elements, coupled with his daring use of revolutionary libretti, turned musical mannerisms into musical gestures and enabled music, by inference, to become *of itself* political. It often proved difficult to disassociate music from its political associations. As art became larger than life, it also became the touchstone of aristocratic tradition, increasing in pretentiousness and confirming the 'morality' of a love of beauty.

The first directly artistic challenge to this spurious notion of artistic morality came from Charles Ives. From America, Ives could see that European art was irrelevant to the cultural mores of his time because its manner conditioned *and limited* its substance: he therefore regarded all aspects of his musical ambience as potential substance for composition. In Europe, the reaction of composers to the atrocities of the First World War provided a further challenge to any residual notions of artistic beauty and morality. While traditional ideas concerning melody and harmony became undermined, popular musical styles were exploited. At the same time, opera and ballet libretti were often taken out of their traditionally heroic settings into ones that were primitive or bawdy.

Throughout the twentieth century, musical art has experienced a period of unprecedented instability, presenting the listener with a bewildering diversity of musical style and content, all of it claiming to represent modern music. Education has a responsibility to explore and attempt to account for radical changes in musical style and to steer society towards the more positive, affirmative aspects of contemporary musical art.

These considerations suggest the following musical objective:

To establish a historical perspective on musical styles and on the social and political factors that have conditioned them.

Audience response to music

Ironically, the importance attached by the West to the composer (due to the precise nature of Western musical notation) causes audiences to devote a disproportionate amount of attention to the performer. The degree of technical virtuosity of which the performer has become capable has made him, more than the composer, susceptible to 'stardom'. This, with its intrinsic subsuming of artistic principle on account of deference to market forces, poses a threat to genuine musical artistry. The performer can often appear in opposition to the composer, sometimes making demands upon him individually and frequently determining the extent to which composers of all periods receive public hearing.

Whereas in India the composition is chosen to suit the season and the time of day so that the audience's mood is already tuned to the style of performance and its attention is not distracted by extramusical causes, in the West, this precise relationship between the mood of the music and the predicted mood of the audience is not possible. Audiences therefore respond as much to the actual performance as to the music performed, often focusing on what they have been told about the performer and often not questioning the value of the music itself. Musical responses have become ritualized by means of applause, even though spontaneous bursts of applause can destroy the mood created by the music that preceded them.

This situation is complicated by the reluctance of many listeners to understand and accept the radical changes in musical style and content that have necessarily taken place during this century, causing them to look for the 'moral truths' of music in past romanticism, careless of any distinction between truth and morality or between art and mere decoration. Such listeners have tended to ignore the social stigmas that have become attached to classical and popular musics, brushing aside the latter along with modern music and the many ethnic musics that have profoundly affected it.

Audience reaction to music is still largely affected by an endemic form of cultural conditioning that, so far, education has proved unable to penetrate. The problem is that re-conditioning is not sufficient: a degree of indoctrination in different cultures is essential before such differences and changes within cultures can be assessed and reacted to spontaneously and with intrinsic benefit.

These considerations suggest the following musical objective:

> To impart such knowledge of musical theory and practice as can assist in eliciting personal and emotional (rather than conditioned) responses to musical performance.

Cultural conditioning and indoctrination

It is important to distinguish between cultural conditioning and indoctrination, for the exercise of both is essential to social stability, even though their use must, of necessity, be only partial if we are to avoid political oligarchy.

Human exploitation has always led to cultural antithesis, even before 'race' became an obvious factor among present social injustices. Differences in cultural habits, to a large extent exemplified in artistic approaches and responses, require full recognition by all parties if peaceful understanding is to prevail. Aspects of one culture may prove inimical to another and can actually be the cause of intolerance. Schools cannot and clearly should not attempt to enforce cultural change. However, they have an obligation to present and define relevant cultures so that these cultures contribute to rather than detract from racial and cultural harmony. This involves a degree of cultural conditioning: and it cannot be achieved without some indoctrination.

Any attempt to understand alien culture involves the exercise of value judgement. This depends upon knowledge and understanding of doctrine, though it does not and cannot require acceptance of doctrine: we do not live in a doctrinaire society — nor can we so long as we are genuinely multi-cultural.

There is, however, a need for a degree of indoctrination. The musics of different cultures can only be understood and assessed in relation to each other if they are presented in their original form and not watered down for the classroom. Only then, and in the course of time, can it be seen whether integration is possible or even desirable. Integration, if it happens at all, should lead to a strengthening of the veracity of the art product.

This suggests the following objective:

To impart knowledge and understanding of the musics of all the various ethnic and social groupings within contemporary culture.

Genius as the guiding spirit of art and culture

Western culture, as a result of imperialism and technological superiority, is dominant on a global scale, often overpowering other ethnic cultures in its midst. As art is one of the most positive products of this culture, it is an indispensable guide to understanding the present and should therefore be nourished and strengthened.

The individuality of Western culture caused the notion of genius to be transferred from being guardian of the individual household to being the guiding spirit of art and culture. In music, it gave to the composer total ascendancy over the performer.

The greatest musical art ritualizes emotion by reflecting the infinite variety of mood to which emotions give rise. It achieves this by integrating the various musical elements *independently* of the mood created by any one of them. To achieve this rare condition, a composer of genius must have proved himself capable of manipulating past musical forms and styles into ones appropriate to the present, of developing these forms and styles with sufficient confidence to reflect and expose the truths of his culture and, subsequently, of establishing his own, exclusive, visionary world. Only thus can the composer of genius be entirely true to his art and rationalize, in his own musical terms, the irrational power of his medium.

The politics of the twentieth century have created cultural problems of such complexity that they have virtually overreached the capacity of musical art to achieve this kind of perfection. The explosive revelations that the twentieth century has brought about in the understanding of the human psyche, coupled with the awareness of human atrocity that technology has imposed on our senses, has challenged any lingering notions of artistic beauty and has encouraged the destructive rather than the affirmative instincts in composers. European art has been pitted mercilessly against the art of quite different cultures which can seem more pertinent to our modern society.

Education has tended to respond to the variety of musics within our present society by seeking the lowest common denominator. This is evident in the current fear of the historical élitism of Western art and in the propensity for offering that which appears most readily assimilable. Instead of strengthening musical roots with genuine expertise, education has encouraged a cosmetic integration of musical cultures. In fact, useful integration can only be achieved by the most acutely creative musical minds we have. In this sense genius, for all the problems that have diluted its effectiveness, is still a valid concept and a potential guiding spirit of art and culture.

This suggests the following objective:

To inculcate understanding of the artistic capability of music.

Music as a means of communication

The personalized nature of Western music enabled it to acquire a dialectical element that could define and disturb its cultural ambience. The composers of genius who made this development possible acquired an exclusive, visionary quality that distanced their music from their public. Thus, although music's power is such that it can appeal directly to people regardless of their understanding of it, the fullness of their response to the music of such absolute genius will vary according to their musical experience, skill, and general artistic susceptibility.

As art music reflects, defines, and even conditions culture, its content must, in some way, reflect its social milieu. Although changes in society have been the major catalyst for changes in musical style and content, any musical composition, if it is to communicate meaningfully, must show some recognition of its musical inheritance, because known aesthetic conventions provide a necessary focus for the listener's attention and understanding. The need for this was proved when, after the Second World War, many composers felt a cultural need to reject totally their musical past, thus causing an unprecedented estrangement between their music and their public. Since then, the technology of the twentieth century has actually ridiculed traditional Western art, while it has expanded our knowledge of quite different cultures — to the extent that the relevance of our classical music tradition has been questioned.

Artistic communication through music is further beset by a host of extra-musical associations, of which the most obvious are religious, social, and racial. The music of fundamentalist religion, of popular social protest and of racial groupings has usually aimed to communicate at a popular level and has seldom aspired — let alone risen — to the condition of musical art. Nevertheless, it is imperative to recognize the social and political importance of these musics and their influence on culture generally.

Art is by definition a directly active medium and continues to exist because people recognize that it still contains a unique means of communication and of emotional fulfilment. The role of education should be that of 'enabler' of artistic tradition, so as to help restore art to being a major cultural force of and *for* our time.

This leads to the following objective:

To encourage the use of music's emotional communicative power as a means towards self-understanding and fulfilment.

PART THREE

METHOD — The Practical Background

A creative minority is always small in numbers but, if it is in tune with the majority, and is always trying to pull the latter up and make it advance, so that the gap between the two is lessened, a stable and progressive culture results. Without that creative minority a civilization must inevitably decay. But it may also decay if the bond between a creative minority and the majority is broken and there is a loss of social unity in society as a whole, and ultimately that minority itself loses its creativeness and becomes barren and sterile.

Jawaharlal Nehru: *The Discovery of India* (1945).

10

Elitism, Egalitarianism, and Method

In any consideration of methodology for music in education, there is really only one question that needs to be asked: how do children gain knowledge and insight into music? Atarah Ben-Tovim, a former professional flute player who has subsequently dedicated her life to providing musical training and performance for children, provides a positive answer:

There is really only one way to come to understand music: by learning to play a musical instrument, whether an external one like the piano or flute or by training the human voice to become an instrument.[1]

Few musicians could disagree. But music in education is not always controlled by musicians, and the economics of providing instrumental tuition make it inevitable that instruction on skilled instruments can be offered only to a minority. This, as I described in Chapter 4, has led to an insistence on the unlimited usefulness of music in the classroom as well as to methods which bypass instrumental skills and appear to eradicate the need for individual specialisms. It has also caused a widespread unwillingness to distinguish between rigorous instrumental skill and the creative use of easily mastered pitch-percussion instruments commonly used in the classroom.

The Schools Council's Report *Music in the Secondary School Curriculum*[2] is unfortunately equivocal on this matter. While admitting that the musically talented must be encouraged and provided with opportunities for developing skills, it is nevertheless concerned that a teacher might appear more of a trainer than an educator, putting forward his own ideas rather than drawing out ideas from the children. This equivocation is entirely understandable: the resources available will not enable us to provide or achieve all that we would like. Hard choices have to be made. For all its attempts to be even-handed, the report — perhaps by the very nature of its brief — often appears obsessional about the need for individual decision-making and the importance of the classroom in this respect. And although it encourages the special development of talent, it castigates those who would appear to be doing so at the expense of music for all in the classroom. Though helpful in many ways, the report fails by attempting to be all things, musically, to all people. More importantly, the underlying justification for its argument leads to a fundamentally false musical argument. However valuable, educationally, creative activities in the classroom may prove, the contention that 'creative' and 're-creative' approaches are two aspects of the same thing and cannot flourish without each other is disproved by all observable facts. How many of to-day's distinguished composers or performers started their musical training by improvising music on mass-produced pitch percussion instruments in the classroom? For many of them, classroom experiences in music may seldom have departed far from the singing of ditties from *The National Song Book*.

Unfortunately — though inevitably, given the inherently élitist nature of music as described in both Chapters 4 and 6 — there can be no satisfactory reconciliation of the conflict between the pursuit of high instrumental standards and the desire to encourage instrumental activity for all in the classroom. It is virtually impossible to provide classroom music which will be attractive, stimulating, and practicable for those with little or no instrumental training, while at the same time being worthwhile for those with more advanced skills. Any attempt to involve high-level instrumentalists practically in the general work in the classroom can have the effect of making them thoroughly disillusioned with school music. Nor is anything to be gained by abandoning the traditional extra-curricular forms of choir, orchestra, and band in order to encourage rock bands, reggae groups, folk music groups, new music ensembles, and other less traditional forms. Apart from the fact that such groups are obviously equally worthy of encouragement in their own right, the performers in such groups need individual instruments and guidance in just the same way as do those in the more traditional formats.

This point is made clearly by Paul Crawford, a professional rock musician and co-founder of the Central London Youth Project Music Workshop which teaches children, on a voluntary basis, to become expert in the performance of popular music:

The individual lessons are the heart of the music programme . . . Most important of all are the personal relationships developed between teacher and student. Crucial in this is the teacher's credibility in the eyes of the student: the confidence of the student in his teacher is transferred to his own performance. If the teacher can play an Eric Clapton or Jimmi Hendrix solo note for note, the student has faith in the teacher. If the student can play some of the solo by the end of the lesson, he has confidence in himself.[3]

It is interesting to note that the 'élitist' argument is as relevant to the practice of popular music as to that of classical music; for a potential dichotomy between these apparently separate forms of music has become entwined with that between the curricular and the extra-curricular — or, as music teachers tend to see it, between provision of instruction in skills for the few and creative experience for the many.

Keith Swanwick, Professor of Music Education at London University, has made a brave attempt to rationalize the issue in his *A Basis for Music Education*.[4] He has devised for that basis the mnemonic CLASP (Composition, Literature, Audition, Skills, Performance) with particular emphasis on CAP, (Composition, Audition, Performance). This mnemonic provides a neat encapsulation of the aspects of learning that should emanate from the classroom — an ingenious compromise between the need for individual skill and the need for instruction to all. However, it has the effect of down-grading skill by suggesting that composition and performance can *precede* skill. It also fails to recognize that skill acquisition is a basic factor in motivation. Unfortunately, subordination of skill to other musical processes can have the effect of negating the very essence of musical experience. It is, of course, difficult to describe music without referring to specific things about it: technique, style, history, etc. I have already suggested that music is essentially its own description because, at its best, it says things that can only be said in music. However, as technique is an essential prerequisite for this to happen, it at least must be talked about. Any suggestion that technicalities such as 'watch the dynamics', 'use less bow' do not contribute to our personal response to musical experience denies, at least at one level, the very process that leads us to genuine musical experience. For example, one of the most lugubrious aspects of *ad hoc* professional orchestras (let alone school orchestras) is the frequent inability of conductor and players to achieve the magic of a real pianissimo or fortissimo. And at least half of the rhythmic inaccuracies emanating from young string players are caused quite specifically by using too much bow. (At a more elementary level, rhythmic inaccuracy in young children playing pitch-percussion instruments in class can arise as much from clenching the sticks as from any inherent lack of rhythmic awareness.)

It is of the utmost importance that the potential dichotomy between the need for individual and small group instruction in specific skills and the extenuating claims of the classroom is clearly recognized if there is to be any rationale for a realistic distribution of musical resources. Any attempts to deny it — to rationalize away the need for individual instruction — creates a far more serious dichotomy: one between school music and the living world of music outside. The classroom has an important place in any scheme for education in music and I shall point to ways in which it can be put to best use in the next chapter. Meanwhile, I will simply reiterate Atarah Ben-Tovim's statement that the only way to come to understand music properly is by learning to play a musical instrument; and I would be glad to hear from any *skilled* music teacher who, considering carefully his or her own past, believes this not to be so.

Of course not all children prove equally susceptible to the mental and physical demands of playing an instrument or to the artistic ethos or aesthetic beauty of classical music. Some children identify immediately with pop music and have a compulsive desire to participate in it. Some children identify deeply with classical music and feel a similar desire to participate in it. Many identify with both, with or without wishing to be actively involved, and some identify only marginally with either. In any event, there is no sense in which sensitivity to music need be restricted to an élite. As with any field of study or activity, it is all a matter of degree. Instrumental tuition enables children to discover the extent of their ability and interest in music and, where appropriate, to be able to develop it.

For certain people, music is the most elemental source of motivation: the strength of music's communication through an ever-growing understanding of its language provides a constant spur to further endeavour and to a resultant sense of wholeness in life. From the earliest desire to sing or to play a specific instrument to the maturing sense of the finest details of musical architecture, conviction — the sense of musical values and the need for a technique with which to express them — enables true musicians to mature and subsequently to inspire and develop another generation of young people who share this inherent and unquantifiable conviction about music and art.

There is a sense in which any compulsive involvement in music is therapeutic. Emotional energy and nervous energy often act as cause and effect. Many of the most 'musical' musicians are social misfits of one sort or another, whose nervous energy, hypersensitivity, and clarity of perception place them at some odds with their fellows and with society. Music provides an alternative means of communication — through the emotions: it also provides an active social environment where such people can work with others of similar ilk. The emotional 'tear-away' is often searching for something just like music — not the craft of the classroom, but that very special sense of achievement and fulfilment accruing from the emotional and technical disciplines combined in musical performance. For such people, music is not an option but a life-giving necessity. For other young people with highly developed aesthetic receptivity, musical performance provides, if not a life-giving necessity, an extremely benefiting disciplined activity. For yet others, musical performance provides pleasurable occupation throughout life, for which classroom activity may provide motivation but is no substitute whatever.

In many of these instances, the level of music-making is unlikely to rise above the level of aesthetic craft; but it is a highly disciplined craft, requiring co-ordination of mind and body and there is absolutely nothing wrong with that. The Newsom Report, *Half our future*, made the point in 1965:

Brass band work, for example, has often proved more successful with pupils of quite limited general ability, and a practical approach through instruments can be much more effective than 'appreciation' classes . . . Music can clearly be a potent force in the lives of many young people. It is a natural source of recreation, and one form of activity which can be carried on from school through adult life; its contribution to both the school community and the larger community can be notable. It deserves generous encouragement.[5]

Controversy over the relative importance of classroom and instrumental teaching has led to a common failure among the parties concerned to recognize the different nature of their respective complementary roles. Too often the classroom teacher is actually unwilling (or unable) to help identify the children who have most to benefit from instrumental instruction. Not infrequently a feeling of animosity is generated because the classroom teacher feels, rightly, that his objectives are quite different from those of the instrumental teacher and, wrongly, that the instrumental teacher is at best an unnecessary parasite and at worst a threat to his hold on the able musicians. The same can be true in reverse. The fact is that, if classroom and instrumental teachers are to do their jobs properly, their respective abilities, interests, training, and experience are likely to be very different. Nothing is to be gained by attempting to paper over these differences or pretend they do not exist. Nor is anything to be gained by requiring instrumental teachers to work in classrooms or to take half classes of beginners. The class teacher has everything to gain by encouraging instrumental teachers to train children to a standard which enables them to take academic examinations as well as to assist with school concerts.

If music is to survive as a living subject within education, there needs to be a fundamental re-thinking over the use of human resources, based not just on aesthetic, egalitarian argument, but on an equally fundamental reassessment of the effectiveness of different aspects and stages of musical provision within education. To do this it will be necessary to recognize that there are four essential means for fulfilling the declared aims and objectives which, in the context of current educational organization in Britain, are complementary and mutually interdependent:

1. The inclusion of musical activity somewhere within the time-tabled, classroom curriculum.
2. Provision of skilled instrumental instruction.
3. Provision of special ensemble opportunities offering challenging levels of training and performance.
4. Exposure to live musical performance.'

11

Music in the School Classroom

The range of musical activities possible in a classroom is sufficiently wide that it can vary substantially not just between primary and secondary schools but between individual schools catering for the same age range. Furthermore, very different methods pertaining to very different content show little correspondence in their success rate: indeed, criteria for defining success are likely to be as variable as method and content. It is therefore appropriate, at this juncture, to consider what particular aspects of musical learning and experience can be accommodated within the classroom situation and in what sort of depth they can be provided by this means.

At its best, class music teaching, whether in primary or secondary schools, might hope to achieve the following:

1. An elementary awareness of the basic elements of music — melody, rhythm, harmony, counterpoint, motor speed, dynamics, timbre, density, etc. — and of ways in which composers have used and combined them. (This will be achieved largely through group experimentation on classroom instruments, backed by recorded or live performance of pre-composed music.)

2. An elementary awareness of the variety of musical styles that exist and have existed: the Western tradition from the early Middle Ages to the present day; the popular tradition — folk, pop, and jazz; music of other cultures, particularly of those to be found in this country. (This will involve some experimental work as in (1) above and some other forms of direct performance, but it will rely very largely on recorded performance and a teacher's ability to relate the various musics to aspects of life today.)

3. An elementary understanding of the relationship between different art forms. (This will be done largely through practical work, such as devising music for drama, creating music in

127

response to art and literature, writing and painting to the
accompaniment of music, moving to music, inventing music
for movement, etc.)

4. An elementary understanding of musical history in relation to
   social history. (This can be effected through relatively simple
   activities such as the singing of English and Jamaican folk
   songs, or through more sophisticated general studies.)
5. An elementary knowledge of voice production and some
   experience of vocal repertoire.
6. Elementary experience of instrumental performance:
   recorders, guitars, open strings and first position of violin
   family, classroom pitched and unpitched percussion, keyboard or strings of acoustic piano, electric keyboard,
   synthesizer, auto-harp, etc., plus any other instrumental skills
   available.
7. Elementary experience and knowledge of musical electronics.
8. Elementary knowledge of musical notation.
9. Incentive to further study, whether through skilled performance, examination work, or both.

It can hardly have escaped attention that Items 1 to 8 have been
preceded by the word 'elementary'. There is, of course, nothing
wrong with elementary study — providing everyone clearly understands that it *is* elementary. What is wrong, is when elementary
study, unknown to the students, turns out to be a cul-de-sac: when
it has not properly paved the path to more advanced study. And it
is precisely because this is so often the case that the possibilities of
content just described apply equally to primary and secondary
schools.

I have based the foregoing classroom content on the assumption
that music teachers will be confronted by the usual size of full class.
Let us now suppose that, through ingenious timetabling, all class
sizes were to be cut by half, that the amount of time given to music
for these half classes were to be doubled and that an option scheme
would enable these half classes of children to attend the music
lessons voluntarily. What more would then be gained by those
attending these music lessons? Depending upon the musical skills
of the teacher, some extra activities might ensue. For example, the
singing of songs might develop into general choral singing; or, if
sufficient instruments could be made available, brass band work

might be initiated; children might be given a rudimentary skill on the violin or flute, etc.; or, again, given the necessary electronic equipment, children might be given a rudimentary ability at keyboard harmony and improvisation. Apart from this, although Items 1 to 8 would be accomplished with much greater thoroughness, the actual *standard* of work attempted could not be greatly increased. Or, in other words, although the content of any syllabus could be substantially thickened and the results of any consequent student assessment considerably improved, the actual objectives could not be greatly extended. In addition, Item 9 — incentive to further study — could be substantially eroded, because the inherent limitations would be the more obvious and could be destructive in the frustration they could cause.

Why should all this be so? In a sense, the answer is what the whole of this book has been about. In a nutshell, it is contained in Item 8: an *elementary* knowledge of musical notation. Anything more than a superficial insight into music requires a thorough ability to read and hear it and this ability is acquired through playing an instrument. Without this ability, real progression in music is impossible. The classroom can encourage and support instrumental work but it cannot satisfactorily replace it. For this reason alone, classroom music is fundamentally more important in primary rather than secondary schools.

It is commonly assumed that the musical qualifications required for teaching in a primary school need not be as high as those required for teaching in a secondary school. This assumption is based as much on expediency as on musical or educational logic. As the British education system places the total teaching responsibility for a class of primary children in the hands of one person, music specialists *working specifically in their specialist field* tend to be found only in secondary schools. This is the more true as cuts in expenditure coupled with falling rolls in schools have made the luxury of a full-time 'floating' music teacher, once afforded by some of the larger primary schools, largely a thing of the past. The music curriculum of the primary school is becoming increasingly subject to the availability of specialist staff.

As always, 'music educators' have not been slow to turn necessity to advantage and to invent a range of simple musical activities (often misnamed 'creative') that can be handled by teachers lacking musical expertise. As a result, in-service training involving such methods has been seen as an almost definitive solution to this situation. There are, however, two factors which limit the usefulness of this solution. One is that many non-specialist teachers do not prove receptive to music: if they were going to do so, the chances are they would already have done something about their lack of musical ability. What they assimilate from in-service training is severely limited, and the lack of conviction with which many of them subsequently present the ideas and materials in the classroom often cancels out the little good that these ideas can effect. The other problem is, quite simply, that it leads to an *assumption* that primary school music must be thus limited. Primary school music need not be limited by anything other than the ultimate ability of the children. It certainly does not require less musical skill from teachers than secondary school music. Practical ability, breadth of musical knowledge, musical imagination, an ability to arrange music, an ability to inspire children to sing — these are all as necessary in the primary school as in the secondary school.

In some ways they are more necessary, for children tend to be more receptive to music at primary level than at secondary level (though this dichotomy can be ameliorated to some extent where middle schools act as a bridge between primary and secondary educational practice). This has partly to do with the more formal structuring of secondary schools; it also has a lot to do with the effects of puberty.

Pre-puberty children are usually willing and glad to share in the enthusiasms of their teachers. Post-puberty children are suddenly self-conscious, acutely aware of the reactions of their peers, and choosy about what to be seen to be doing and enjoying. The typical combination of singing, percussion, and recorder playing to be found in many primary schools is often of only immediate rather than lasting value: the traditional repertoire of songs is not easily made relevant to secondary children, percussion instruments soon seem like childish toys, and the school recorder's general limitations become all too apparent.

The effect of puberty on musical motivation creates problems for both primary and secondary schools. The best solution is for children to develop sufficient *skill* at primary level to *want* to continue some form of disciplined musical activity throughout adolescence. Participation in school, area or central music ensembles and festivals can add to this incentive. The greater the availability of instrumental tuition in primary schools, the greater the number of children who will be directly motivated to continue active musical involvement at secondary school. However, instrumental teachers cannot, on their own, solve the problems of general primary music.

I do not propose to describe in detail the many ideas and methods concerning class music teaching in primary and secondary schools that have evolved over the past fifteen or so years, from the pupil-orientated ideas of Orff to the teacher-orientated disencumbrance of Silver–Burdett. I suspect that by now enough theory, methodology, and actual music relating specifically to 'music education' in the classroom has appeared in print for it to stretch without gap from Land's End to John O'Groat's. Many of these publications have proved valuable, although the success of any method depends largely on the personality and musical inclinations of a particular teacher.

Our current obsession with methodology (just one of many cultural phenomena with which we have been infected by the United States) is having one disastrous effect: it is blinding us to content. It has become a 'manner' conditioning the 'substance' (see the discussion on Charles Ives, Chapter 7). The musical *substance* being offered to children as a result of this publication fever is largely dominated by pop, third-rate functional composition, and classics distorted by context and arrangement to such an extent that the *spirit* has been destroyed with the letter. The artistically exciting, the emotionally gratifying aspects of music have often escaped attention — and this almost without notice. The very fact that this situation has been able to come about serves as a sharp reminder of the serious lack of skilled and perceptive musicians working in schools. Music specialists are often appointed on the basis of their knowledge of educational gimmickry rather than on their innate musicality. The former may well effect immediate short-term interest but only the latter will ultimately be able to infect children with a deep sense of music's emotional and artistic capability.

In these circumstances, it is all the more important to consider the appropriate content, or 'substance' of the music curriculum, particularly that of the primary school. The possible range of activities I listed earlier can be contained within four basic components which should, I suggest, form the core of primary school music:

1. *Skilled* use of the voice.
2. Creative exploration of the basic elements of music, leading to compositions by groups of children.
3. Exposure to a wide variety of different musics (which can be effected in conjunction with (2) above, creative writing, painting, movement, and drama).
4. Systematic training in musical literacy (which can be developed from (1), (2), and (3)).

All these are complementary to each other. Music reading of itself is of little value unless it is seen to have purpose (choral singing, instrumental playing, etc.). Choral singing is unlikely to be greeted with enthusiasm unless it is seen to be a challenging skill and unless the content is found appealing, relevant, and a stimulating extension of musical experience. In any case, no music syllabus is likely to have lasting value unless it attempts to obviate the class and cultural distinctions that have become attached to different forms and styles of music (see Chapter 15). If the above components are presented meaningfully, with the musicality of the content constantly in mind, they should encourage children to continue exploring music after primary school, whether through the secondary school curriculum, through area or central activities, or on their own.

In theory at least, it is quite possible for a teacher with specialist musical training to implement this kind of curriculum. It could therefore prove a more productive use of in-service resources to assist music specialists in doing just that, rather than forever trying to make it possible for non-specialists to be responsible for their own music. A music specialist trained in this way could then encourage non-specialists on the staff to assist with (2) and (3) above, particularly if he or she has the responsibility of general class teaching. Any re-thinking over deployment of human resources must take into account the fact that no amount of in-service training can atone for the lack of an able specialist on the staff of an individual primary school. Acquisition of musical skill is something that, as we all know, should ideally start at an early age. The best teachers excel largely because of the ease with which they can read, think, and play music (thus leaving the majority of their attention for monitoring the class) and this is usually the result of over ten years regular training from childhood. Such teachers are to

be found mainly in secondary schools, tied to a classroom-orien-
tated timetable. Very often their abilities are being squandered.

The role of music teachers in secondary schools varies substantially according to the structure of secondary education within the
LEA and the academic structure of individual schools. This, in
turn, is often related to the type of pupil intake. Secondary music
teachers may be required to spend the majority of their time
teaching classes or they may spend much of their time on examination work. They may do a mixture of both. They are likely to be
involved in a large amount of extra-curricular work which could
involve rock groups, folk groups, steel bands, electronics, instrumental ensembles, choirs and/or operatic productions. They may
be given compensating time off for this extra work load or they
may, because of a full timetable of class lessons, have to skimp or
curtail the extra-curricular activities. In any event, they may well
find the need to arrange music for special ensembles or they may
feel the need to compose. They will almost certainly be responsible
for detailed organization of whatever instrumental music there may
be. They will spend much time negotiating the maintenance and
purchase of complicated equipment; and if they are in schools with
a community brief they may well find themselves involved in
anything from male voice choirs to record clubs. Clearly, this kind
of work load is more than most individual people can bear and its
variety is likely to outstrip the abilities of the most eclectic teacher.
Occasionally it all works well, quite often it works in part and
equally often it doesn't work at all.

Where it does work, the secondary music teacher is likely to have
a significant influence on the style and content of the music curriculum. Or, put the other way round, the style and content of the
music curriculum is likely to be at the mercy of the particular
interests and abilities of a single music teacher. An extraordinary
variety of musical activities takes place from school to school. This
would be fine if the musical needs of children differed substantially
from school to school. I do not believe they do. I do not believe, for
example, that the fundamental musical needs in six different
schools should be rock music, brass bands, jug bands, steel bands,
madrigal groups, and 'creative music' respectively. Yet music in
secondary schools still, to a large extent, reflects the particular
interests of a particular teacher. Of course the ideal teacher does not
allow this situation to arise: but 'ideal' teachers are thin on the

ground. An educational structure that allows this degree of diversity to exist must at least be open to question.

An early task facing any Head of Music in a secondary school will be to establish priorities. In many instances a decision will need making on the relative importance of general class work, examination work, and extra-curricular activity — for something usually *has* to give way. In fact, however, if the class work is to show *progression* in terms of skill and knowledge acquired, the whole syllabus will need to be seen in terms of a pyramidal structure, leading to examination work and including care of actual and potential instrumentalists, who will set the tone of music in the school by virtue of genuine accomplishment.

The secondary teacher's role is complicated by the variety of musical backgrounds of the primary schools that supply his clientele. He will need to win over the new arrivals and, if he is resourceful, he will have an armoury of tricks up his sleeve for this purpose. With these he will hope to establish a rapport with the children who will, in turn, hopefully establish a rapport with music. However, such a rapport can only last in meaningful terms if the teacher is leading the students to ever increasing endeavour and accomplishment. And how is he to do that in classes of thirty children of mixed musical ability and motivation? It can only be done if somewhere along the line a sufficient body of children are involved in some form of performing, reading, composing and/or analysing music. This can and has been achieved by very exceptional teachers, and the methods and results of some of these exceptions are recorded very usefully in the small print of the Schools Council's *Music in the Secondary School Curriculum.*

These accounts of creative approaches to musical understanding will amply repay study, though they are likely to prove most useful to successful rather than struggling teachers. For while some teachers cope and some do not, the majority *do* struggle. If and when they have learned to cope it is often because they have learned to live with the musical mediocrity that is generally intrinsic to the secondary classroom situation. They then find it safer not to question their objectives or assessments too far. If they did, they would perhaps observe substantial differences between the kinds of music and music-making with which they are concerned in school and the world of music outside school to which many of them will return with relief when their school work is done. In short, they would find that their work in school is lacking in *musical* idealism. It frequently happens that the fundamental concern of the teacher — as of the Head of the school — is for the children to be kept in order, occupied, and reasonably content. Teachers who achieve this in problematic comprehensive schools deserve genuine congratulation. It is not their fault that, in *musical* terms, their success *can* only be partial. Nor is it their fault that their necessary daily preoccupation with the classroom, with all the hard grind that entails, often prevents them from assessing the value of what they do in the light of the broader spectrum of music. Too often music teachers are made mediocre in outlook by the situation in which they are ensnared but which familiarity causes them to take for granted. To this extent, mediocrity usually wins. The most musically sensitive teachers usually sink or swim spectacularly. More often than not they sink.

The role of the secondary school music teacher depends fundamentally on the type of children with whom he or she is dealing and the philosophy of the school that houses them. (A teachers' equilibrium throughout the whole of his career can depend upon the ambience of the school first encountered.) In depressed areas, it will prove harder to break down music's class associations; indeed, this may never be achieved. In this kind of situation, the teacher may opt immediately for a popular form of musical culture: the teacher may well have been appointed on account of his or her ability to do that very thing. If the teacher is successful, it will again have been a partial success arising from *necessarily* limited horizons in a similarly blinkered situation.

There is no reason why the content of the secondary school music curriculum should be greatly different from that of the primary school, provided that increased fluency in musical literacy combined with more complex creative exploration and more analytical exposure to musical styles leads to an enhanced perception of music. It has to be admitted that this very seldom happens. Generally low entry figures for music examination courses have less to do with syllabus content and job requirements than with the drastically uneven amount and quality of music teaching in primary schools and with the limited value of three years' *compulsory* attendance in the music classroom. The sense of progression that is vital to continued motivation seems always to be at a premium, if not entirely absent. This is in striking contrast to the very clear-cut sense of progression that inspires the instrumentalist and that is reflected in the graded instrumental examinations, whether or not the instrumentalist wishes to use them. As is the case with primary schools, the 'manner' of secondary classroom teaching frequently obscures the mediocrity of the 'substance'.

The situation is not helped by the generally inadequate equipment available. 'Orff'-type glockenspiels and xylophones are sufficiently common in primary schools now that they are regarded as little more than toys by growing adolescents. Many demonstrations of successful creative work in secondary schools use real xylophones, vibraphones, marimbas, large percussion instruments, and electronic equipment that cannot normally be made available unless a school has been specially equipped for experimental work or is a centre for LEA orchestral work. Quality of sound is perhaps the most important ingredient in the creation of musical excitement. From violins to sitars and from electric guitars to classroom instruments, much active music-making in secondary schools is forced to take place on instruments whose sound quality is utterly lacking in potential.

The microchip revolution is also having its effect on the quality of musical sound. In addition, it is further discouraging the teaching of genuine musical skills. Now that the electronic keyboard can be linked with the BBC 'B', or 'Beeb', and other school computers, a whole new range of instructional opportunity has become available. Unfortunately, the marketeers of this technology know all too well the commercial value of alleviating rather than stimulating work. The computer keyboard is being pushed as a development that obviates the need for learning the traditional musical skills: only learn to handle it exactly according to its pre-packaged instructions and it will produce, for example, its own — emasculated — version of 'Yesterday'. I have yet to see a programme that involves students in feeding a computer with the actual musical information that would *enable* it to play 'Yesterday'. Yet this activity could actually involve students meaningfully in learning about musical notation and harmony.

At a simpler level, the possibility of a realistic means of enabling students to teach themselves to read musical notation and to translate it orally is at hand. Software for musical instruction applied solely to computers has been limited by the absence of a keyboard (the use of the conventional typewriter format for indicating the names of musical notes reduces such ingenious games as 'Note Wars' to exercises in typing skills) and by the awful bleep of computer sound. Now that electronic keyboards can be linked to computers, the possibility of adapting software to keyboards and combining this with a varied (if still somewhat emasculated) polyphonic sound world, means that a sensational break through the music-reading barrier could be at hand.

Unfortunately, microchip technology is being pursued *primarily* as an aid to musical creativity — a short-term and a short-sighted view of its use. (While it will undoubtedly *involve* pupils in creating musical structures, the limitations of electronic sound will remain: the *artistic* capability will be roughly that which the BBC Radiophonic Workshop made available years ago, but in compact and virtually idiot-proof form.) The stranglehold of 'creativity' in the classroom, with its implicit tendency to obviate the need for skills, is such that it is extremely difficult to elicit from manufacturers of the new technology interest in its potential for increasing — rather than mitigating — musical skills. This again reflects the mediocrity of expectation that secondary school music, so often defined by the limited possibilities of the classroom, frequently inflicts upon its music teachers.

I am well aware that these remarks may elicit howls of abuse from schools to whom it will be considered that most of these criticisms do not apply. To such schools two questions must immediately be addressed: to what extent is the provision of general music within the school at the expense of suitable opportunities for advanced musical instruction and to what extent is the musical activity in a particular school typical of schools in the area. Thereafter, a third question is almost certain to be necessary: to what extent should an individual school pride itself on the success of any aspect of its curriculum if its administrators recognize that this success is due to exceptional circumstances that cannot be expected to obtain in most other schools — or, put more pungently, whether, in such circumstances, a school is justified in upholding such success as an example of 'good practice'. Unless 'good practice' is the rule rather than the exception, something must be wrong with the system.

When a teacher has spent a substantial part of his or her life *coping* with problems that would daunt the average citizen, whatever the training, it is not easy to accept that there could just be something wrong with the very *raison d'être*, that the obsession with overcoming the difficulties of the task in hand may have caused the teacher to *refuse* to see the subject, music, in a wider educational or social context. Yet, if we are to make any sense of music in our present educational system, this is precisely what must happen.

In the context of mounting financial stringency, reduction of staffing levels, the need for specialist teaching in primary schools, and the need to provide challenging outlets for adolescents in an increasingly volatile society, the common suppositions that determine musical provision in secondary schools must be called into question. The persistently *involuntary* nature of musical instruction, often over three or even five years of secondary schooling, the general lack of modern equipment and suitable spaces, and the common need for the classroom to be forever motivating its students rather than responding to its students' motivation, all combine to suggest that compulsory music in the secondary school needs minimizing. Radically new outlooks, strategies, and pooling of facilities are needed if music in schools is to lead to progressive ability and is ultimately to prove 'accountable': if it is not to appear 'frivolous or futile to people who belong to a more severe or ambitious culture' (see Chapter 1). Too much of what does appear accountable, from rock groups to choirs and from steel bands to school operas, seems wholly unconnected with the secondary classroom. Yet all too often it is the classroom that is seen as 'school music'.

12

Instrumental Music in Schools

Thirty years ago, no one ever thought that instrumental teaching should — or could — cater for a majority of children: the problem was to persuade enough children to give it a try. The function of instrumental teaching was — as it still should be — to provide opportunity for in-depth study and involvement for those who respond to it with diligence and aptitude.

The concerns that have since been expressed over the provision of instrumental teaching have sprung, paradoxically, from its success. Youth orchestras proved to be a great incentive. Increasing numbers of children opted for instrumental instruction with the result that the peripatetic services in the country were unable to cope satisfactorily with the demand. Many peripatetic teachers were then encouraged to teach more children than they could possibly teach thoroughly. This discouraged the right sort of people from becoming peripatetic teachers, while it encouraged the more successful pupils to seek tuition from private teachers. As this situation became increasingly erosive, the *ethical* status of instrumental teachers was called into question. Was it right for children to receive small group and individual instruction? Above all, was it right for some children to receive it while others did not?

The fact that this last point reflected so precisely what happened throughout the whole examination framework was hardly considered relevant. The irrational confusions of function that have bedevilled Western music since the fifth century BC again came into full play. Schools that had been obliged to gear their curricula to academic success on account of prevailing parental opinion saw in music an egalitarian vehicle with which to redress their imposed élitist stance. ('I want my school to be permeated by music,' said the Head of one such school to me. My suggestion that he might permeate it more successfully with chemistry was not greeted with enthusiasm.) The result of this confusion was that by the early 1980s, many instrumental teams were being reduced or even obliterated and in some areas instrumental teaching remained available only if parents paid for it. Because many LEAs had allowed their instrumental services to attempt to be all things to all people, these services had failed in their original, more limited objectives.

In contrast to the tokenism that had characterized so much classroom music teaching, instrumental teaching had already proved its value, not just in educational terms but as a lasting benefit to the community. Before LEAs started appointing instrumental teachers, instrumental tuition had been available only privately. Outside the Greater London and Manchester areas, where the established Music Colleges offered 'Junior Exhibitions', this had been very thin on the ground and of generally low quality. Because, in the smaller towns, the parish organist tended to be the resident musician/conductor, the piano and organ were the instruments generally taught and they were, of course, taught to the children of the parents who could afford the tuition and who considered such tuition worthwhile.

I remember when, in my small town some thirty-five years ago, the new resident organist attempted to assemble an orchestra (as a substitute for the organ) for the annual ritual of performing *Messiah*, he was hard pressed to find, in the whole area, half a dozen scratchy violinists — such was the state of community music-making and the musical milieu in which various forms of music teaching, privately and sometimes in class in the grammar school, took place. Today that small town boasts good choral and instrumental activity and a wide range of professional concert-giving, and it can recruit from the young and from the residents for its local orchestras without difficulty. Outside London, there is considerable geographical stability amongst the British population. Where energetic and enlightened schemes for school music were initiated, involving introductory activities in class and separate instrumental instruction for those able and willing to profit from it, the subsequent musical impact on the community generally was sensational. It is therefore particularly ironic that the general failure of the secondary school classroom to meet basically impracticable objectives should sometimes be blamed on instrumental teaching. Musical provision will only succeed in disentangling itself from the net in which it has allowed itself to become entwined by educational ideology if it separates its various components in a musically realistic way, clarifies its aims, objectives and methods and distributes its resources accordingly. Instrumental teaching represents a critical component within those resources.

It should never be forgotten that instrumental playing is a skill. If learning an instrument is to lead to a lifetime of enjoyment rather than a lifetime of frustration, it is necessary that the skills of any instrument be taught correctly and thoroughly from the start. Only specialist performers on the various instruments can give the necessary instruction. Too much instrumental teaching fails because it is carried out by people who lack the necessary skills and insights themselves.

If instrumental teaching is to be programmed satisfactorily, it is clear that only a small percentage of the school population will be able to receive this specialist tuition. Class teaching of violins can be successful in the early years and, in the right circumstances, small groups can be continued in the middle years. But ultimately the committed instrumentalist needs individual lessons of up to one hour's duration and, unless this is provided, instrumentalists of good and lasting ability will not be produced. More importantly, children with real talent will be denied the opportunity to realize it fully.

Any act of high endeavour must be élitist in the sense that only a few have the ability to achieve the end results. Accepting this fact does not prevent large numbers of young players from reaching a sufficient standard for gaining enjoyment from taking part in a wide range of musical ensembles. However, this middle part of the complete musical pyramid will only work successfully if standards are high at the top, to act as an incentive. Standards cannot be pushed up from the bottom: they have to be *pulled* up from the top.

The basic difference between instrumental and classroom work is that the former requires a degree of commitment from the students that the latter, by its very nature, cannot demand. Clearly this kind of commitment will not seem desirable to many children and the degree of commitment obtained will depend to some extent on the musical milieu within a particular school and — perhaps more importantly — within a particular area. It will also depend on the skill with which the opportunity is presented and on the ability and conviction of the instrumental teacher. Some of the initial learners are bound to drop out, others will succeed to a large degree through sensitivity, intelligence, and application, while others will discover a *need* for music that will lead to genuine flair. How then can children with the potential for that motivation and ability be identified?

If it were possible to answer that question definitively, many of the problems besetting instrumental instruction would never have arisen in the first place. Ironically, it is the attempt to categorize such characteristics that has helped to give instrumental music its mistaken 'élitist' status, for it has encouraged a predominantly middle-class clientele. Intelligence, we might say, perseverance, a good ear, reliable home support — these would be the identifying characteristics. Let us therefore consider the usefulness of these definitions as criteria.

Definition of intelligence is, of course, a complex and tortuous subject. Suffice it to say here that *conventional* intelligence (for example, the ability to pass academic examinations) often exists in musicians to a high degree but is not a basic criterion for musicality. Many *emotionally* intelligent children find conventional (written) intelligence hard to master and seek other means of communication. The realization that they can communicate emotionally *through music* often causes a new competence in conventional intelligence. Conversely, some conventionally intelligent students display this intelligence in abundance, precisely because they are late to develop emotionally. As they do mature emotionally, they find an increasing need to develop an emotional means of expression. To them, intelligence without emotion then becomes meaningless and frequently — through lack of intrinsic motivation — they decline in conventional academic success.

Some children persevere in *nothing* until they discover their need for music. Once this is discovered, they will often persevere in music, initially to the exclusion of all else. The child, therefore, who appears to lack perseverence may be the very one who is looking for music. The ability to persevere *in music* is essential but may be unrelated to any general tendency in this respect.

As for the ear, it is almost invariably measured through the voice. (Can this account for the fact that so many string players are paranoid about singing?) I have known 'tone deaf' children become first-rate violinists. The ability to succeed in vocal tests relates largely to a natural or acquired vocal facility. Over twenty years of auditioning large numbers of young children, I have continually observed that pre-puberty, primary children respond to the tests much better (i.e. more naturally) than secondary, post-puberty children, who respond self-consciously. Rhythmic tests yield no more conclusive results. Many natural young musicians, because they react with emotion rather than reason, are badly co-ordinated physically and mentally: a condition that music will eventually cure. They may appear, at first hearing, to be unrhythmical. Initially, sound rhythmic sense may be more obvious in conventionally intelligent students: but the professional musician may perhaps notice greater potential rhythmic excitement in a badly co-ordinated adolescent, who may be at least eighteen before the various physical, intellectual, and emotional factors come together to create an outstanding instrumentalist.

As for reliable home support: it is certainly an advantage. I can only comment on the vast number of really musical children I have known who have been musical almost because of the *lack* of understanding and tolerance at home. This, again, is often because of a clash between the conventional intelligence of the parents and the emotional intelligence of the young musician. With children from poorer homes there can also be a clash between the parents' desire for early employment and the child's desire for further musical study. 'Good home support' is often taken to mean a middle-class background. The point to make here is that the middle-class has no monopoly whatever on the emotional intelligence required of a musician.

Intelligence, perseverance, a good ear, and reliable home support are all useful attributes for a successful instrumentalist and, as such, can provide modest guidelines to assist teachers in searching out suitable pupils. They are not, however, of any use as criteria for spotting exceptional musicality. Successful musical talent-spotting among children requires expertise, perception, and experience. Two general and related points can, however, be made.

Firstly, one of the most important indications of ability is how much music actually *means* to the child. In this respect, general class music activity can prove a useful help in selection, though even here there may be problems. It is quite possible, for example, that playing a recorder or banging a drum may appear to mean very little to a child, simply because that child is sufficiently musical to recognize the inadequacy to him or her of that particular sound. Sometimes, reactions to a professional performance may give a better guide. In any event, this sense of the importance to a child of music may be something only a musician can judge, because the reaction may be one of fear; fear that the listening adult may pour scorn on the child's participation in something that to him or her, means so much. And that very fear may cause the child to show diffidence rather than confidence.

Related to this, the second general indication of talent is conviction. The child who knows he or she *needs* a particular instrument will eventually come forward (though sometimes terribly late) *providing there is someone to whom to come forward*. Often, such youngsters have been badly taught in large groups and from schools where there is no one taking a sensitive interest in childrens' deeper musical responses. Providing suitable expertise is to hand, it is never too late to help such pupils — though it is obviously desirable to eliminate the necessity in the first place.

One further point needs to be made concerning the nature of so-called 'talent'. Almost any student with reasonable intelligence, sensitivity, and co–ordination can be 'manufactured' into a musician of professional competence *if the student desires it* and has access to appropriate instruction and musical opportunity. There is nothing markedly different about this from the production of lawyers, accountants, dentists and so on, who can be manufactured satisfactorily as professionals without being exceptionally talented. (The only difference is that these professions do not usually have the potential to become enriching, lifetime hobbies.) Talent in music, as in any subject, is relative. While those opting for music as a career are very few in number (and not always the most talented), thousands of children in any geographical area have the potential for receiving a stimulating educational discipline leading to a lifetime's purposeful recreation. For LEAs to renege on their musical responsibilities on the grounds that the few national specialist music schools can accommodate the 'musically talented' is to deny this essential fact as well as to prevent those from less privileged homes ever being in a position to discover or demonstrate their musical talent.

There is an in–built conflict of objectives within the provision of instrumental teaching. On the one hand, there is a need for as many children as possible to be taught in order to create a musical milieu which will keep schools enthusiastic about music and from which talent can emerge. On the other hand, there is a need for the minutiae of up to thirteen different skills to be taught correctly by specialists at an early age if talent is to be *enabled* to emerge. Because much instrumental teaching is carried out by musicians who have more enthusiasm than skill and whose objectives tend to be for quick results more than sound pedagogy, instrumental schemes have increasingly come to be aimed at quantity rather than quality: a situation that has been exacerbated by current political and economic pressures. In fact, there should be no reason why quality cannot grow out of quantity. Any instrumental staff is likely to contain teachers of medium playing ability whose usefulness will be in arousing enthusiasm and who should be used for teaching at the lower grades. It should also contain teachers of more advanced playing ability, able (and often more suited) to teach advanced pupils. The aim should be for there to be an available teacher in this category for every instrument. It is then important to ensure that instrumental teachers are apportioned the tasks to which they are most suited and that they are discouraged from teaching beyond their own performing ability and experience.

Although quantity has, to some extent, to be geared to quality, there is no reason why, given an average-sized staff of instrumental teachers, large numbers of children cannot be given the opportunity to try out their ability on an instrument. It is essential, however, that there should be some sort of screening system for isolating students who show particular aptitude from those who, for various reasons — lack of inner motivation being the most likely — will probably reach a plateau around Grade 5 or 6. This is particularly important, as the starting of large numbers of children may result in some bad technical habits being acquired. If talented children are to reach their full potential, these faults will need correcting by more specialist teachers at as early a stage as possible. In this way it should prove possible to determine appropriate levels and modes of study for different children, as is the case with other subjects in the curriculum.

Music is almost unique among curricular subjects in the single-mindedness it attracts and requires. Frequently this single-mindedness cannot be exercised in a normal school, either because appropriate staffing cannot be made available or because the practice needs of music students conflict with the general ethos and running of the school. It is therefore appropriate to structure some sort of special provision to meet the exceptional needs of committed musicians. The need for this provision is from the age of 16+, for it is only by this age that one can be reasonably sure that even the most talented students really wish to pursue the subject as a career. Young musicians develop in musical sensibility and conviction at different rates and stages. It is as possible for a potential star at 13+ to lose interest in music by 16+ as it is for a potential musician merely to emerge by 16+. Despite all the advantages of an early and meticulous start, nothing leads to success so much as conviction. Given this kind of conviction coupled with the necessary talent, and given the time, the teaching and the right environment, 16+ is still not too late for a player with limited or faulty technique to succeed. Equally, it is possible for the most docile of musicians at 16+ to kick the academic and family traces, as maturing sensibility revolts against restrictions on what suddenly becomes an all-consuming occupation. Because music usually goes hand in hand with exceptional sensitivity and emotionalism, many talented young musicians can only find their potential outside school in an environment which places them in company — and friendly competition — with young people of similar abilities and interests.

There are, of course, as many different ways of organizing instrumental teaching as there are LEAs and each will have its own geographical, logistic problems. Nevertheless, it would be desirable, pragmatically and politically, to have a common set of objectives informing all these endeavours. I suggest therefore that, from the various points discussed in this chapter, the following objectives for the instrumental side of the music service would seem both logical and practicable:

1. To create within an area a musical milieu that encourages children to undertake the task of learning to play an instrument.
2. To ensure that all children have an opportunity to apply to learn an instrument.
3. To use the widest possible criteria in making the initial selection and to offer the facility to as many children as can reasonably be accommodated within the staffing structure.
4. To ensure that there is a screening process in the early stages which selects children with obvious potential for individual tuition with appropriate teachers.
5. To ensure that instrumental teachers are encouraged to teach at a level consistent with their technical abilities.

6. To ensure that professional expertise is made available on every instrument to service the more talented players as and when they come to light.

7. To structure special in–depth study at 16+ for exceptionally motivated students.

8. To ensure that any scheme provides sufficient flexibility of operation to allow for the sudden emergence of talent and for changing degrees of commitment to music throughout students' school lives.

13

Centralized Ensemble Opportunities

The need for balancing the numbers of children taught instruments with the quantity of teaching available affects the structuring of suitable orchestral opportunities. It can also affect relationships between school-based music teachers and county or area-based instrumental teachers, emphasizing the differences in their roles — the former working largely with children who have not already been motivated. The satisfactory programming of instrumental teachers may make it impossible for schools to operate their own orchestras successfully. The most important factor for consideration is that the middle layer as well as the upper layer of ability is provided with access to ensemble activity, whether it proves convenient to organize this as an area-based or school-based activity.

I have repeatedly referred to education — of which school is the most significant factor — as being an 'enabling' medium. There should, therefore, be no questioning the fact that a school exists to serve its students and that if the needs of any of its students can be met more satisfactorily elsewhere, the school should encourage them to go elsewhere for the purpose. That said, however, it must be recognized that schools may well need to retain the abilities of certain students in order to encourage the generality of its students in that subject area. This is, of course, the nub of the comprehensive argument and it is rightly based on the notion that the able lift the standards of the less able.

Despite this, there have always been a minority of students and a minority of subjects for which comprehensive education has found it difficult to make entirely adequate provision. Music, with its multiplicity of skills and extraordinary variety and level of activities, has often been conspicuous among these minority subjects. It is for this reason that county-based instrumental schemes and centrally-based orchestras evolved in the first place. Children who have tasted the better fruits of a county-based, evenly matched ensemble do not necessarily enjoy — or profit from — concurrent

148

attendance in school orchestras. This is partly because they would be participating in something below their standard, partly because the conductor may be relatively unskilled in orchestral training and partly because such students may have come to see 'school music' as being something largely removed from their own living world of music. It is questionable whether there is any other school activity in which students of such widely differing levels of attainment can be deliberately grouped together — where, for example, students between the standards of Grades 2 and 8 can be placed in the same group, creating a wider gap than that between first-year G.C.S.E. students and second-year A level students.

It is reasonable to postulate one general principle with regard to centralized orchestral provision: that there is no justification for structuring any activity centrally if it can be provided or made to be provided *equally effectively* within individual schools. To this principle a rider must be added: that necessary central activities should be structured, as far as possible, so as not to prevent these activities taking place, albeit at a lower level, within individual schools. If centralized activity *should* result in the demise of that activity within an individual school, this fact needs recognizing from the start by all concerned and accepting as a rational if regrettable decision.

In any event, school or 'schools' orchestras should not exist as show-pieces or as ends in themselves: they should exist as an indispensable corollary to instrumental instruction. Orchestras should act as the same kind of incentive to young musicians as do, for example, football teams to young footballers: they should present clear goals to which students can aspire and, by virtue of their very existence, demonstrate the standards that it is possible to reach by dint of good tuition and hard work.

It is not only the top schools orchestras that are important. Ensemble work, properly structured, should provide a corollary to instrumental tuition from the earliest stages. Proper structuring involves a reasonable matching of standards among players, careful attention to individual seating among sections, careful selection of repertoire that challenges but does not surpass the ability of the players, provision of sectional coaching, and direction by people whose knowledge and experience fits them for the task of orchestral coaching and training. All of this can rarely be found within a single school. Nothing can do more harm than to create a school orchestra of widely differing standards, averaging around Grade 4 or 5, but with a few advanced players leading and pulling sections in music that is above the average capability. It does harm to the less able players and it does harm to the leaders. In the early stages, it is much more appropriate to structure separate string, wind, and brass groups. It takes many years to build up a tradition of orchestral playing but, from the very start, it is worth looking at some sort of structure that will include a junior string group, a junior brass group, an intermediate orchestral group that is not too large, a training orchestra performing and rehearsing selections from the easier classical repertory, and, at the top of the structure, a schools or youth orchestra.

The argument as to whether or not conservatoire students should be included in such orchestras is a vexed one. As far as this country is concerned, with its long tradition of orchestral playing in schools, I am absolutely convinced of the error of including students in schools symphony orchestras. Among school students, it is quite possible to regard all advanced instrumentalists as potential professionals, in the sense that they can be expected to take their music with a seriousness of purpose, regardless of whether they are going on to study music or not. Normally, those who do not go on to study music when they leave school lose the facility of instrumental instruction and, when this happens, their approach becomes essentially amateur. Conservatoire students, on the other hand, spend their whole week on music and soon become geared to the minimal rehearsal time imposed by the profession. The advantage of restricting LEA orchestras to those of school age is that a consistently dedicated approach (with the quantity of detailed rehearsal that, at this stage, is required) can be maintained throughout the whole system. Senior school players will be less frustrated by the less able players than would conservatoire students, who already have eyes on professional playing.

Naturally, it is sad to lose good students — this applies to any level or sphere of education — and it is often difficult to see where their replacements are to come from. But if a tradition is established, the very need to find new section leaders will create them. In twenty years' experience, I have never known a year when there have not been two or three principal positions that have seemed virtually irreplaceable; nor have I known a single instance where the challenge has not been met, at least adequately, by appointing players who show the potential. The challenge that these situations present to individual players is vastly beneficial, personally and musically. By far the larger problem to the schools orchestra director is the bottle-neck situation where the continued existence of outstanding players sometimes prevents this kind of challenge being given to students obviously in need .of it: which is exactly what happens when conservatoire students are permitted to stay in youth orchestras.

At whatever level instrumental ensemble activity is structured, the most important aim should be to develop an atmosphere of enthusiasm for the highest possible standards with an understanding of the very hard and disciplined work that this requires. Such an atmosphere cannot be created quickly and it is therefore of great importance that goals are right from the start. This makes it essential for the players to be coached by specialists on their instrument. Indeed, the single most important aspect of training a schools orchestra lies in the sectional coaching. Good coaches are hard to find, both from the performing and teaching profession. Sectional coaching is certainly an art that needs to be acquired and it is acquired best by player-teachers who have some knowledge of the players in their section. Thus, an ideal system is one where the sectional coaches are also the teachers of the able children. Not only does this help the process of sectional tuition: the familiarity with the players enables the sectional coach to start with the right psychological approach and to handle delicate problems, such as re-seating of the section, with the necessary tact and decisiveness.

If a top schools orchestra is to be effective, it must have a proper balance of players. I have always worked with quadruple woodwind and one or two extra brass players to provide that essential respite for the tender and as yet undeveloped lips of the young players. I have tried to work to a string section of eight desks of first violins, seven of second violins, five or six of violas, five or six of cellos, three or four of basses. This is not always practicable and, within reason, it is always preferable to reduce the numbers and maintain the technical competence. It does no good to anyone to put into a schools orchestra players who cannot play the music technically or who are too immature, physically, to cope with the long hours of heavy rehearsal. Sometimes the existence of a smaller chamber orchestra, specializing in the 'classical' repertoire, can provide musically challenging but physically less demanding experience for younger players of talent.

For any orchestra, weekly rehearsals are invaluable in order to keep alive the incentive and to remind players of aspects of orchestral discipline. However, by far the most useful form of rehearsal is that of a concentrated five or seven-day course during a school holiday. I have found it is possible to work young players for up to eight or nine hours a day on such courses. It is better to concentrate upon sectional rehearsal for the first half of the course at least. Without this, full rehearsals only consolidate mistakes. All string parts need bowing and fingering and the players need to practise these parts collectively and individually before being asked to repeat them incessantly in full rehearsal. A course of this intensity can do a certain amount of short-lived damage to an individual technique. But any tension can quickly be eradicated by the right teacher and by the pupils doing the right practice — and the gains in terms of commitment, incentive, and musical experience are incalculable.

There are, of course, countless individual schools where ensemble activities in a wide variety of musical styles are well coached, provide valuable learning situations, and lead to high performance standards: the annual 'Festival of Music for Youth' provides ample evidence of this. From all the schools in the country, it is quite possible to assemble many concerts' worth of very varied and accomplished musical performance. The vital question that has to be asked is whether children in *all* schools of any area represented have the same opportunities to develop their musical skills and enthusiasms. Another question follows: does the variety of styles in which different children are involved result from the choice of the children or the teacher — do children really have the opportunity to develop skill for purposes that to them are musically and culturally relevant, and indeed to discover what these are?

The subject of music is so wide that answers to these questions are likely to be negative. And because the subject is so wide, perfect solutions are unlikely to be found. Nevertheless, the fundamental aim should be to ensure that children receive equality of opportunity. This aim cannot be achieved unless the overall *content* (as well as the activity itself) is subject to validation. As content can so easily condition (and limit) the physical activity, it is crucially important that objectives should be defined *musically*. Unless this is effected, there is a danger that music in schools will exist *only* at the level of handicraft and entertainment (a danger that is to some extent reflected in the monotonous activities of the professional musical establishment and the conditioned responses of its clientele). There is nothing wrong with music existing at the level of handicraft and entertainment providing there are clearly defined objectives that transcend this state, objectives which motivate children to develop skill and understanding in such a way as to experience music as art. Given the exceptional breadth of the subject and the eclectic nature of the school music teacher's task, it is inevitable that many musical objectives can only be achieved through centralized activity.

14

Vocal Music in Schools

At the beginning of Part Three I quoted Atarah Ben-Tovim as saying that the only way to come to understand music is by playing an instrument 'whether an external one like the piano or flute or by training the human voice to become an instrument'. In the last two chapters I have concentrated on 'external' instruments because the logistics of providing instruction on them are far more complex. The problems with choral music have more to do with motivation than logistics: youth choirs tend to be very much less in evidence than youth orchestras.

To the young child, singing does not offer the attraction of physical activity that is offered by 'external' instruments. Where instrumentalists can frequently allow their involvement in the actual business of playing to take over from critical attention to the value of the music itself, a process that encourages motivation and does no lasting harm, singers are likely to need motivating to want to sing by the actual music they are asked to sing.

Unfortunately, a mixed class of thirty children of similar age is a completely unsuitable group for the performance of any vocal material in existence (except for the largely vacuous offerings of 'music educators' written expressly for the purpose) especially when that class also contains an ethnic mix. Classical songs and arias were written for soloists; choruses were generally written for combinations of sopranos, altos, tenors, and basses; folk songs were usually sung by solo singers as and when the mood took them; and popular songs were and are generally written to be sung down a microphone with electric backing. The words of traditional English folk songs are somewhat obscure in relation to the average perceptions of the modern child: only American folk songs fit into the class situation with any ease and they depend upon the guitar as opposed to the piano for accompaniment.

The question of *what* to sing is further complicated by being inextricably intertwined with the question of *how* to sing it. Ever since, in the late 1930s, Bing Crosby sang down a megaphone in front of Swing Bands, artificial means of vocal amplification have come to characterize popular singing. And if Bob Dylan's challenge to formally accepted notions of vocal timbre has seemed short-lived, the current prevalence of ethnic musics, with their very different manners of vocal style, has resulted in a further gauntlet being thrown to the 'approved' tradition. Even within our own cultural norm, the increase in operatic activity over the past two decades and the elevation of British singers to rank with the world's greatest operatic stars has challenged the somewhat phlegmatic sound that characterized the British ecclesiastical choral tradition. And while many a successful singer at some time must have strained the vocal chords on the back of a school bus or at a football match, the vocal production of, say, a typical lead tenor from a Welsh male voice choir could unnerve the most resilient of 'traditional' singing teachers.

So far as the school classroom is concerned, problems of style and repertoire are largely intractable and any solution must involve some element of compromise. Nevertheless, this compromise need not exclude some basic vocal instruction, if only in breathing and vowel production. Vocal style, more than almost any other form of musical production, is conditioned by example; and one reason why singing in primary and secondary schools tends to be so mediocre is that a large majority of music teachers lack any sort of vocal skill or confidence themselves. There are therefore two urgent needs: one is for music specialists to develop vocal skills themselves in order to present singing to children as a *skilled* activity; the second is for children who have been sufficiently motivated to be placed in separate, specialist choral groups, in order to study a repertoire more geared to skilled singing than is usually possible in the classroom.

Solo singing is a very personal activity. Unlike even a brass instrument, the whole of the mechanism for producing the sound is invisible; there is less agreement over voice production than over technique on any single 'external' instrument. To complicate matters further, local musical circles appear to be riddled with semi-professional (or, more accurately, quasi-professional) singers, whose egos are continually inflated by local Operatic Societies and a line-up of mature pupils with potentially similar egos awaiting similar inflation. Voice production has traditionally rested very largely in the hands of private teachers, whatever their degree of competence in teaching it, while school education has tended to bypass the whole business. The reasons for this are:

(*a*) the problems of motivation,

(*b*) the reluctance of schools to recognize the need for skill in music,

(*c*) the problem of finding suitable material, particularly in relation to the classroom,

(*d*) the lack of vocal ability and conviction among most music teachers.

It is significant that wherever schools have produced outstanding choirs the music teacher responsible has nearly always been a knowledgeable and confident vocalist.

Vocal repertoire, even in primary schools, need not be restricted to what is immediately popular: classical repertoire can be interspersed judiciously with simpler and more immediately accessible songs. Two points arise from this. One is that this will only work effectively if the more accessible material is chosen for its 'human' appeal rather than for cant musical gimmickry: for the basic difference between folk and classical musics of any culture is that the former gives precedence to the words (a fact that rules out all rock cantatas as being folk) and that the latter gives precedence to the music. The other is that it will only be possible to teach classical vocal music in the classroom if the teacher is able to demonstrate the music and introduce simple instruction and exercises in vocal production.

As with any other form of music teaching, it is fundamentally important that skilled approaches, opening the way to progressive endeavour, should be introduced at the primary school level. Children must be encouraged to sing, not just because the words are funny or the tune derivatively catchy, but because singing is seen to be a skill worth acquiring and because the music chosen has intrinsic meaning and merit. Thanks largely to the co-operation of many vocally skilled music teachers, I have had the privilege of directing up to 300 primary school children at a time (chosen from a wide social mix of schools) singing, amongst other things, Bach arias in two parts, Verdi choruses and Schubert songs, accompanied either authentically by a chamber orchestra or adaptively by a mixture of acoustic and electric instruments. I make the point only to indicate that, given ability and hard work on the part of the teacher, skilled singing *can* be developed in the primary school. For boys in particular, it is vital that this kind of experience should exist at primary level.

Once singing has been established as a basic skill within the primary music curriculum, it is of crucial importance that it should be taken seriously at the secondary school. Because of the difficulties intrinsic to classroom singing there will be a need to form a first year choir to encourage immediate continuity. Boys near to the change of voice can then be put straight on to an alto or baritone part so that the *habit* of singing can be preserved; for once this habit is allowed to lapse it is very difficult to resurrect. Secondary teachers need to be aware of children who have shown ability in skilled singing in primary schools, just as much as they need to be aware of children who have shown ability in playing instruments. They need to capitalize on previous experience chorally as much as instrumentally.

I remarked earlier that the logistics of providing for choral instruction are less complex than those for providing instrumental instruction. Excluding, for the moment, the extenuating circumstances created by ethnic styles of singing, vocal music does not involve thirteen or more different specialist skills. Furthermore there is no reason why music teachers should not learn basic vocal skills: indeed there is every reason why they should. Given the present state of vocal insecurity among many music teachers, regular instruction in vocal skills should be a priority for in-service training.

The only long-term solution to the vocal problem, as to most other problems concerning music in schools, is to effect a greater input of expertise within the teaching service, both in primary and secondary schools. The shorter-term solution is to appoint to the central staff a few trained and experienced singers with the vocal and human perception to be able to encourage teachers to take their own standards of singing seriously. Primary and secondary school choirs can be brought together for 'Singing Days' or trained for choral festivals, while teachers can be encouraged to join choral groups which will further their own choral skills. Activities of this sort can pave the way for the establishment of central or area youth choirs and for the elevation of choral singing to the same status as orchestral playing.

Instrumental teaching has frequently been made the scapegoat for the deterioration in choral activity, just as it has been made the scapegoat for non-success in the classroom. The real scapegoat is of course education itself which has so frequently discouraged real expertise in music. Success in instrumental teaching is usually in direct proportion to the expertise of the teacher. This applies equally to any musical activity. The gap in musical ability and perception that so often exists between performers and teachers is symptomatic of the gap between school music and the living world of music. This, more than anything else, is the cause of the desultory nature of choral singing in schools and it will only be remedied once it is realized that singing, like any other worthwhile musical activity, is a skill requiring expert instruction.

15

Popular Music in Schools

It is commonly held by classical musicians that popular musics are inferior to the music to which they subscribe. To hold such a view is to mistake the very different functions of classical and popular musics. As I have already suggested, the distinction between popular and classical musics have, throughout history, helped to delineate a multi-cultural society. The only thing that has changed over the past few decades is that adherence to popular musics by the bourgeoisie has sometimes been adopted as a political stance. This, taken in conjunction with the social attitudes and responsibilities of education, has made the use of pop music in schools a somewhat emotive subject. Were it not for the social attitudes that popular musics have come to represent, it could be assumed that these musics could and should form a legitimate part of classroom and instrumental content. However, in the context of the consider-ations and practice so far outlined, it has to be decided where, and to what extent, inclusion is appropriate. It is necessary, therefore, to consider briefly the background to the use of pop music in schools.

Fifteen years ago, no one had published a rock opera for schools: indeed no one had thought that this was really what rock was about. The Beatles were creating a universal awareness of rock, as their perceptive but well-tempered commentary on current social affairs created for pop-rock a respectability that crossed class and even national barriers. The Rolling Stones were offering a similar message with rather greater polemic and aggression, though with less of it than the heavy rock groups from the West Coast of America such as The Grateful Dead. Rock had developed out of rhythm-and-blues to become a universal pop music, transcending the latter's colour bar and establishing itself as a fact of life that no one could really ignore.

Many teachers were taken unawares. It had not generally been thought that pop music was relevant to school music. The Beatles forced everyone to be aware of pop — at least of its presence as an incontrovertible musical force — and pop music started to enter schools. 'Troublesome' early-leavers could sometimes be heard singing 'All my loving' in four parts, proving not only that they could be occupied purposefully in music but that music of this sort could offer an agreeable antidote to the asperity of George Self's *New Sounds in Class* and other modern classroom methods that were replacing traditional courses of singing and 'music appreciation'.

Concurrently with pop's new-found academic status, classically trained musicians started turning to pop, jazz and/or minimalism (no doubt largely as a relief from the relatively ungratifying music of integral serialism and clustural composition that was then fashionable) and The Who produced their seminal album (subsequently filmed) 'Tommy'. The appearance of this rock opera gave added impetus to the notion that rock could be more than musical wallpaper and that it could vie with classical tradition as an art form. Many schools started encouraging children to bring their guitars to school and to compose operas and cantatas in a rock style. This was sometimes achieved most effectively — and genuinely creatively — with a kind of immediacy particularly appropriate to the style. But the immediacy was short-lived. Rick Wakeman and others developed the rock-album format with a pretentiousness that eventually forced rock, already a tired style, back on to its own original devices. The result was that many of these devices became clichés.

In the sixties, when I was suggesting to groups of teachers that Beatle songs would soon prove to be the urban folk songs of our age, the suggestion was often greeted with as much incredulity as horror. Although folk was beginning to be practised in a more 'folksy' way, it was still regarded as being essentially 'pure'. However, the folk music currently hitting the headlines came from America, where chord twanging and vamping had for a century been characteristic of its folk music. As a result, attempts were made to inflict similar kinds of techniques on English folk song, regardless of the fact that real English folk song was centuries older, originally unaccompanied, largely modal, and singularly unsuited to this treatment. It was harder to align the earthy style of English folk, then to be heard in suitably guttural vocal manner in many a pub basement, with the needs and presumed ambitions of a class of thirty children. Folk music in schools ceased to be English and became largely American — until American songs started to vie with Jamaican songs which, in turn, became identified with reggae. Meanwhile Christianity (which in America had always retained a strong link with folk through gospel songs and white and black spirituals) availed itself of the guitar vamping medium to preach a new liberal form of social Christianity (Faith, Folk, and Clarity, etc.). Ten years after the heyday of The Beatles, many of these new songs, along with songs by The Beatles themselves, began to find their way into school song books. In such fast-changing times The Beatles had already acquired historical status.

Much earlier in this book (Chapter 4) I remarked somewhat disparagingly that, ten years too late, rock operas started appearing in schools, usually written by the teachers rather than the pupils. The problem was, quite simply, that the times were changing faster and faster: too fast for education, folk or rock to keep up with them. For as the sixties (most of the exciting things about which in fact took place in the early seventies) passed, somewhat unfairly, into folk-lore as a period of indulgent moral and intellectual laxity, the 'modernized' songs for schools to which they had given rise began to acquire a sense of *déjà vu*. Rock music itself lurched from fashion to fashion and style to style, trying desperately to create something new out of relatively unchanging musical formulae and instrumental and vocal sounds. Changes in fashion and style were not always synonymous: the music itself had such in-built limitations that changes became more obvious through verbal attitudes and clothing habits than through musical style. At the time of writing, the general poverty of invention in pop music has caused the charts frequently to be topped by golden oldies, professional instruction in rock music to look more to the past than to the present for its materials, and rock stars to acquire a disconcerting habit of switching (or attempting to switch) from rock singing to film acting, once their names have become known.

It is therefore unfortunate, though not entirely uncharacteristic, that it should have been over the past decade that there has been a growing insistence on 'the place of pop music in schools'. It is unfortunate because this was the very time when pop was particularly lacking in genuine originality and, after such a promising recent past, was becoming particularly hard to define; it was not uncharacteristic of education because the clichés of pop were then evident as never before and could be transferred to the classroom and to pupils' consciousness with relative ease. Many teachers have now acquired the kind of musical fluency needed to produce their own, home-grown cantatas and operas, based on the more obvious clichés of pop and scored for combinations available at the time of composing. Since the first appearance of Herbert Chappell's *The Daniel Jazz* (which in the wake of its following now seems something of a mini-masterpiece) religious, moral, folk, and socially-conscious themes have been spuriously 'rocked' or 'jazzed' to the extent that 'jazz' or 'rock' cantatas and operas have come to occupy an extraordinary amount of curricular and extra-curricular time in many schools. In these circumstances, the words 'jazz' and 'rock' have become virtually synonymous, rock tending to have taken over from jazz, as jazz has attempted to reassert itself by attempting new musical paths.

A recurrent theme of this book has been the need to adopt a critical approach to the *content* of music in education. Criticism must inevitably lead to value judgement; yet to establish value judgements in the context of the very different functions of classical and current popular musics could properly be seen as an impertinence. And if popular musics would seem to be somewhat directionless at present, bound by a number of verbal, melodic, rhythmic, harmonic, and timbral characteristics that define their very nature, much the same can be said for the a-melodic, a-rhythmic, atonal, clusterized or pointillist devices that so often seem to define contemporary music. Yet popular and contemporary musics still largely represent different ways of life, in the sense of different views of culture and the values associated with it — and this despite the efforts of so many trained musicians to bridge the gap. It is therefore important that education should recognize the existence of this gap and subject it to some scrutiny, rather than pretend that it does not exist or plump solely for one side or the other. Given the customary classical training of music teachers and the general pop-orientated musical preferences of unselected classes of children, there is usually an intrinsic wariness between class and teacher: an unstated need for rapprochement — for a kind of negotiated settlement. As with any negotiation, the start should be with areas of agreement rather than disagreement. The 'you bring your records and I'll bring mine' kind of approach can only succeed if it is used to point initially to areas of similarity.

There is of course much in common between the materials of popular and classical musics. The 'three chords' round which it is often claimed (and with sime truth) that a great deal of rock and pop music is structured are usually the same three chords round which Mozart's operatic ensembles were structured; and the frequent modulations in rock and pop, if rather more violent, reflect nevertheless the need for tonal variety felt in the eighteenth century. The tendency for current pop music, particularly that with ethnic or other social associations, to emphasize a harmonic *stasis*, forcing melodic patterns on to chords with which they are not in conventional agreement, is reflected in the musical manner of 'minimalist' composers, whose minimalism often springs from socialist concerns. The need for variety of rhythmic density, motor speed, etc., is common to musics of most cultures; and, of course the strophic song is almost as ubiquitous and universal as man himself. All the traditional elements of musical construction can be used for comparison.

Having pointed to the similarities, it is important to note the differences. Like classical musics the world over, popular musics all derive in some measure from folk forms; unlike classical musics, however, they generally aim to avoid sophistication or, at least, to present an ambience of easy accessibility. Unlike classical musics, too, they tend to avoid notation and depend upon improvisation or the recording of successful pieces of improvisation.

With this in mind, it is important to distinguish carefully between the various forms of so-called popular music: jazz (whose history is at least as complex and interesting as that of classical music of the last century and which is at present a minority interest), rock (which virtually turned rhythm-and-blues into a universal pop music and now occupies a somewhat equivocal place in the pop music syndrome), pop (which seems to have reverted to being a music aimed at immediate accessibility), folk (which, after a period of heady popularity in the early seventies, now seems to be more exclusive or associative), reggae (which has taken some of the ground from rock as the clearer, distinctive rhythms of Caribbean folk music have provided some relief from the heavy poundings of kit drummers), disco . . . punk . . . Culture Club . . . fashions come and go. But there is one clear distinction that can generally be made between different forms and styles of pop: it is between music that attempts to gear itself specifically to 'the market' and music that attempts to gear 'the market' to itself. To whatever extent the marketeers dictate the style (the manner dictating the substance yet again) there are always likely to be musicians of interest reacting against this stranglehold.

Such musicians are more likely to be found in the field of jazz than rock. As rock has grown out of its quasi-artistic heyday of the late sixties, jazz has increasingly adopted this quasi-artistic role. As the distinctive formulae of jazz have succumbed their originality to a predominantly white rock industry, becoming debased through the materialistically orientated rock production line, jazz has sought new forms of sophistication and has become a more minority interest. While Big Bands continue to exist, smaller groups, taking their cue from such widely different sources as, for example, Charlie Parker, Miles Davis, John McLaughlin, and Terje Rypdal, continue to search for new forms of improvisation, thus retaining the original ethos of jazz, though not the distinctive musical characteristics which made its style possible. Importantly, some jazz musicians are looking directly to Africa for sources of inspiration: a factor which could produce a distinctively British jazz sound.

With popular music as with classical music, the only way to come to understand it thoroughly is by performing it. And here I refer not to the singing of popular songs in class (because songs susceptible to such treatment have, almost by definition, virtually entered the world of folk) but to the skills of vocal and instrumental performance. The problem with many home-grown bands is that they are self-taught and, consequently, if ever they reach the level of public performance, they only succeed in perpetuating the mindless cant and kitsch so common in the pop world today. The days when a group of raw, talented musicians could get together and work their way through to a distinctive sound, constantly improving their technique in the process, seem to be gone. The various permutations of the acceptable formulae of pop music have become virtually exhausted: *acquired professionalism* is now a prerequisite of success.

There may still be talents around of the order of a Jimi Hendrix or Eric Clapton able to acquire prodigious technique mainly by themselves, but the motivation — the sense that there is still something urgent to say within the medium — has largely evaporated. Most aspiring youngsters are increasingly content to play their own versions of other people's tunes. For the kids who really want to get up and perform, however, professional instruction is usually necessary. There are, in fact, many young people for whom such instruction would prove a mental therapy and consuming occupation, but the desirable noise level alone makes this very difficult to accommodate in a school. There is an urgent need for more centres like the Central London Youth Project Music Workshop (CLYP) (see Chapter 10). Pop appreciation in the classroom, more even than that of classical music, can be little more than tokenism. Those who want to get into it deeply will need to learn to play it; they will probably do this on their own anyway, but there is no doubt that professional instruction would help them greatly and purposefully along the path.

The case with jazz is rather different. Although many of the early jazzmen were largely self-taught, picking up what they could from any musician who happened to be around, jazz, even at its most improvisatory, has now become highly sophisticated. Most of the instruments commonly used in jazz are also used in symphonic music. In terms of basic instrumental tuition, therefore, the normal instrumental tuition (which should, in any event, include the saxophone) can do double duty. The question simply arises as to how far developing young musicians can and should be taught the common improvisatory techniques of jazz. This is a debatable point. On the one hand, in-depth involvement in this particular style at an early age can create a more concentrated awareness. On the other hand, it can also lead to a blinkered, single-track view of music and, like the creation of child prodigies in classical music, can prove musically self-defeating, technically inhibiting or both. As with classical musicians, conviction frequently provides the key: the player of outstanding talent will know he is a jazz player and find opportunity to develop as such. Nevertheless, conviction can only grow through awareness. Education generally provides too little exposure to jazz styles, new and old: in this sense, jazz has not only a rightful but a necessary place in the classroom.

There is of course an intrinsic conflict between the detailed conformity to the written symbol required of classical music and the controlled improvisation required of jazz. It is difficult for musicians to travel wholeheartedly in both directions at once, even though there are famous examples of classical musicians being accomplished jazz musicians and vice versa — interestingly more commonly the former. (The imaginative, fluent classical musician can more easily imitate the stylistic conventions of jazz than can a jazz musician train himself to read music with the precision required of classical music.) Education should at least provide the opportunity for young players to find out whether or not they have a talent for jazz: a task which can be fulfilled relatively easily through regular workshop sessions. The true jazzman may well become a loner, adapting his technique to his personal sense of the jazz style he wants to cultivate. The mindless, technique-less indulgences of many 'improvising' groups, or 'co-operatives' as they often like to be called, provide no model whatever. Nowhere, in the whole world, has worthwhile, durable music been created without technique and discipline — and this applies as much to popular as to classical musics.

Wherever jazz goes or is going, knowledge of and about it remains pitiably small. It is a sad reflection on education's approach to music that it has frequently allowed the common clichés of rock-turned-pop to dominate its popular thinking. In the popular field, no less than in the classical field, education needs to re-examine its musical objectives and the musical content of its activities in order to distinguish between what is distinctive and purposeful and what is already common and urbane.

16

Ethnic Music in Schools

One of the first questions to arise when considering the inclusion of ethnic musics in the school curriculum is the extent to which the ethnic musics explored should be limited to the ethnic populations in a given area. The answer will depend to a large extent on the immediate function of the exercise. If the function is to provide a global understanding of music, there is obviously no limit to the musics that can be involved. However, study of comparative musics is no less complex than that of comparative religions: indeed, it is very closely allied to it. The global view of music is likely to appeal mainly to an intelligentsia and one that is more white than ethnic. This is because ethnic groups are still fighting to establish their own musical cultures while Westerners, often disillusioned with their own music, can find a new stimulus in the music of other cultures. To a skilled, Western musician, such stimulus and interest can be superficial, for the difference between Western and other musical cultures is so vast (see Chapter 8) that deep involvement in an outside culture can almost necessitate the abandonment of Western cultural mores. This is hard for a Western musician to accept. Yet this very difficulty should at least provide an awareness of the problems faced by people from other ethnic backgrounds who have deep artistic sensibilities, yet may be starved of the musical art which is intrinsic to them. Studies of, for example, Balinese, Japanese, or Chinese musics have a general value and can throw new light on Western culture. They will tend to be more theoretical and philosophical than practical and their function will be to supplement the overall study of music within Western culture. The objective in studying them is and should be very different from that of studying the dominant ethnic cultures in our midst.

For Indians, Africans, and Afro-Caribbeans, study *about* their musical culture is not sufficient. School music should provide opportunity for them to develop knowledge, understanding, and *skills* in their own musical arts. The intensity with which such musics are pursued in any given school or area will obviously depend to some extent upon the size of the local ethnic populations. As in Chapter 8, I shall deal here only with the two largest ethnic communities in this country: the communities from the West Indies and those from the Indian sub-continent.

Much of what I have said about tokenism in the classroom and professionalism in performance applies as much to ethnic as to Western classical and popular musics. There are, however, two major differences: the sounds of ethnic musics (certainly in their classical forms) tend to be unfamiliar; and the improvisations involved in the classical forms of Indian and African musics are subject to strict, traditional procedures. There is clearly a need to create a familiarity with these musics and their procedures — and this can, to some extent, be done in a classroom. However, this by itself can have little lasting value. The essence of a culture can only be established if children have the opportunity of learning the actual skills of the music.

As I showed in Chapter 8, the social and musical conditions of Caribbean and Indian cultures have very different parameters and lead to different basic objectives. The methods for dealing with them in education must also be very different.

West Indian music can be performed as well as listened to in the classroom. Much of the folk music lends itself unusually well to the classroom situation and there is an increasing amount of such music available in print. If, however, this music is to be treated with the dignity it deserves, it must be seen within its social context: too often Jamaican songs provide just another vehicle for 'fun' activity with which to fill slots in a timetable. While a sense of fun permeates much of this music, representing an applied resilience and gaiety in the face of oppression, much of it is also a reflection upon injustice and ponders a happier and more humane society, whether it be in Heaven, in the land of adoption or, latterly, Ethiopia. Yet listen to recordings of almost any Afro-Caribbean music, whether it be of primitive cult music, revivalist music, country folk music, or the tightly disciplined choral arrangements now performed competitively, and the thing that strikes hardest and most consistently is the rhythmic exuberance. This is usually missing in the classroom, for inculcation of a real Afro-Caribbean rhythmic exuberance would inevitably present to the modern British school teacher the kind of potential problems that the street drumming and Tamboo Bamboo did for the white authorities in Trinidad. As is the case with Western music, Caribbean folk music introduced in the classroom needs complementing with the formation of specialist vocal and instrumental groups under specialist instruction. So far, extra-curricular Afro-Caribbean music has been largely restricted to steel bands — a situation which tends to project a very one-sided view of Afro-Carribean music.

Where there is rhythm there is usually the dance: this is very much the case with West Indian music. Yet the teaching of Caribbean dance has scarcely begun in our schools. I have had opportunity to witness the speed and vigour with which an unselected group of West Indians — and Indians — responded to the tuition of a visiting expert from the Jamaican School of Music and Dance, and I could only regret that this dancer and others like him, along with trained drummers, could not be brought to this country for substantial periods of time so that a much wider experience of Caribbean culture could be provided.

In Chapter 8, I referred to the need for black people in this country to experience skilled African as well as Caribbean music, in addition to being increasingly encouraged to participate in Western arts. The largest single obstacle to providing real experience and skill in ethnic musics is the lack of British residents who have acquired these skills. There is an urgent case to be made for importing such musicians as teachers in *schools*, even though this may lead to considerable problems relating to induction into Western culture and school activity. The teaching of Indian and African classical music is very much more complex than the teaching, for example, of steel band music, for the former remains pure and opposite to Western musical culture whereas the latter represents an adaptation to it. It is a sad commentary on the dichotomy in function and understanding between our school and higher education systems that induction into these musics has tended to be through the university intelligentsia rather than through the general school and community milieu.

Nowhere is foreign expertise more urgently needed than in the teaching of Indian music, for there is a real danger of a substantial majority of Indians in this country becoming divorced from their musical culture; and those who do have some appreciation of it often respond with alarming rapture to the virtuoso histrionics

with which many visiting performers have learned they can easily
seduce their Western audiences. It is, alas, as true of Indian music as
of Western music that the only way of gaining knowledge and
insight into it is by performing it. There are, nevertheless, ways in
which Indian music can be introduced in the classroom by teachers
willing to learn about Indian music, providing the necessity of
complementary specialist peripatetic tuition is clearly recognized.

Indian music is commonly thought of in this country as being
performed primarily on the sitar. In fact, India has as great a variety
of instruments as the West and one way to introduce Indian music
would be to compile tapes contrasting the sounds of Indian and
Western instruments: the sitar with the lute and cittarone, the
sarangi with the viola d'amore, the veena with the psaltery,
the santoor with the dulcimer, the Indian violin with the European
violin, the shenai with the shawm, the tabla with the tambour —
for many have common Middle-Eastern roots. It would also be
useful to compile tapes of different forms of Indian music: *Alāpā*
from a *raga*, folk music from Gujurati, children singing a Bengali
folk song, part of a *khayal*, a modern *ghazal*, part of a *thumri*, etc.
Shops selling suitable records can usually be found in the centres of
Indian population.

Certain practical activities can also be undertaken. Specific *melas*
and *ragas* can be learnt and children can explore various melodic
patterns, if possible comparing them with the *pakads* (catch-
phrases) prescribed by Bhatkande. *Ragas* have two specially
important notes — *vadi* and *samvadi* — and the surrounding notes
can be explored in their relationship to these main notes, as in *alāpā*
of a *raga* performance. Children can also learn tala cycles, clap and
wave the appropriate beats and improvise around them. It must,
however, be emphasized that these exercises have only limited
value, partly because of the limitations of the classroom instruments available (there is no Indian instrument that corresponds to
the idiophones of Indonesia, now pervasively bastardized as
'classroom instruments') and because the all-essential microtonal
ornamentation will be missing. The importance of related listening
cannot therefore be over-emphasized.

The constant use of different types of ornamentation in Indian
music is the most obstructive element in any attempt to notate such
music in Western style or indeed to produce it on Western instruments. (Only the violin, among Western instruments, has proved

suitable for this kind of music.) This use of ornamentation also frustrates attempts to notate and reproduce Indian vocal music in a classroom. Indeed, Indian vocal style is so entirely different from ours, with its emphasis on agility, range, and ornamentation rather than on tone quality (Indian singers are never too old to sing), that any attempt to sing it in Western style is likely to destroy its essence. Nevertheless, it *is* possible to make approximate Western notations from Indian singing, particularly of more 'modern' songs (such as those by Rabindranath Tagore), and group singing of such songs can provide an elementary sense of the kinds of melodic patterns in Indian music. Nevertheless, all these activities are simply 'creative' in the way I defined the word on page 42: they provide a method towards achieving our objectives and are not an end in themselves.

If the objective is to propagate a real knowledge and understanding of Indian music, this can only be achieved through specialist teaching of vocal and instrumental skills to small groups of children and to individuals. Here again, the greatest obstacle is the lack of suitably skilled musicians resident in this country. But there are other obstacles as well, intrinsic to the nature of the music. As I have described it in Chapter 8, Indian music is learned as a mother-tongue at the feet of gurus, and it has no sophisticated grammar. Bhatkande's classification of *melas*, *ragas*, and *pakads* have made it possible for Indian 'academies' to form syllabuses which nominally enable students to follow a progressive course but, in practice, are too imprecise to be of any great service. Most of the students at these institutions are female — a little knowledge of music being considered good for marriage prospects — while students with real talent and dedication follow their guru and learn at his feet in his family *ashram*. Even Indian universities are only just beginning to consider the need for a methodology. Unless some progress is made in this direction there is a danger that knowledge of Indian music will die out even in India, as changing social and economic conditions render the *guru-shishya-parampara* increasingly impracticable and every guru that dies takes a body of knowledge with him to the grave.

To develop a systematic methodology for teaching Indian music may have rather different implications for this country than it does for India. In India, the musical tradition is all around — even though to the perceptive it is starting to die on its feet. Indian gurus will for the most part be unwilling to accept the possibility that a musical 'grammar' *could* exist: it is in distinct contradiction to their whole training and sense of culture. Fortunately, through the International Society for Traditional Arts Research, there are a number of Western musicians in India applying computers to reams of recorded tape, attempting thereby to analyse incidences of phrase and rhythmic structures in an attempt to arrive at a systematized 'grammar'. This is all at a fairly esoteric level and the results may produce a useful teaching aid for the many skilled classical musicians prevalent in India.

Our needs in British education at this time are more humble; we need to send children away from their lessons with clearly delineated and attractively presented materials for personal practice, in order that they may develop the technique with which to expound their traditional music. These materials need relating imaginatively to *rag* and *tal* theory and to do so will involve new and special forms of composition to that end. It will also require a knowledge and skill not prevalent in this country and the kind of humility and flexibility that is not in keeping with the guru tradition in India. The problem is virtually intractable: the only solution seems to be the recruitment of some young and imaginative skilled musicians from India who can be inducted into the mores of British society and education and, hopefully, persuaded to assist in this task.

It is commonly upheld by Indian musicians in this country that it is the British and not the Indians who respond to Indian music. In my own Education Authority, this argument has been disproved. Generous assistance from the Gulbenkian Foundation has enabled us to bring over a carefully chosen leading sitarist to give demonstrations in schools and stimulate interest in learning. A further grant enabled us subsequently to bring over two younger musicians to develop, among other things, Kathak dance and to assist our peripatetic Indian musicians in the task of providing suitable materials and, it is hoped, a progressive methodology. Western notation is being introduced as an approximate *aide-mémoire* for practice. The skills being taught are limited to sitar, tabla, vocal, and kathak dance but there is no shortage of customers. Furthermore, the Indian community has founded its own music circle and, despite high ticket prices for concerts, has a general membership (mainly of Indians) that would be the envy of many a Western music club.

All this leads to the same basic conclusion that emerged from discussion of Western music in education: that without carefully structured teaching of genuine skill and the recruitment to education of people suitably qualified for the task, there will be no sense of achievement, no relating of school music to the living world of music, and a general dissipation of musical energy and artistic commitment. So long as there is a chronic lack of highly skilled musicians able and willing to demonstrate and pass on these skills to the young, music within multi-cultural education will be no more than a token gesture and self-defeating.

In my own work I have tried:

(*a*) to prove that there *is* a desire among ethnic communities to hear and perform their own music, and

(*b*) to prove that it *is* possible for children from ethnic communities to develop substantial skill in their own musical art.

I hope thereby to prove to the politicians (national as much as local)

(*a*) that there *is* a proven need to take active steps to recruit carefully musicians from abroad to work within education in this country, permanently or on extended contract, and

(*b*) that, following from this, there is a corresponding need to set up induction courses to enable such recruits to familiarize themselves with what to them will appear a totally alien culture.

It is time for the educators to lobby the politicians. The pressure for work in this country is such that the political will is more to put people in jobs than to face the reality of job definition. British residents can only be trained to fulfill necessary tasks if the expertise is around to do the training. If 'multi-cultural' music in education is to be more than a cosmetic sheen and is to contribute towards the cultural identity and self-respect of our ethnic communities, the politicians must not just face the music — they must actually bring it in.

17

Listening to Music

Musical experience does not have to be active: listening to music is a crucial component of any musical method.

Listening to music in the classroom has tended to receive a low priority in recent years. This is partly because the old style 'music appreciation', with its dogmatic assertions of value judgement, has been somewhat shattered by the newer perspective on Western culture emanating from the communications revolution and the natural onward march of history. It is also because the newer 'creative' methods of teaching, pioneered in the early 1960s, proved very much more demanding on teachers, to the extent that the playing of records to children was made to seem like an easy option for lazy teachers.

Over the past two decades, much has been written about stimulating 'aural awareness' through 'creativity', and there has been much professional scientific and psychological research into the phenomenology of aural perception. There is an endemic truth in the argument that 'creative' work leads to enhanced aural awareness; though I am not convinced that this enhancement has any endemic connection with artistic discrimination. The arguments of the music educators are usually in response to what they see as a habit of uncritical listening induced by pop music. To this doubtless accurate response two points need making. The first is that classical music is also listened to uncritically: as much by the 'music-loving' bourgeoisie as anyone else. (I well remember the Headmistress who complained that her girls were allowed to do their homework while Mozart was being beamed at them for their edification and who, when she had later shared with me her delight over her new home hi-fi system which so eased the burden of writing reports, was surprised to realize that there was an exact correlation between her report-writing and her girls' homework.) The second is that the aural awareness of the average listeners to classical music — and I am afraid that includes a majority of music

174

teachers — is also severely under-developed: their reactions are to a large extent preconditioned. The really discriminating listener *cannot* tolerate music as a background to any concentrated activity because he is hearing (and mentally transcribing) every note and therefore cannot shut it out.

If encounter with musical performance, recorded or live, is to have impact on the young, it is not going to be because it has been suitably prepared by creative exploration or didactic explanation, but because a particular piece of music is able to move an individual susceptible to such motivation by its irrational, primeval power. That is why it is so important that children should encounter the real world of music — preferably live as well as recorded — in as much variety as possible, and why assumptions about taste in relation to pop are dangerous. I personally was first 'turned on' to music when I heard Parry's 'Jerusalem' being played on the local church organ (and that was after some years of hopelessly unsuccessful piano lessons). I make no apology for this apparent early error in taste: it set me going — and I moved on from there.

Unfortunately, many children go through their whole school lives without ever experiencing face-to-face encounter with expert musical performance. And because of the way this is often presented, those who do are not always turned on by it. Indeed, over the years, children have used their unique collective capacity for disruption to prevent this particular form of edification conferring upon them its intended benefit.

The notion that adequate musical experience can be contained within a classroom developed partly because it was discovered, many years ago, that children did not always take kindly to being made to sit through performances of Beethoven symphonies, *et al.* The problems with these school concerts in fact arose not from the nature of the concept but from the style of content and manner of presentation.

It was naturally considered that 'schools concerts' could be made more palatable if preceded by some verbal explanation. The Ernest Read and Robert Mayer concerts for children pursued this approach with considerable success. However, the seats cost money (subsidized though they were), the performances were mainly on Saturdays and the audiences consisted largely of middle-class children — or at least, children who, through family background or musical activity on their own, had come to believe in the relevance and veracity of musical performances of this sort. Understandably, such concerts were seen by some educators as bastions of musical élitism.

Presenting musical performances to unselected groups of children during school-time does present problems — and challenges — that the promoters of the Saturday concerts have not had to face. The sense of wariness between teacher and class, to which I have already referred, is magnified substantially when the teacher becomes a conductor with a ninety-piece orchestra or a whole opera company and the class an audience of 2,000 to 3,000 children of mixed ages and abilities. The results of such endeavours can be catastrophic. Consequently, the daunting nature of the task, together with the considerable costs of hiring orchestras for the purpose, has tended to discourage the presentation of this type of musical experience and to encourage the smaller, workshop approach within individual schools or in small central venues. Although there is much to commend this latter approach, it would be a pity if it were to replace entirely the larger type of format.

There is a psychological as well as an artistic need for children to receive musical experiences *outside* the confines of school. However attractive the architectural surround of the school and however friendly and co-operative the atmosphere within it (I put it this way round — schools, as we all know, can vary quite astonishingly in this regard) school, like home, is a place where people remain for large periods of time; and the opportunity for an outside visit, rather like a holiday away from home, provides a useful psychological break. If the visit is to a visually exciting Arts Centre, it contains an in-built double-plus from the start. From this vantage point it should prove possible for children to receive stimulating and memorable musical experiences. Success will depend largely upon four things:

(*a*) the variety and style of the programme,
(*b*) the manner of presentation,
(*c*) the intrinsic merit of the music performed,
(*d*) the excellence and commitment with which it is performed.

Educationally, the most important of these aspects are the last two, yet it is the first two that make the last possible. And from small-scale workshops to symphonic presentations, manner — yet again — is apt to condition the substance. It should be expected that children will leave a musical performance with a stronger memory of a deep musical experience than of a humourous, slick entertainer.

The following points may help to encourage the provision of such opportunities in a purposeful way:

1. The fundamental aim should be to provide artistic experience rather than musical knowledge. It is, in any case, always desirable that experience should precede knowledge.
2. Any tricks or jokes used by the compère should not be ends in themselves nor prevent the music from speaking for itself. They should be used to amplify the musical experience rather than alternate (and thereby collide) with it.
3. The impact of a visual image is always stronger than that of the spoken word. The use of slides can eliminate a great deal of verbiage and be more effective in providing a context for the listening experience.
4. Whisperings among the audience (particularly with primary children) are not necessarily indicative of inattention. (Young children have a natural desire to respond verbally to an experience and their concentration span is very limited.) Compères should allow for this reaction and ensure that programmes do not require over-long periods of concentration. (The judicious 'cutting' of a symphonic movement will not be noticed by young children and may make all the difference between eliciting excitement and boredom.)
5. The pieces in any programme need to be varied in length as well as style. The most important consideration is that the content should have artistic integrity. Jokes, whether musical or not, can often interfere with this. (There is, for example, a world of difference between the 'Trumpet Voluntary' played on the hose-pipe and the purely musical humour that is to be found so frequently in music by, say, Haydn, Beethoven or Ives.)
6. The unfamiliar is always likely to receive an excited or even virulent response: 'modern music' does not automatically appeal to children. However, if modern music is carefully introduced and set in a suitable context, children will often find a greater affinity with it than adults. Music that is extrovert rather than intellectual in its approach is likely to prove more acceptable. (I have frequently used the 'Dance of King Kastchei' from Stra-

vinsky's *The Firebird Suite* to introduce primary schoolchildren to the full orchestra and almost invariably young children have laughed at the first 'sforzando' chord. This is simply an excited reaction to the unfamiliar and the laughter usually subsides after the third 'sforzando' chord.)

7. Primary and secondary schoolchildren show very different responses and have different concentration spans. This has a great deal to do with puberty and self-consciousness. In fact, secondary and primary children do not necessarily need separating and the attendance by some secondary children can have a helpful effect upon the attentiveness of primary children.

8. Descriptions of instruments are often redundant in these days of visual communication and, if allowed to precede the music, can prove boring. In small group concerts, displays of instrumental acrobatics can be usefully stimulating; but it is important that, once enthusiastic interest has been elicited, this kind of display is followed by music of real artistic substance.

9. 'Workshops' have an in-built danger, for they imply by definition that explanation should precede experience; indeed, that experience *benefits* from prior explanation. It is the background and social ambience of the music — and musicians — that benefits from explanation more than the music itself.

10. 'Workshops' need to be clear in their objectives: as to whether they exist to sell the notion of musical performance, the actual performers, the actual music, or an actual performance. I suggest that only the first is relevant. (The music should speak for itself, initially at least.) Frequently what is needed is *not* an explanation of, say, the evening's performance, but an entirely different programme, geared to the particular age range of the audience — a point frequently neglected by performers of contemporary music. Experience should precede explanation so that the art object can be perceived before its layers are stripped away (see quotation on this subject from Professor David Aspin, p.45).

11. The more programme content and explanation can relate to commonly understood *and felt* human issues, the greater will be the general appreciation.

12. Last, but by no means least, the response of the young audience will depend upon the intensity and commitment of the performers. Unfortunately, schools concerts given by

professional orchestras and smaller groups do not always receive the rehearsal time needed for suitably adventurous programmes, the experienced expertise that is needed for devising them, *nor the commitment from the players that is fundamental to success*. The common day-time orchestral dress of suits and dark tie hardly creates the ideal image from the start. I have to say that the most successful orchestral schools concerts I have ever given have been with the Leicestershire Schools Symphony Orchestra (dressed in jeans and plain coloured shirts) because the players share with me the unnerving sense of performing, as it were, on a high-wire. *They* know the kind of response that can ensue if the programme does not hit the mark and the performance is not up to standard — and *they* share with me a concern and a determination that our music *will* be accepted and appreciated by their peers. Concerts of this sort are ones which a quality 'schools' orchestra can be uniquely qualified to perform.

The perpetual diatribes that come from Arts Councils about the need to educate in 'The Arts' usually result from a mixture of muddled altruism and commercial necessity. The latter has caused the word 'marketing' to be used in the arts field: a development which has inevitably undermined the status of art by encouraging attention to be fixed on aspects of musical performance that may be least related to its intrinsic merit. Arts Councils seem perpetually to ignore the historical fact that art *is* education — or, at least, a form of education. The misguided concern for 'education in the arts' results largely from the fact that responses to musical art have ceased to be modern (see Chapter 6.) It also results from the disinclination of educational institutions to come to terms with the living world of music. For all the reasons that I have outlined in these last eight chapters, there is a general refusal to recognize that a great deal of school music tuition has actually resulted in increasing hostility among children to the living world of classical musical art. The unfortunate result of this is that Arts bodies find it necessary to approach educational institutions in education's own terms: with workshops, rather than performances, with explanation rather than experience.

Artistic encounter should be a prescribed part of educational provision and, ideally, it should take place in artistic surrounds. In a world of insensate materialism and violence, the sensitive young

are showing an increasing need for artistic pursuits while government and employment opportunities point increasingly to
technology as a basis for education. Education has the power, and
therefore the responsibility, to create a balance. As increasing
numbers of artists of all sorts find themselves rejected by the
already replete established Arts organizations, they will, if they
have genuine artistic perception and determination, discover their
own less orthodox means of bringing their arts to other people.
There is a whole body of unemployed young musical talent which,
for want of a comparatively small financial outlay, could be mobil-
ized to bring artistic encounter to the young. Provision of genuine
artistic encounter in music tends to be haphazard, depending upon
facilities, finance, and inclinations of different schools. This is yet
another area where there will need to be a greater sharing of
resources among schools if music is to continue to justify its place
in school education. Living musical performance is not, as is commonly supposed, the icing on the cake but is a vital ingredient of it.
It will need a prominent place in any scheme of resource rationalization designed to make school education an enabler rather than an
emasculator of the living musical art.

18

Priorities in Relation to Resources

By now it should hardly need reiterating that music is a particularly diverse and complicated subject. It can exist in all manner of forms, at all manner of levels of sophistication, and for all manner of purposes. It can function as art, entertainment or political agitation: it can be regarded as a humanizing agent, an élitist perversion, a symbol of social superiority or a means of losing consciousness. For some it is emotionally indispensable; for others it is a moral agent. Practically, in terms of instrumental activity alone, it contains at least thirteen specialisms that can take up to ten years of concentrated study to master — and that does not include instruments of ethnic minority cultures.

It follows that music is a particularly difficult subject to administer educationally. Its resource demands are potentially exorbitant while the resources under which it is required to work are usually minimal. Under the impact of ever-widening musical horizons and of socially more liberal attitudes as to what constitutes suitable music for school, it has allowed itself to become too diverse a subject to resource. Unless this crisis is resolved intelligently and selflessly by all concerned, so that what is essential to the subject and educationally purposeful is separated from what is peripheral to the subject and basically entertaining, and so that what can and must be provided in every type of school is distinguished from that which can only be provided effectively on some centralized basis, music could disappear from school education faster than many people might imagine. It is imperative to rationalize needs and priorities with a cogency that neither education nor the nature of music itself has generally encouraged in the past.

It will be pertinent at this point to make a précis of the main evidence before us.

Aims

1. To create an awareness of the power of music as a resource for the emotions.
2. To encourage the practice of the art of music.
3. To enable children from all backgrounds to discover interest and talent and to reach their fullest potential.

Objectives

1. To establish a historical perspective on musical style and content and on the social and political factors that have conditioned them.
2. To impart such knowledge of musical theory and practice as can assist in eliciting musical and emotional (rather than conditioned) responses to musical performance.
3. To impart knowledge and understanding of musics of the various ethnic and social groupings within contemporary culture.
4. To inculcate understanding of the artistic capability of music.
5. To encourage the use of music's emotional communicative power as a means towards self-understanding and fulfilment.

Methods

1. Inclusion of musical activity somewhere within the timetabled classroom curriculum.
2. Provision of skilled instrumental and vocal instruction.
3. Provision of special ensemble opportunities offering challenging levels of training and performance.
4. Exposure to live musical performance.

Each of these methods suggests its own more limited objectives and creates its own specific problems.

The classroom

1. Objectives

(*a*) To bring elementary knowledge and experience of music to all children. (For overall content see Chapter 11.)
(*b*) To provide incentive for further study.

(c) To provide more advanced musical study in the later years of schooling.

2. *General organization*

(a) Classroom teaching is most urgently needed between the ages of eight and twelve, normally covering the last three years of the primary school and overlapping the first year of the secondary school.

(b) Specialist teaching in primary schools can be augmented in certain content areas by non-specialist class teachers.

(c) Shortage of staffing usually necessitates children in the lower age ranges receiving musical experiences from general class teachers.

(d) Classroom teaching again becomes vitally important in the fourth year of secondary school for selected examination pupils, though this can often be provided on a centralized basis.

3. *Problems*

(a) Musical specialists working specifically in their specialist field are found mainly in secondary schools and very rarely in primary schools.

(b) It is difficult to provide *progressive* stages of learning for large classes of mixed musical ability and motivation.

(c) The consequent need to be continually motivating students tends to influence the determination of the content.

(d) Classroom teaching needs supplementing by specialist instrumental teaching in order to accommodate advanced examination work.

(e) There is a general lack of suitable equipment in secondary schools.

Instrumental teaching

1. *Objectives*

(a) To provide opportunity for interested children to discover whether or not they have the inclination and ability to succeed in playing a musical instrument.

(b) To provide in-depth musical study and involvement in music.

(c) To provide a musical resource for the community.

2. General organization

(*a*) Relatively large groups of children need selecting for initial teaching which will be largely diagnostic in effect.

(*b*) A screening process is needed to enable those with proven potential ability to receive more specialist and detailed instruction.

(*c*) Specialist expertise is needed for tuition in each instrumental specialism.

(*d*) Special facilities are desirable for intending musicians at 16+.

3. Problems

(*a*) Potential conflicts of interest and understanding can arise between classroom and instrumental teachers.

(*b*) Selection processes can cause resentment and can easily be mismanaged.

(*c*) Political pressures combined with under-resourcing can lead to more pupils being taught than can properly be handled, causing a decimation of the upper end of the teaching.

(*d*) Under-resourcing can lead to teachers being required to teach beyond (or perpetually below) their technical abilities or to teach instruments on which they are not properly qualified.

Ensemble opportunities

1. Objectives

(*a*) To provide through music a form of disciplined endeavour involving co-operative team work where mental and physical processes combine with emotional responses.

(*b*) To complement instrumental tuition by providing instruction in orchestral skills.

(*c*) To provide clear goals and incentives.

2. General organization

(*a*) Need for a structure of ensembles in which standards are well matched.

(*b*) Need for regular weekly rehearsals and holiday courses.

(*c*) Need for regular sectional coaching by suitably experienced staff.

(*d*) Need for ensembles to cater for interests not geared specifically to the classical tradition.

3. Problems

(*a*) There are potential conflicts of loyalty between area and school ensembles.

(*b*) Insufficient quantity of suitable players can cause harmful mismatching of standards and problems of balance within sections.

(*c*) The need for competition for places can cause discouragement among otherwise keen players.

(*d*) There is a possibility of ensembles being used for show rather than for their intrinsic educational benefits.

Exposure to musical performance

1. Objectives

(*a*) To provide face-to-face encounter with artistic musical performance.

(*b*) To provide instruction in musical style and performance through direct experience.

2. General organization

(*a*) Performances and workshops in individual schools.

(*b*) Performances and workshops in area centres.

(*c*) Large-scale performances in Arts Centres.

3. Problems

(*a*) Possibility of encouraging the imparting of knowledge to precede experience.

(*b*) Possibility of the compère attracting excitement more by his own style than by the actual musical performance.

(*c*) Possibility of the programme misfiring and eliciting hostility rather than appreciation.

Needs relating to other musical matters

1. Greater attention needs paying to the development of vocal skills in primary schools, follow-up in secondary schools, and to teachers' vocal knowledge and ability.

2. There is a need for Centres and Workshops for promoting skills in Rock music and Jazz.

3. There is a need for peripatetic teachers of Indian, African, and

Afro-Caribbean musics, and for knowledge and live experience of these musics to be disseminated generally.

Conclusion from Aims

The opinion held in some political, educational, and musical circles that the first priority within State Education should be to provide regular *classroom* teaching *at all levels* and that the 'talented few' can be catered for, if necessary, through private tuition or through the national state-aided specialist music schools, contains an intrinsic contradiction (unless, within these circles, it is the deliberate intention to ensure that the 'talented few' become fewer and fewer). Talent cannot emerge unless it has the opportunity to emerge. Once it has the opportunity to emerge and to do so within an encouraging milieu, the 'talented few', though still a small percentage of the school population, nevertheless become the 'talented many'.

In referring generally to 'musical talent' it is not unreasonable to make comparisons with A level entries in other subjects. A one-year sample of students in their second year 6th taken over *all* the secondary schools within my LEA indicated that the number of 'talented musicians' — by which I mean those of an average Grade 7 or 8 standard, continuing purposefully with instrumental or vocal lessons and attending musical ensembles regularly — was approximately one fifth the number taking English Literature, nearly five times as many as those taking English Language, about half as many as those taking French, nearly one and a half times as many as those taking German, a little under one third of those taking History, over four and a half times as many as those taking Classics and Ancient History, well over twice as many as those taking Art History and those taking Music itself. Were I able to double the present strength of the Instrumental Staff (whether of Western or ethnic instruments) I am convinced there would be double the number of the 'talented few'. Were a large part of the secondary teaching strength to be redeployed in order to spend the majority of their time in primary schools, I am equally convinced that there would be a dramatic increase in the numbers of the 'talented few' (because the selection and preparation of pupils would have been so much more effective and thorough) and that there would be a considerable increase in choral singing and musical interest generally. Were the teaching strength for class teaching within secondary schools to be doubled, many new, musically peripheral activities would emerge, but I cannot see that there would be any great increase in the 'talented few'. Hidden talent would remain hidden because of lack of suitable opportunity *at the right age*.

Musical ability of the sort I have described is not something God-given to an eccentric minority: it is something which lies dormant in vast numbers of children, awaiting appropriate encouragement and opportunity. Why else do some individual comprehensive schools appear to have a monopoly on musical talent? Not because there is something special in the water, but because their children, for one reason or another, have had suitable opportunities for developing musical skills within an appropriate musical milieu. To decimate instrumental teachers would be, within a short space of time, to decimate school music. Besides, without visible and audible accomplishment to establish its cause, music could soon be jostled out of its curriculum place by new technological subjects. *The a priori conclusion to be drawn from the aims I have suggested is that there needs to be a fundamental turn-around in priorities regarding classroom and instrumental tuition.*

Conclusion from Objectives

Although my list of objectives is basically concerned with the musicality of the content of any curriculum, it embraces the extremes of culture: from imparting 'knowledge and understanding of the musics of various ethnic and social groupings' to encouraging the use of music 'as a means towards self-understanding and fulfilment'. While the former can be contained within the classroom situation, the latter can only accrue from very deep and high level involvement with music. The common essence of these objectives is the need to investigate the purpose of music: to know 'why' before declaring 'what'. Music, as we have seen, is essentially an irrational medium and there will be many questions concerning it whose answers must inevitably remain equivocal. To account for music is like trying to account for human nature: which is precisely why the attempt should be made. For unless music stirs the imagination and provokes the emotions in some way, it is both as useful and as useless as wallpaper. Unfortunately that is how it is to many people, including some music educators.

My objectives suggest not only that music teachers should themselves have 'lively enquiring minds', but also that they should have considerable musical expertise. Musical expertise is, as we have seen, the touchstone for deep musical experience. You can stir the imagination through creative classroom work but you are unlikely to touch the emotions with it — not, at least, in a *musical* manner. In any case, you personally cannot pass on a musical experience you have never had; and although the music itself can often do this for you — if the recipients have natural musical sensibility — you may be unaware that a deep, inexplicable message has in fact been passed on. Without musical expertise, music teachers are unlikely to develop musical intelligence or musical imagination, either in themselves or in others. School education, blinkered by its social obligations, often appears afraid of real subject expertise: witness only the content of M.Ed. courses, to take which many teachers are able to gain a year's secondment. *The one inescapable conclusion to be drawn from the objectives I have listed is that school education cannot contain music purposefully within — or without — its curriculum unless it finds satisfactory and satisfying teaching employment for musicians with genuine expertise and sensibility.*

Conclusion from Methods and their individual objectives and problems

Assuming there is a staffing structure that includes classroom and instrumental teachers, most of the listed *objectives* for particular methods can, in theory at least, be achieved. Those that may not be so easily achieved come under 'Exposure to musical performance'. Schools' workshops and concerts have not normally been regarded as an integral part of musical provision: any adaptation of present staffing structures should take this into account.

Many of the specific *problems* I have listed are soluble by increased human understanding and endeavour: in other words they do not cost money to solve. They do, however, require a willingness on the part of many educators to re-think their attitudes and priorities in actively musical rather than ideologically educational terms — a willingness to prevent educational theory from subsuming the actuality of musical practice and effect.

The more intractable problems exposed by the above analysis centre upon quantity of staffing, staffing structures and the kinds of specialisms required within them. They also relate to the general exiguousness of spaces and equipment. I shall deal with each of these in turn. *First it is necessary to draw one inescapable conclusion from the Methods listed and the individual objectives arising from them: that meaningful solutions to current problems can only be realized if individual schools and centralized authorities work together co-operatively rather than competitively* — and that that means viewing falling rolls as a challenge for new, creative, and constructive thinking rather than as a cause for self-centred scrapping over a dwindling supply of pennies.

Staffing problems

1. Balance of available expertise between secondary and primary schools
The present pupil teacher ratios that govern the quantity of individual school staffing often make it difficult for secondary schools to 'lend' their teachers to primary schools. Nevertheless, in the hope and belief that the new economics of education will enforce a more flexible system of operation, it is worth examining ways by which this imbalance might be overcome. The effectiveness of any such schemes would depend upon the extent to which secondary head teachers are prepared to recognize the importance of providing specialist musical expertise for the primary classroom; and the degree of any teacher exchange would be affected by the structure of schooling in a given area and by the extent to which music is already given emphasis.

Assuming that the change to secondary school is at 11+, one year of general class teaching for all in the secondary school is desirable to provide continuity and to enable the Head of Music to get to know the new intake. (An effective alternative where the age of transfer is older, is to make music part of a faculty structure that gives in-depth experience of a particular Arts or Design subject over, say, half a term: the teacher is able to use all his tricks at once, to perfect, package, and repeat a proven course and to be able to deal only with those who have specifically chosen to return to him and his subject in future years.) After the first year, music can with benefit be made part of an option system so that the music teacher effectively deals with the equivalent of only one class per school year. This, in some school structures, could save up to two-thirds of a music teacher's timetable.

A common economic measure (as much curricular as financial) has been to have CSE and O level taught at once. The common examination at 16+ will solve this particular aspect of the examination problem, though it will almost certainly necessitate devaluing performance skills and consequently the level of expertise required generally. Some music teachers find themselves obliged to teach 5th year examination music outside normal curriculum hours. In many areas, it would make sense to prescribe such teaching as an *extra-curricular* subject: for it to be provided centrally through Further, Community or Continuing education. Music at A level (along with other minority subjects) absorbs a vast amount of teacher-time. Moreover, if it is to be taught effectively, it requires the teacher to have a particular type of musical outlook that is not always compatible with the rather different type of outlook needed in the general classroom. The teaching of music at A level could with profit be set up in areas. Students *needing* music at A level would be directed to the schools that teach it; the only losers would be those few who choose music A level as an elective study — and they would almost certainly be instrumentalists who would receive continuing musical experience through centralized choirs and orchestras.

Effective teaching of public examination work in all appropriate years can take up the best part of a complete timetable. Substantial savings in time could be made if all this teaching were to be centralized. The resulting slack in the timetable could then be used for teaching in primary schools; and if overall syllabus guidelines were to be provided for general primary teachers, all concerned would stand to gain.

In some areas it is quite possible that, by these means, between half and a whole of a specialist music teacher's timetable could be spent in primary schools. Throughout the year he or she could probably visit at least the third and fourth year class in all primary schools once a week for one term in the year, assist other teachers in the school in providing certain types of musical experience and co-ordinate joint performances, productions and/or festivals at the secondary school. In some areas this kind of arrangement could provide systematic coverage of primary schools. In other areas the problems would be greater. Nevertheless, I hope these remarks indicate that it *is* possible to achieve a considerable turn-around in emphasis between secondary and primary class teaching.

2. *The expertise needed for class teaching*

Although many apparently effective class teachers lack genuine musical expertise, (their expertise often consisting of easy relationships with pupils and an ability to be entertaining through music) a great deal of in-service training in music is concerned more specifically with detailed classroom methodology than with the acquisition of musical knowledge and skill. The real need, for many music teachers, is the reverse: to be able to develop and augment their actual musical knowledge and skill — including, of course, vocal skill. (One of the largest handicaps to effective 'creative' teaching is the average teacher's lack of general musical knowledge. The most 'creative' teachers usually turn out to be the most complete musicians, because they possess a whole armoury of musical knowledge from which to draw small but relevant items as required.)

Experts in primary educational practice are apt to be horror-struck at the thought of secondary teachers being let loose in Primary Schools. (It is an indication of education's fundamentally theoretical nature that it should so delight in creating for itself such tiny boxes.) My response is to state categorically that it is much easier to train a teacher lacking knowledge of primary education in current primary school practice than it is to impart to non-specialists in music the skills required for teaching music. With the former, one would be dealing with trained musicians. Although this training could well need adapting in order to relate it specifically to the abilities and responses of primary children and to primary educational practice generally, the fundamental skills of music — virtually unteachable through in-service training — would already be there. If primary schools were to be able to depend upon input from specialist music teachers, general primary teachers could be provided with in-service training aimed at more limited and realistic objectives and thus enabled to complement the work of the music specialists.

3. *Supply and recruitment of instrumental teachers*

All the above remarks concerning the proportion of specialist teaching between primary and secondary schools are related broadly to the existing staffing structure for classroom music: although they involve an element of redeployment they do not reduce existing staffing levels for classroom teaching — nor can they if music in primary schools is to be given the importance it deserves. However, one major reason for treating primary school music with this degree of importance is that it can pave and ease the way for the development of musical skill and create appropriate foundations for the development of musical experience. Unless there is opportunity to develop skill (and that must include instrumental skill, however much new emphasis is given to vocal skill) much of this work will prove moribund in the long term and school music will decline to a point at which it ceases to be accountable.

It must therefore be assumed that, in whatever quantity, instrumental teaching will be available. The cost of maintaining a staff of peripatetic teachers is small in comparison with the enormous benefits involved, both to individuals directly and to communities generally. Where peripatetic forces appear too small to meet the demand, other remedies may need to be sought. Virtually all specialist music teachers have one *instrumental* specialism: this may be an orchestral instrument or an orchestral instrument may have been a second study. Either way, some regular tuition and training may enable these teachers to start off groups of beginners satisfactorily and, in many cases, take them to a fair standard.

Under present structures, and where there are shortages of peripatetic teachers, which instruments are taught in any one school may depend entirely upon the specialism(s) of the staff in that particular school. Worse still, the staff may be tempted to start children on instruments on which they have no skill whatever. If the importance of imparting instrumental skills is recognized by all concerned, it should prove possible for a number of such classroom teachers to be brought together on some sort of centralized basis, which would at least increase the variety of skills on offer.

Ideally, of course, there will be a sufficient supply of peripatetic teachers for this situation not to arise. And if we can hear less of the classroom 'anti-élitist' talk from some music educators (whose own proper background of musical élitism should cause them to know better) and more of the importance of musical skill through performance, the situation may not have to arise. At all events, it is a minimum necessity that any area should have access to instrumental expertise on piano and all orchestral instruments and in roughly equal proportion to their use in the symphony orchestra.

Whether they are recruited on a full- or part-time basis, to work individually in schools or in centres or in both, will depend upon local circumstances. What is crucially important is that these instrumental teachers should contain an upper layer of expertise to complement the beginner and less advanced tuition. For this task, good orchestral experience is of more value than the customary forms of teacher training.

Ideal instrumental teachers may have vital qualifications that are rather different from those of classroom teachers in some other subject areas. The best sportsmen, actors, and dancers, whose services could be of immense use in schools, do not usually take a one-year course in teacher training; nor, usually, do the best musical performers. (How many members of professional theatre, music, and dance companies who give successful workshops in schools are 'qualified' teachers?) Professional performers of some years' experience who choose to turn to instrumental teaching are seldom in a position to take a one-year course in teacher training; and even for the many promising young players who do not find a place in the performing profession and who are glad to devote themselves to teaching, conventional teacher training is not greatly relevant. Their teaching job is best learnt on the spot where help and in-service training can be given immediately by advisers and senior colleagues. Much the same applies to teachers of rock and ethnic music except that, in the case of the latter, some training in general British educational mores may be a necessity.

4. *The proportion between classroom and instrumental teaching*

There is no final resolution to the problem of teacher supply, but there is a principle that could be established concerning the proportion of instrumental to classroom teaching: that the amount of skilled instrumental instruction (whether it comes from classroom or peripatetic teachers) should be in *at least* equal proportion to the amount of classroom teaching. In support of this contention I would quote the example of a 10–14 High School[1] where, until recently, out of approximately 800 pupils on roll, 125 played band or string instruments and 185 sung in extra-curricular choirs. The Head of Music had some knowledge of all wind band instruments and was also an accomplished singer and conductor. Because success breeds success, he had a second full-time music teacher. The classroom was regarded to a large extent as a jumping off ground: singing and band work was introduced and the latter provided a diagnostic process, prior to more specialized tuition. Pupils with sufficient aptitude and industry were taken on by the senior peripatetic staff and were thus able to reach their fullest potential. Because the classroom was used partly for the development of musical skills, it engendered a great deal of extra-curricular activity which necessitated the teachers giving very freely of their spare time. Taking this into account, at least half of their time was spent teaching and organizing choral, band, and orchestral activity.

In a sense there is — certainly should be — nothing exceptional about this kind of situation. However, what is less than usual about it — sadly — is simply that objectives were ambitiously but realistically defined and that they were carried out with expertise and dedication. It should surely be the aim to make this kind of situation the norm rather than the exception.

5. *Providing exposure to live musical performance*

With the demands being placed on an already over-extended and rapidly dwindling budget, it is not easy to see how additional finances can be made available for presenting live music. Yet this aspect is a crucial ingredient of the motivational and instructional process. Assuming that a central budget for this work is inadequate or even non-existent, there are a number of ways in which this kind of resource can be provided:

(*a*) Large numbers of workshops are available at subsidised rates through Regional Arts Associations and through regional and national Arts Council networks. Even without subsidy, the cost of hiring a small, suitably selected group need not be great if it is shared between a number of schools and presented at a central venue.

(*b*) Various Youth and Music schemes exist throughout the country and teachers can encourage students to take advantage of these and assist with transportation.

(*c*) Teachers can do a great deal simply by bringing local concerts to the attention of students and encouraging attendance.

(*d*) Suitable instrumental teachers can be encouraged to devise and present programmes for children. If, say, five schools send parties of interested children to one central school, a staff group giving three presentations in one day can cover fifteen schools.

(e) Similarly, advanced school or conservatoire students, introduced by a teacher or adviser, can give suitably devised concerts.

(f) Schools orchestras can also be used for presenting special schools concerts.

Spaces and equipment

The continued financing of music in education as we have known it is presenting educators with substantial problems, often requiring radical solutions. One radical solution that could work in all but the most rural areas would be to take music out of *individual* secondary schools entirely (except, perhaps, for the first year) and place it all in centres. There are precedents for classes visiting local centres on a regular basis: for example in most urban areas all outdoor sports activities require buses and outside visits. Many LEAs already have experience of centralized music centres for instrumental work, A level work, etc.

It is likely that individual schools with the best available provision of spaces and equipment would be selected as such centres, though existing Arts Centres, Colleges of Further Education, redundant schools, churches, etc., could also be considered. Block timetabling of, say, a 'music' half-day as part of an Arts option could make complete centralization of this sort possible. The centres could well be combined with existing instrumental and examination centres and could possibly serve up to six different secondary schools. There is no reason why primary schools should not also be encouraged to use such centres.

To implement this suggestion successfully would of course require considerable vision and magnanimity on the part of Head Teachers: they would need to recognize that while their *school* might appear to suffer, their *students* would have a lot to gain. A list of these gains should make the point:

(a) *Staffing:* Interests and abilities of different staff would be pooled and, if the centre were to be attached to Youth or Adult services, tutors of instruments from flutes to string basses and electric guitars to steel pans could be hired for small, voluntary, after-school classes, building on the work done during school hours. 'Head of Centre' could be made into an attractive post.

(b) Space and Equipment: Other subjects might be similarly centralized so that spaces released from music in one school might cause another school to allot *more* space to music. It becomes very much more feasible to consider making special provision for *one* centre rather than *six* schools. Similarly with equipment: it would become feasible to think in terms of equipping such centres with great thoroughness if it were understood that they were to act as *the* musical resource for up to six secondary schools and make possible genuinely musical results.

(c) Variety of activity: Students could have access to a range of opportunities that no individual school could begin to offer. The list is almost endless, but the following could be a sample: Instrumental tuition, including electric guitar and ethnic musical instruments, orchestral work, choral work, creative composition with a professional range of percussion, electronics, theatre music, examination work, concerts.

(d) Variation in depth of commitment: All the activities just listed have the potential for large group tuition and activity by day, or small group or individual tuition voluntarily after school. One student may simply gain a short-lived experience by experimenting with a brass instrument or creating with electronics; another may become an expert in either.

(e) Flexibility: There would be a sufficient variety of activities for students to discover for *themselves* which aspects of music interest them most — if at all. The Rock Band, Brass Band, Jug Band, Steel Band, Madrigal Group, and Creative Composition (see Chapter 11) — and much more besides — could all happen at the same place, at the same time and the students would not be dependent upon the interests of one particular teacher for deciding towards which activity they felt most inclined. The problem of motivation would be greatly diminished.

This suggestion for centralization may be considered to have merit, to be an absurdly impracticable vision of Utopia or to be a graphic vision of educational Hell, depending upon the point of view. Clearly it presents timetabling and staffing problems within schools and the actual centres that could take considerable experimentation and experience to resolve. There could be no norm for the degree of centralization or the range of activities that could be provided: this would vary greatly according to local circumstances. Any implementation could only start on a 'pilot' basis and the details could only be determined after lengthy discussion by all concerned. The problems and caveats are too obvious to need listing.

If then the notion is so beset by problems, why introduce it as a penultimate thought for a book of this length? Precisely because my aim has been to analyse in detail the components and attitudes of education and music in relation to each other, historically and as they appear in current practice, and to draw conclusions from them. And I am left with two fundamental and irreconcilable conclusions: that music, in the wild disparity of forms in which it currently appears in education is crying for the moon at a time when its resource requirements need to be shrinking; and that the net in which it is thus ensnared is in fact being stretched to a point where virtually every satisfying aspect of the subject is capable of slipping away. Music Departments are trying, impossibly, to be all things to all people: they are already out of date. If they do not start to share their resources, music in schools — and that, I actually suggest, means 'music', as most of us have known it and some of us have tried to love it — will also become out of date.

Educational institutions and a love of music

In Chapter 5 I proposed a criterion for aims: *provision of musical resources in education should be geared to the known needs of children and students rather than to the ability of music to enhance public and religious occasions.* Throughout human history music has been used and/or abused for such occasions; and the degree to which it has incited the spectators to ecstacy or simply provided extraneous pomp has depended upon the cultural ambience. For example, music's present day use in Indonesia as catharsis to prevent injury as a result of ritual self-mutilation is in curious contrast to its use in Western society to adorn royal rituals — or, for that matter, the rituals of educational institutions. Schools are still apt to feel deprived if there is no home-grown music with which to adorn communal occasions such as assembly or prize-giving. They are still apt to weigh this use of music more heavily than its use as a form of general therapy to individual students. They are, in other words, still inclined to create a symbol out of an essentially non-symbolic medium.

Music is of benefit to individual schools only in so far as its presence can provide encouragement to other children to learn musical skills and to spur them to further endeavour. The degree of centralization I have proposed need not prevent this from happening: indeed, it could even increase the chances. For if centralization enables more children to reach higher standards, individual schools are more likely to find themselves with musical resources to tap, both for special occasions and as an incentive to others. Nor would that resource be purely instrumental: a whole variety of skills could be made available for public display — if public display is needed.

This is the nub of the problem. The current obsession with the importance of the classroom and the apparent willingness to destroy all that seems best in school music for the sake of pursuing an unattainable egalitarianism — between schools themselves as much as between individual students — is not only at odds with the age-old desire for music to adorn public occasions; nor is it caused just by social conscience or financial expediency. It reflects a deeper contradiction within the musical process itself that has something to do with artistic *déjà vu*, with the modern artistic problems discussed in Part Two: a sense that perhaps, after all, there *is* an inbuilt élitism — and I mean *social* élitism — in the very notion of 'loving music'. The obsession reflects a spurious guilt emanating from a sense of over-possessiveness: a compulsive need to share a musical something whose intrinsic value is not to be questioned. This theme has been addressed with persistence and penetration by John Berger with reference to visual art, and it is worth quoting him here for, as he suggests, his thesis is applicable to other art forms.

A love of art has been a useful concept to the European ruling classes for over a century and a half. The love was said to be their own. With it they could claim kinship with the civilizations of the past and the possession of those moral virtues associated with 'beauty'. With it they could also dismiss as inartistic and primitive the cultures they were in the process of destroying at home and throughout the world . . .

The usefulness of the concept had to be paid for. There were demands that a love of art, which was so apparently a privilege and was so apparently and intimately connected with morality, should be encouraged in all deserving citizens. This demand led to many nineteenth-century movements of cultural philanthropy — of which western Ministries of Culture are the last, absurd and doomed manifestations.

It would be exaggeration to claim that the cultural facilities concerned with the Arts and open to the public at large have yielded no benefits at all. They have contributed to the cultural development of many thousands of individuals. But all these individuals remain exceptions because the fundamental division between the initiated and the uninitiated, the 'loving' and the indifferent, the minority and the majority, has remained as rigid as ever. And it is inevitable that this should be so; for, quite apart from the related economic and educational factors, there is a hopeless contradiction within the philanthropic theory itself. The privileged are not in a position to teach or give to the underprivileged. Their own love of art is a fiction, a pretension. What they have to offer as lovers is not worth taking.

I believe that this is finally true concerning all the arts. But . . . it is most obvious in the field of the visual arts. For twenty years I have searched like Diogenes for a true lover of art: if I had found one I would have been forced to abandon as superficial, as an act of bad faith, my own regard for art which is constantly and openly political. I never found one. Not even among artists? least of all. Failed artists wait to be loved for themselves. Working artists love their next, as yet non-existent project. Most artists alternate between being one and the other.[2]

For twenty years, I too have searched for a true lover of music. I can also say that, if I had found one, it would have shaken my fundamental belief in the supernatural power of music which, in a necessarily less tangible way, is also intrinsically political. I, too, never found one. I have searched in European and North American concert halls, in theatres, pubs, barns, and cellars, where a love of music has appeared at best to be ritualistic and affected and at worst socially conscious, contrived and pretentious. I have searched among parents and discovered that loving music is closely related to the relative position in the local youth orchestra of their child to that of the child next door.

I have searched among educators. 'The School of Music taught me to love music' said one Headmaster to me. 'I never went to concerts before my daughter joined the orchestra; of course, I don't go to concerts any longer — my daughter left the orchestra ten years ago.' Recently, I attended an important educational concert — not very well performed, as it happened — and found myself sitting behind a distinguished general educator. I therefore had a particularly clear view of his neck muscles which, during the first piece, were thoroughly relaxed. (His mind was clearly on other things — like musical glory?) After this piece, *he* noticed me.

During the second piece his neck muscles contorted in horrid confusion as his head nodded out of time with the music and his ears pricked obviously to what he considered special musical sounds. Did he love music? He said he enjoyed the concert . . .

I have searched among young people and occasionally thought I had found a real lover of music: the guitarist who temporarily lost consciousness in the joy of his performing dexterity, the oboist whose every sound was a source of joy, the violinist tearing out his and the music's heart in a neurotic fever of white heat. And then I knew I had not. These people love *playing*; mostly they love themselves; mostly they love the music *they play*: they also love the applause: that moment of appreciation of their agonizing hard work. But they will become bored with playing; they will become bored with most of the music; they will become bored with the applause and possibly with themselves. And then they will react in different ways. Some will continue to love their playing — they will become less self-critical, but to themselves — lucky them! — they will bring joy and satisfaction; they will love their activity but they will not love music. Others will become music 'doers': they will play for their daily bread. Boredom will give way to routine while self-imposed reliability and efficiency will severely temper musical excitement: they will not love music — they would be as unlikely to take their instrument on holiday with them as a doctor would be to take his stethoscope. A few will become musical artists, whether as performers or composers. Theirs will be the agony, punctuated by the occasional moments of ecstasy when — because of the daemon inside them — this thing they love yet so often hate (because they have attained the humility to learn that it is always bigger than they are) becomes, to echo Xenakis again, 'beyond objects, emotions or sensations — as Beethoven's Seventh Symphony is beyond music — leading to realms that religion still occupies for some people'. These people will feel music so deeply that they will not dare to love it.

Music was not made for being loved. That is something that man, particularly in the West, has foisted upon it in justification for its persistent — and continuing — use as the badge of an élite. This contradiction is at the heart of the crisis of musical objectives within education. The actual *love* of music that caused the sharing in the first place may have been 'a fiction, a pretension' that was in fact 'not worth taking'; but the music itself (and the act of becoming a musician) was and is quite different from the *love* that has been foisted upon it. For whatever initial reasons, thousands upon thousands of children have been encouraged in musical *activities* that, for them, have proved immensely worthwhile. In the post-war years, this activity has spread at a colossal rate, across the social barriers and at vast cultural gain. In the process, however, selectivity became integral to the system and, with that, neurosis set in. It is safe to assert that in no other subject in the whole curriculum has selectivity been such a highly charged issue.

Selectivity gave the lie to the false idealism on which this propagation had rested; educational egalitarianism became threatened by the very subject that had provided it with such a convenient symbol of success — just as had happened in ancient Greece. The symbol remained but the art that nurtured it deteriorated: the medium and the function given to it were in fact incompatible. It is now time to change the function rather than the medium for, artistically, music can never be of service to Mammon. The truth is, music, of all the arts, is totally, uncompromisingly self-contained. It is not necessary to institutions: it is an adjunct to the spirit that is necessary only to people. That is the fundamental misconception.

POSTSCRIPT

It is over six years since I started writing this book. During that time there have been considerable changes in education and increasingly diverse views of its obligations to music. Far-reaching changes contained in the Education Reform Bill, new curricular emphases induced by the introduction of a single examination at 16+, significant developments in 'user-friendly' musical technology, and the mush-rooming of a whole arts marketing industry, all have the power to affect the usefulness of education to music. They seem to me also to warrant and endorse the general conclusions I have drawn in the book.

Music's essential irrationality is bedevilling the leglislators of our 'severe and ambitious culture', just as it did in ancient Greece and in many epochs between. The subject is currently considered sufficiently important to warrant a place in a new National Curriculum, but sufficiently peripheral to permit some charging for individual instru-mental instruction, even — uniquely among chargeable 'options' — during school hours. This last is, of course, a slight upon music and musicians, but such slights are nothing new, as anyone who has absorbed Part One of this book will readily appreciate. It appears likely that the attempt to define an inessential and therefore chargeable 'option' within a free educational system will prove completely intractable. This problem of relating competitive excellence to core stability is intriguingly redolent of the situation in fifth century BC Greece.

It is greatly to be hoped that the National Curriculum will include a minimal entitlement to instrumental instruction, if only in group tuition for essentially diagnostic purposes, for there is a serious possibility that the continued existence of some centralized peripatetic instrumental services could be threatened. This is particularly serious in LEAs where professionally trained musicians are available *only* through these peripatetic services. 'Opting out', increasing competition between schools, and a decreasing ceiling of expenditure on centralized services which LEAs are legally permitted to incur, will all threaten the actual availability of access to instrumental instruction. Financial strictures may eventually force LEAs to pass on the costs of peripatetic music services to schools or groups of schools. To whatever extent the competitive spirit may be engendered among schools in the years ahead, so far as music is concerned, there is all the greater reason to heed my plea on p. 189 for co-operation rather than competition; otherwise education in many areas will fail its clientele by not providing access to necessary musical opportunity.

I suspect that, in retrospect, the new GCSE examination in music will seem little more than a bubble in a teacup. There is nothing intrinsically new about dividing music into 'Performing', 'Listening', and 'Composing'. We used to use the terms 'practical', 'aural', and 'theory' — and 'history'. History is now embraced largely within the listening activity, and the new terminology appropriately reflects many of the useful postwar developments in musical objectives and teaching methods described in this book. The essential point of departure is the linking of 'pastiche' writing with free composition, and the insistence that this package is an *essential* part of musical training. In essence this should be welcome. The problems arise in connection with the sheer range of musical ability involved and the extraordinary diversity of what may pass for composition. Creativity, which I have described on p. 42 as a method — a process — has been packaged as a product; or, put more bluntly, GCSE has been used to enforce curricular innovation rather than reflect improved teaching method. It is a classic case of a tail wagging a dog: the standards of some of the group compositions put forward for GCSE could arguably be achieved by fourth-year primary children, were the specialist teachers and equipment generally available.

The range of what may pass as 'Performance' is also very wide: it is difficult to envisage how, for example, average or less than average 16-year-olds can be assessed as conductors, and how it will prove possible to make comparative and meaningful assessment of the ability of individual performers to react to each other in ensembles ranging from rock groups to string quartets. The principle of increasing the range and style of content should, again, be welcome; but, the present result is an examination containing some aspects which are, by normal musical criteria, fundamentally unassessable. Regrettably, perception, imagination, creativity, and musicality are qualities which, supremely important though they are, can be assessed objectively only in the context of skilled technique; and the less the skill, the less they can be incorporated in the assessment — and vice versa. The problem highlights the importance of defining separate roles for classroom and instrumental teachers; for, as the latter have been drawn increasingly into classroom activities, their skill-orientated teaching methods have tended to become correspondingly undermined. My insistence throughout this book on the *complementary* nature of classroom and instrumental teaching seems now to be all the more relevant.

Musical technology has, as predicted, marched on apace. Children usually enjoy working with computer technology; its increased application to music has provided greater motivation for the subject and has been one cause of the large uptake for GCSE music. Useful developments are still progressing in DIY microchip music pro-grammes. (Whether, however, these increasingly 'user-friendly' pro-grammes, creative and instructional, actually require schools and teachers for their operation could be open to question.) The new technology brings obvious benefits, but it also harbours dangers relevant to my comments in Chapter 11; for it tends to provide only *elementary* experience and knowledge. As I write, I have before me a complimentary copy of a tape containing the sounds that can be made by a 'digital horn' — at the press of a button, this remarkable instrument can transform itself from a recorder into an oboe into a clarinet into a . . . Are we finally living in Nibelheim?

Evidently not. I recently saw a poster stating 'Heaven is an evening with Bach'. My remarks on the emergence of Arts Marketing on p. 179 must already sound oddly quaint. The Arts Marketing Brigade is now out in force. It is having a ball. And it is being highly successful. It attracts people to concerts and operas and it is not too squeamish about how it does it. When political elections can be fought and won with substantial help from advertisements some of which have only the most tenuous connection with material truth, it would seem churlish indeed to question whether Heaven could be anything other than an evening with Bach, or whether any and every evening with Bach is truly representative of what we might take Heaven to be. The Arts Marketeers are not first and foremost in the business of artistic discernment. 'It is desperately unfair', warns Rhinegold Publishing's *The Musician's Handbook*, 'but is also helps to be physically attractive.' A rueful thought — but then, perhaps it always did. However, the handy musician of today has some rather different concerns than had, for example, the sixteenth-century disciple of Thomas Morley's *Plaine and Easie Introduction to Practical Musicke*. The new breed may or may not have the compositional ability to 'take a point at his pleasure and wrest and turn it as he list', but he or she is up to the minute in self-promotion techniques, career patterns, financial benefits and any other matters that avoid falling foul of tax evasion or trade description laws.

There is, however, another side to the new marketing imperative: thematic programming. What once seemed an obsession of the Festival industry is now becoming a feature of regular concert life. When Berg can be promoted successfully on equal terms with Mahler, when a Schoenberg Festival can attract large audiences at the Festival Hall, as can an all-Bartók concert given by Solti and the LPO, something of importance is happening.

Political movements come and go and education is one of their carrier pigeons. Art, however, if it truly attests to a culture, remains on as living history. For all the recent upheavals within politics and education and for all the mindless urbanities of our increasingly consumer-orientated society, *music* has followed its own course, led by its own parameters, reflecting at time the debasements and banalities of our age, but fundamentally untouched by anything politics and certainly education can do to it. And this book was essentially about music and the usefulness of education to it.

Cardiff   Peter Fletcher
December 1988

Notes

Introduction

1 H. I. Marrou, *A history of education in antiquity*, Sheen & Ward (1966), pp. 140-1.

Chapter 1

1 M. I. Finley, *Aspects of Antiquity*, Chatto & Windus (1968), p. 198.
2 Oliver Strunk, *Source Readings in Musical History: Antiquity and the Middle Ages*, Faber & Faber (1972), 'Plato'.
3 *A Framework for the Curriculum*, Government Report, HMSO (1980).
4 Aristophanes, *The Clouds*, translated by Alan H. Sommerstein, Penguin Books (1973), p. 152.
5 *A history of education in antiquity*, p. 226.

Chapter 2

1 Quoted in Henry Raynor, *A Social History of Music from the Middle Ages to Beethoven*, Barrie and Jenkins (1972).
2 Quoted in Groves *Dictionary of Music and Musicians*, 6th Edn. article on 'Education in Music', Macmillan (1981).
3 Oliver Strunk, *Source Readings in Musical History: Antiquity and the Middle Ages*, 'St Clement of Alexandria'.
4 Quoted in H. I. Marrou, *A history of education in antiquity*, p. 336.
5 Oliver Strunk, *Source Readings in Musical History: Antiquity and the Middle Ages*, 'Boethius'.
6 Ibid. 'Cassiodorus'.
7 Quoted in Kenneth Clark, *Civilisation*, Harper & Row (1969).
8 Quoted in John Lawson & Harold Silver, *A Social History of Education in England*, Methuen (1973), p. 20.
9 Ibid. p. 50.
10 Ibid.
11 Quoted in Groves *Dictionary of Music and Musicians*, 6th Edn. article on 'Education in Music', Macmillan (1981).

12 Quoted in Bernarr Rainbow: *The Land without Music*, Novello (1967), p. 24.
13 Ibid. p. 36.
14 Quoted in John Lawson & Harold Silver, *A Social History of Education in England*, p. 239.

Chapter 3

1 John Lawson & Harold Silver, *A Social History of Education in England*, p. 241.
2 Quoted in Henry Raynor, *Music and Society since 1815*, Barrie & Jenkins (1976), p. 102.
3 Ibid., pp. 103–4.
4 Ibid., p. 112.
5 Ibid., p. 113.
6 Quoted in Dorothy Taylor, *Music Now*, Open University Press (1969), p. 6.
7 John Lawson & Harold Silver, *A Social History of Education in England*, p. 318.
8 The basic information (as opposed to the opinions) contained in these last three paragraphs is taken from Dorothy Taylor's most useful book, *Music Now*.
9 David N. Aspin, 'The Arts, Education and the Community', *Journal of Art & Design Education*, Vol. 1, No. 1, 1982.
10 One of the chief aims in the Charter of the Arts Council.

Chapter 4

1 M. R. Gautam, *The Musical Heritage of India*, Abhinav Publications (1980), p. 64.
2 Wilfrid Mellers, *Caliban Reborn*, Victor Gollancz (1968).
3 Malcolm Ross, *The Arts and the Adolescent*, Schools Council Working Paper 54, Evans/Methuen Educational (1975). John Paynter, *Music in the Secondary School Curriculum*, Cambridge University Press (1982).
4 Malcolm Ross, *The Arts and the Adolescent*, p. 54.
5 Colin McPhee, *The Music of Bali*, Da Capo Press (1976).
6 Malcolm Ross, *The Arts and the Adolescent*, p. 53.
7 Robert Witkin, *The Intelligence of Feeling*, Heinemann Educational Books (1974).
8 Ibid. p. 120.
9 Ibid. p. 120–1.
10 See note 3 above.

11 David N. Aspin, 'The Arts, Education and the Community', *Journal of Art and Design Education*, Vol. 1, No. 1, 1982.

12 M. R. Gautam, The Musical Heritage of India, p. 58.

13 Michael Tippett, *Moving into Aquarius*, Paladin Books (1974), p. 55.

14 Thucydides ii 37. As quoted in Kenneth Dover, *The Greeks*, BBC Publications (1980).

Chapter 6

1 Quoted in H. C. Robbins Landon, *Beethoven*, Thames and Hudson (1974).

Chapter 7

1 Quoted in *Charles Ives: A Portrait* by David Wooldridge, Faber and Faber, (1975).

2 Ibid.

3 Ibid.

4 This quotation and much of the preceding argument is taken from George Steiner, *In Bluebeard's Castle*, Faber and Faber (1971).

5 Ibid.

6 Merion Bowen, *Michael Tippett*, Robson Books (1981).

7 Iannis Xenakis, *Formalized Music*, Indiana University Press (1971), p. 1.

Chapter 8

1 R. W. Emerson, Journal for September 1862, Harvard University Press (1925).

2 For further reading consult *Hindustani Music in the 20th Century* by Wim van der Meer (Allied Publishers Private Ltd. ISBN 90 247 2066 4) to which I am indebted for some of the foregoing analysis.

3 Peter Fletcher, *Roll Over Rock*, Stainer & Bell (1981).

4 Bryan McGee, *Aspects of Wagner*, Penguin Books (1968).

5 Libretto for Benjamin Britten's Cantata, *Our Hunting Fathers*, Faber and Faber (1936).

Chapter 10

1 Atarah Ben-Tovim, *Children and Music*, A. & C. Black (1979).

2 John Paynter, *Music in the Secondary School Curriculum*.

3 G. Vulliamy & E. Lee, *Pop, Rock and Ethnic Music in Schools*, Cambridge University Press (1983).

4 Keith Swanwick, *A Basis for Music Education*, National Federation for Educational Research (1979).
5 The Newsom Report, *Half our Future*, HMSO (1965).

Chapter 18

1 Sarson High School, Melton Mowbray. Head of Music, Brian Humpherson (now Head of Creative Arts at Guthlaxton College, Wigston).
2 John Berger, *The Moment of Cubism and Other Essays*, Weidenfeld and Nicholson (1969).

INDEX